William Lucas Sargant

Inductive Political Economy

Volume I

William Lucas Sargant

Inductive Political Economy
Volume I

ISBN/EAN: 9783744644877

Printed in Europe, USA, Canada, Australia, Japan

Cover: Foto ©Suzi / pixelio.de

More available books at **www.hansebooks.com**

INDUCTIVE

POLITICAL ECONOMY.

BY

WILLIAM LUCAS SARGANT,

AUTHOR OF

"The Science of Social Opulence" (1856)
And other works from 1857 to 1874.

Volume I.

Good sense which only is the gift of heaven,
And though no science, fairly worth the seven.

Instruire en intéressant.

LONDON: SIMPKIN, MARSHALL, & CO.
BIRMINGHAM: CORNISH BROTHERS.
1887.

PREFACE.

———o———

THIRTY years ago I published the *Science of Social Opulence* (Political Economy under another name): part of the book was devoted to Terms and Definitions; another and more considerable part to expounding the theories of the subject on the supposition that there existed a community which used no money.

Had I been a writer for bread, or if I had desired immediate notoriety, "fame counted in halfpence," I should have chosen a more attractive theme: for this one could not bring me pence or popularity; besides that I deliberately set down what I thought new, true, and useful, and not what would be likely to please the public.

Now, according to the elder Mill, "Mr. Locke declares that he who follows his own thoughts in writing, can hope for approvers in the small number alone of those who make use of their own thoughts in reading: that by the rest, a man is not permitted without censure to follow his own thoughts in the search of truth when they lead him ever so little out of the common road." If anyone supposes that we are greatly changed for the better during the last two centuries, I reply that an eminent London publisher when accepting two of my works, warned me to have nothing in them which would require readers to think; meaning that neglect of this maxim would expose me to the fate of George Primrose, when, as he told the Vicar, he tried to attract attention by dressing up three paradoxes with some ingenuity. "And what did the learned world say to your paradoxes?"—"Sir, the learned world said nothing to my paradoxes, nothing at all, Sir. I suffered the cruellest mortification;—neglect."

Before I risked my volume of 1856, I applied by the advice of a London friend to one of the most intelligent of London publishers, and I received for answer that it was useless to send my MS. since there was no sale for works on Political Economy.

At that time however, the subject was open to discussion in the pages of the *Economist*: the proprietor and editor for example, Mr. James Wilson, wrote in it some elaborate articles on the thorny topic of value. But after his death his son-in-law Mr. Bagehot found it his duty to conduct the paper on commercial principles, and to exclude the discussion of theories as ill calculated to foster popularity. Nor have we any periodical like the French *Journal des Économistes*.

England therefore, has few opportunities for debating theoretical questions. No doubt there is a Political Economy Club in London, and another at Oxford; but as I can testify, the members prefer the consideration of practical questions and proposals for legislation.

Some experts however, have been willing to think of the foundations of their science. The late Professor Cliffe Leslie was always willing to read and learn: he did not look upon his subject as a closed book, but went about trying to verify his opinions. The late Dr. W. B. Hodgson, the Edinburgh Professor, was another of the candid few: he wrote me word that he was teaching his class my heretical distinction between capital and self-maintenance: and not long before his death he spent a day with me to propose certain verbal alterations in my essay, "The Purse and the Cash-box." Professor and Mrs. Marshall of Cambridge are willing to listen even to a heterodox thinker; and in their "Introduction to Political Economy" have liberally acknowledged that they are indebted to me for the substance of one section.

It was in 1856 that I published the "Science of Social Opulence," a book mostly deductive, as was natural, after I had for years laboured through Ricardo and John Mill, to say nothing of Adam Smith, J. B. Say, and a score of other authors. In 1857 however, I wrote and printed my "Economy of the Labouring Classes," which abounds in facts. Here I was more successful than in the previous venture: I was reviewed in the *Spectator*, and so favourably, making allowance for the severe tone of the paper, that an editor said to me "there are authors who would give £100 for such an article." Praise by the *Spectator* was highly valued because Mr. Rintoul, the founder and editor, was a very mastiff in guarding the entrance to literary reputation: it was impossible to cajole him, and to ask in behalf of a friend for a favourable notice, was in his eyes an intolerable insult. I never saw him; and as he knew nothing of me he might commend without any sacrifice of independence.

Next year (1858) Mr. Rintoul died.

Now after the interval of a generation, I reproduce my Terms and Definitions, much enlarged, and altered in form though not in substance.

The body of my work consists mostly of practical questions with induction from facts. One of the chapters deals with Free-Trade: I ask whether we might not extend the narrow area at present under its influence: I show how, as it appears to me, this might be done, in accordance with the advice of Adam Smith, at a cost to our working men of 3d. a week each, with a possible gain of 3s. or 4s. a week. "Protection!" is at once bawled out by men who were protectionist or indifferent when I was, as I still am, an undoubting free-trader. I have ventured to express in strong terms, my contempt for all popular cries and for their idiotic victims.

I have quoted many authors but without giving page or volume. Formerly I gave these particulars; but I found that other writers made use of my references without acknowledgement; I have been unwilling to expose them to further temptation to wrong-doing.

In my "Terms and Definitions," given "For Reference only," I have mentioned the Definitions by Malthus (1827): I must do that distinguished author the justice to say that he would probably have disclaimed my attempts as pernicious novelties; his Definitions and mine being as unlike as the treatises of Sir James Steuart and Ricardo.

I am bound to acknowledge the important assistance I have received from my son, the author of "Farthing Dinners," who suggested many alterations in my MS., especially in the Chapter on "Depression of Trade," where his skill as an accountant added much by improved arrangement to the force of the figures adduced: the final chapter too, on "Over-production," he entirely recast when a troublesome fall had incapacitated me for exertion.

W. L. SARGANT.

To the Opinions of the Press, not arranged by myself, I add the notes mentioned above. I know that authors have been blamed for making use of such communications. But, as it seems to me, a few lines from Lord Derby or from the author of "Friends in Council," or from the eminent Professor Marshall will weigh more than an anonymous article however excellent.

From the Rt. Hon. the Earl of Derby, K.G.

"Knowsley, Prescot, Oct. 21/71.

Sir,
I have to thank you for the 3rd volume of your Essays, which I have been reading with more than ordinary interest. They are full of original thought and practical good sense: rare qualities separately, and very rare indeed in combination. I hope the book may have the success it deserves.

I remain,
Your obed. servant,
DERBY."

"Knowsley, Prescot, Oct. 15, 1872.

Lord Derby thanks Mr. Sargant for the volume of his essays received this day.

Lord Derby can say with truth that he has read all the earlier essays most of them more than once, and that they have materially added to his stock of knowledge and ideas on the subjects of which they treat."

From the late Arthur Helps, Clerk of the Privy Council: author of " Friends in Council," to the late Dr. Charles Badham, the eminent Greek scholar.

Nov. 27/57.

"Will you thank Mr. Sargant very cordially for his kindness in sending to me his book. I have only had time to dip into it; but it is clear to me that it is a very thoughtful and valuable book." ("The Economy of the Labouring Classes.")

"I particularly like the concluding paragraph in Chapter 4. I have been for some time intending to write something on that subject. What he says of Niebuhr is excellent."

From the " Economics of Industry " by Professor and Mrs. Marshall.

"The relation between interest and profits is explained in Book II. Much of this section is taken from Sargant's *Recent Political Economy*."

SUMMARY OF CONTENTS.

Chapter.	Section.	Page.	
			INTRODUCTION.
I.	1	1	The Dismal Science.
	2	3	A. Smith's Successors: Dulness, Selfishness.
	3	6	The Almsgiver classed with the Spendthrift.
	4	9	Poor-law relief necessary though abused.
	5	14	Charity is not Socialism.
	6	17	Censures of even Factory and Mines Acts.
	7	22	Education requires Government Aid.
	8	26	Mr. Spencer consistent: Philosophical Vanity.
	9	29	Mr. Spencer a Visionary.
	10	30	"Not-Socialism" resumed.
	11	35	Summary of Indictment against Mr. Spencer.
2nd Part.	12	36	A Free Government: John Locke: Continuous Relief Works.
	13	41	Are there any Remedies?
	14	44	Discussion as to Direct Action.
	15	46	Higher Wages Wanted: Chinese Immigrants.
	16	49	Higher Wages insufficient: Moral Qualities.
3rd Part.	17	53	Theory of P. E.: Production and Reproduction.
4th Part.	18	59	"Instruct by Interesting."
	19	61	Whately and Jevons repulsive: First Principles for reference.
	20	64	Conclusion.
			INEQUALITIES OF FORTUNE.
II.	1	66	The Gross Inequalities: Facts.
	2	68	Mitigation by National Insurance-Fund. Other Causes of Envy.
	3	72	Mr. Gregg's Fallacy: Matters have been Worse.
	4	78	No Hope then? Machinery: Chinese Immigrants.
	5	84	Means of Rising: County Labourers: New Voters: Limited Democracy.
	6	87	What desirable? America. Socialism. Settlements of Land.
	7	95	French equal division at death.
	8	99	No substitute proposed: Danger as Irish: Weakened Security.
	9	104	Personal Improvement: Education.
	10	107	Capitalists should be moderate.
	11	110	Harrington's Oceana: Limitation of Property.
	12	111	Summary.
	13	117	Conclusion.

Chapter	Section	Page	
			MR. HERBERT SPENCER'S BARBARISM.
III.	1	120	Definitions: Authorities: Adam Smith.
	2	126	Jeremy Bentham.
	3	131	Mr. H. Spencer's Opinions.
	4	137	Facts.
	5	146	Little Sisters of the Poor.
	6	159	Little Sisters of the Poor: Lessons.
	7	170	Further Considerations.
	8	182	Expediency.
	9	194	Conclusion.
			DEPRESSION OF TRADE, 1885.
IV.	1	201	Farmers and Traders distressed.
	2	207	Facts continued.
	3	214	Income-Tax: absolute or comparative? Houses.
	4	216	Ditto Shedules A, B, &c. Retail Trades.
	5	226	Ditto Summary.
	6	229	Causes: Want Field for Employment.
	7	232	Chinese Railways: Wars: Foreign Loans.
	8	239	Enhancement of Gold denied.
	9	251	Our Prospects.
	10	256	Summary of Chapter.
			RETALIATION NECESSARY TO FREE TRADE.
V.	1	264	Adam Smith's doctrine.
	2	267	Application to us.
	3	272	Alleged dear bread: Mr. Bright: Spain.
	4	277	The Cobden Club: Democracy: Treaties.
	5	284	Threats sufficient: Existing Treaties.
	6	286	Fair-Trade: Mr. Bright: Repeal 1846.
	7	289	Summary.
			THE PURSE AND THE CASHBOX.
VI.	1	292	100 sovereigns and 10: Capital and Self-Maintenance.
	2	300	Use of the distinction.
	3	308	Wheat in the hands of Farmer, Dealer, Consumer. Spending and Saving.
	4	315	Workmen: Productive Forces.
	5	322	Reconsideration: if without money: Summary.
			OVER-PRODUCTION: OVER-CAPITALIZATION: GLUTS.
VII.	1	332	Grows out of the last Chapter.
	2	342	Summary.

INDEX

TO

TERMS AND DEFINITIONS.

A

	PAGE
Annuitants	xxxii
Appreciation of gold (see Enhancement)	
Art and Science	xx

B

Bank Notes	xxxvii
Barter	xxxiii
Bastiat	xvii
Business	xxiii, xxxii

C

Capital	xxii, xxiii
,, and Self-Maintenance	xxii, xxiv
,, fixed	xxvi
,, unfixed or circulating	xxvi
Capital-Rent	xxx
Cheques	xxxvii
Coin	xxxiv
Commodities, cheap, said = gold dear	xxxv
Consumption	xxv

D

Demand (see supply)	
Depreciation of gold	xxxvi
De Quincey	xxix
Desirability	xxxviii
Devoted (capital)	xxii
Differential Rent	xxxviii
Distribution	xxxi
Division of labour	xlv

E

	PAGE
Economics	xx
Effects-Rent	xix
Effectual Demand (supply)	
Enhancement	xxxv
Exchange	xxxiii
Extravagant prices	xxxviii

F

Final Self-Maintenance	xxv
Fixed Capital	xxvi
,, Property	xxvi
Foreign words	xlvi

G

Gambling	xxxiii, xxxiv
Gifts of Nature	xxi
Gold a commodity	xxxv
,, dear = commodities cheap	xxxv
,, depreciation and enhancement	xxxvi
Gratification	xxii

H

| Hobbes | xvii |
| Human Productions | xxi, xxii |

I

Improvements-Rent	xxix
Income	xxvii
Interest	xxvii
Investment	xxxiii

INDEX TO TERMS AND DEFINITIONS.

L

	PAGE
Labour	xliii
,, is it capital?	xliv
,, productive	xliv
,, reproductive	xliv
,, unproductive	xliv
Laissez-faire	xlvi
Land not capital	xxiii
Luxuries	xlv

M

McCulloch	xix
Malthus	xvii
Marshall, Professor	xx
Mathews, William	xviii
Mediate Self-Maintenance	xxv
Money	xxxiv
,, value of	xxxix
Monopoly-Rent	xxx

N

Necessaries of life	xliii
Not-Capital (Self-Maint.)	xxiv

P

Parasites	xxxii
Partition	xxxi, xxxii
Patriots	xxi
Pleasure	xxii
Political Economy	xix
Price	xxxix
,, of gold	xxxiv
Prices, three classes	xl
,, extravagant	xxxviii
Principal	xxvi
Produce, to	xliii
Productive	xliii
,, forces	xliii
Profit	xxxiii
Property	xx
,, fixed	xxvi

R

Rent	xxviii
,, capital or principal	xxx
,, differential	xxviii
,, improvements	xxix
,, kinds of	xxviii
,, monopoly	xxx

	PAGE
Rent, spontaneous prosperity	xxxi
,, ,, adversity	xxxi
,, theory of	xxix
Reproduction	xxii
Revenue	xxvii

S

Satisfaction	xxii
"Science of Social Opulence"	xviii
Seignorage	xxxiv
Self-Maintenance	xxii, xxiv
,, ,, Mediate	xxv
,, ,, Final	xxv
Services	xxii
Speculation	xxxiii
Spending	xxv
Spontaneous	xxx
Stock	xix
Suez Canal	xxxi
Superfluities	xlv
Supply and Effectual Demand	xli

T

Trade	xxxii
Transport	xxxii
Truck	xlii

U

Undertaker	xxxiii
Unearned increment	xxx
Unfixed capital	xxvi
Unproductive	xliii
Utility	xxxviii

V

Value	xxxvii
,, -in-Use	xxxvii
,, -in-Exchange	xxxvii
,, of Money	xxxix

W

Wages	xlii
,, real (wheat)	xlii
Walpole, Sir Robert	xxi
Wealth	xx
What is a pound?	xxxvii
Whately	xvii
Wheat, prices	xl

FOR REFERENCE ONLY.

TERMS AND DEFINITIONS.

"By this it appears how necessary it is for any man that aspires to true knowledge, to *examine* the *definitions* of former authors; and either to correct them, where they are negligently set down, or to *make* them himself. For the errors of definitions multiply themselves according as the reckoning proceeds, and lead men into absurdities, which at last they see, but cannot avoid, without reckoning anew from the beginning, in which lies the foundation of their errors."

"So that in the *right definition* of names lies the first use of speech; which is the acquisition of science: and in wrong, or no definitions, lies the first abuse; from which proceed all false and senseless tenets; which make those men which take their instruction from the authority of books, and not from their own meditation, to be as much *below* the condition of *ignorant* men, as men endued with true science are above it."

"For words are wise men's counters; they do but reckon by them; but they are the money of fools; that value them by the authority of an Aristotle, a Cicero, or a St. Thomas, or any other doctor whatsoever, if a man."
HOBBES: *Of Man.*

"The great defect of Adam Smith, and of our economists in general, is the want of definitions."—WHATELY quoted by CAREY.

"Les définitions sont au bout de la science, et non pas à son origine."
(Definitions come last in a science and not first.)—*Revue des deux Mondes.*

"When we employ terms which are of daily occurrence in the common conversation of educated persons, we should define and apply them *so as to agree* with the sense in which they are understood in this ordinary use of them."—MALTHUS, *Definitions, 1827.*

"Political Economy has not had the advantages of most sciences, as chemistry for example: it has not invented its own vocabulary. It treats of matters which have occupied men's minds since the beginning of the world, and which are habitually talked of; thus its expressions have been found ready made, and have been adopted by necessity."—BASTIAT.

"Economists have certainly not been backward in claiming indulgence for their definitions, on the ground of the *extraordinary difficulty* of obtaining them."—Professor ADAMSON.

These quotations supply us with lessons from the pens of several considerable or great thinkers, as to the requirements of true definitions. Hobbes tells us that in "right definition of names lies the first use of speech," and that without it, bookish men fall "as much *below* the condition of ignorant men as men indued with true science are above it." A professor has recently said that economists have confessed the extraordinary difficulty of finding good definitions. The cause of their difficulty, said the ingenious Bastiat, is, that they have not had the opportunity, as chemists for example, of inventing their own terms, and have therefore had to use the ordinary language of the world. In using that language, Malthus tells us, we must take care to apply it so as to agree with the practice of ordinary men of education. A French author holds with many noted Englishmen, that sound definitions are not possible in an unripe science, but are of necessity deferred to the period of maturity. We cannot therefore wonder at the criticism of Whately when he says that the defect of Adam Smith, the founder of Political Economy, is a want of definitions. Two observations may be added: I. those persons are wrong who maintain that a scientific writer may adopt what names he pleases, provided that he tells his readers what he understands by each name: the objection is that this practice gives the readers the trouble of constantly recalling the arbitrary definition; besides that the author is in danger of sometimes forgetting it: II. names should as far as possible be connotative: *i.e.* should denote the thing meant; thus, in fixing on all productions of labour the name of stock, we have to remember that houses and steam engines as well as food and clothes and materials are stock; but if we fix on them the name of "human productions," we shall never be at a loss as to the things intended.

A great part of the following Terms and Definitions, and the most important part, are what I proposed in my *Science of Social Opulence* (1856). Scarcely any of them have been sanctioned by other authors: the only important exception being Self-Maintenance, which, as well as the distinction it indicates, was adopted by the late Professor Dr. W. B. Hodgson of Edinburgh: I should add the less important term Differential Rent (as distinguished from Monopoly Rent and Capital or Principal Rent) which Mr. William Mathews has used in a valuable paper upon "The Influence of Taxation on Rent."

Since 1856 I have made some changes, but more in form than in substance. What I then called Realty I now call Gifts of Nature (Land, Streams, &c.).

"Stock" I have changed into Human Productions (Crops, Manufactures, &c.).

"Effects Rent" has become Capital or Principal Rent.

In 1856 the word reproductive did not appear: I now regard it as of great importance. All labour well directed is productive: even a butler renders, or produces, services. But these services are not *re*productive: they do not furnish the means of future production. They do not replace capital.

"Definitions come last in a science, and not first," and they are most difficult to find. I have done my best; but the imperfections of my attempts are painfully shown by the fact that after having rewritten my MSS. many times, I find further alterations wanted every time I read them.

POLITICAL ECONOMY.—I now come to the question what Political Economy is.

Forty to fifty years ago, J. R. McCulloch was the representative of the "high and dry" school. Just as the orthodox church at that time was high in its dogma, and dry as remainder biscuit in its sermons, so the M'Culloch school was unreasoning in its creed and repulsive in its teaching. Here is an example.

McCulloch says:

"Political Economy is the science of the laws which regulate the production, distribution, and consumption of those articles or products which have exchangeable value, and are either necessary, useful, or agreeable to man."

A beginner might ponder long over this sentence: he might ask whether land is one of the things intended; if so, is it an article or a product? it may be distributed, but not produced or consumed. "Exchangeable value" he finds to be a clumsy substitute for "price." Then again McCulloch's last clause seems unnecessary, since nothing can have a price unless it is either necessary, or useful, or agreeable.

Adam Smith's title is far more attractive:—"An Inquiry into the Nature and Causes of the Wealth of Nations." Nor can any one doubt what it means.

Taking wealth in the sense of weal or well-being, and especially of material well-being, Smith's title is very nearly the definition we want. Political Economy is an Inquiry into the Nature and Causes of the well-being, and especially the material well-being, of nations.

Bastiat says that Political Economy is the study of the *mechanism* of society. With limitations, this appears true. Some would say "the mechanism of the means of living," and not of society generally.

It has two branches, the art and the science: the art which is intended to teach the duties of governments and philanthropists; and the science which assigns the reasons for the instruction. For example: the art tells Parliaments and private managers that they should leave men and women to settle their own affairs: the science explains why it is better: it shows from history and recent experience, that men and women treated as children contract childish notions and habits, while those who are duly left to themselves become self-reliant and trustworthy.

A distinguished Professor has in a certain short treatise used the word Economics. If the subject were a new one this might be an excellent term, remembering Xenophon's use of that word and adopting it in a wider sense. But the term Political Economy is now rooted in the language, and is found in hundreds of books: to extirpate it in favour of another term would be as difficult as to substitute Wakefield's "distribution of employments" for the popular "Division of Labour."

WEALTH.—The word wealth has been used carelessly: sometimes in its proper sense of opulence and at other times in the sense of the matter which when abundant constitutes opulence. Adam Smith in his title speaks of the Wealth of Nations, meaning opulence. Other writers tell you that all the wealth of the ancient poverty-stricken cave-dweller consisted in a few flint implements. Now to talk of this wretch's wealth is misleading: why not say, the cave-dweller's possessions?

Again; a certain man has 10,000 acres of good land, well situated: he is a wealthy man. It is the land which makes him wealthy: surely then, the land is wealth: no! says a critic, it is only the means of producing wealth. At any rate it is better to call the land property and not wealth.

PROPERTY.—In defining Property, we are concerned with the

thing and not with the right *(jus utendi et abutendi).* It might be defined:—everything which has a price. True, Sir Robert Walpole, pointing to the Patriots (the discontented Whigs) said, all these men have their price: yet these men were not property. An answer is easy; but still the fact remains that the word price is used by educated people of existences which are not property.

Another plausible definition of property is:—everything which is possessed and can be transferred. It is sufficient if the *title* is transferable: a landed estate cannot be sent from the Lothians to London, but the title may.

According to this second definition, if I root up a dock by the road side, it becomes property, because I possess it and can transfer it. Yet the law does not recognize it as property; a man who took it from me could not be indicted for stealing; and I might die a pauper though I possessed a million dock-stalks.

Perhaps it is better to combine the two definitions, and to say that Property is everything which is possessed, is transferable, and has a price. When Sir Robert Walpole gave a member of Parliament £1,000 for his votes and influence, he did not take possession of the creature, nor could he transfer him: the creature did not become his slave. He was not property though he had a price.

GIFTS OF NATURE
AND
HUMAN PRODUCTIONS
} are the two great classes of property.

This distinction is essential; because Gifts of Nature (land, streams, natural forests) are absolutely limited in quantity, while Human Productions are not absolutely limited. The two classes differ in the laws which regulate their price: as population increases Gifts of Nature rise in price; land and streams pay an ever-growing rent; forests sell for more and more. On the contrary, Human Productions constantly fall through increased coöperation and division of labour. Rent rises, profit and interest fall.

GIFTS OF NATURE are things which men find existing: land, streams, beds of minerals, natural forests. Certain persons or governments take possession of these things, which thus become property if they are transferable and are worth any money.

If they are not worth any money, they are possessions but not property.

Some Gifts of Nature are not Property. Before 1848 to 1851 the gold in the soil of California and Australia was not property, *i.e.* was not the property of individuals. Gold in the depths of the sea is not property even to a nation.

HUMAN PRODUCTIONS come into being by human effort, *i.e.* by human thought and labour. The cave-dweller, when he chipped a stone into an axe, exerted thought and labour. James Watt, when he fashioned the steam engine with its condenser and its parallel motion, exerted much thought and little labour: his foremen and smiths and fitters, in carrying out his instructions, exerted some thought and great labour.

Human Productions have in them an element of the Gifts of Nature. The table I am writing on is made of mahogany brought from a natural forest in Honduras: the screws in it have their origin in a natural bed of iron ore. The table therefore, consists partly of Gifts of Nature, though its predominant character is that of a Human Production.

PLEASURE. \
GRATIFICATION. } Why are Human Productions brought into being? Why do men produce? The
SATISFACTION. / common answer is:—in the expectation of pleasure. I object to the word pleasure as ambiguous: pleasure, like the Latin *voluptas*, frequently means sensuality. I prefer satisfaction or gratification. Self-denial gives gratification, but to the man of pleasure self-denial does not give pleasure. Eating and drinking give pleasure: abstinence, frugality, saving, give gratification. Men often labour and produce that they may have the gratification of saving.

Gratification includes pleasure and a great deal more.

SERVICES.—Are services Human Productions? they are certainly Human Products: but I have defined Human Productions as one division of Property; and services not being Property, are not, for our purpose, Human Productions. In ordinary language, services are rendered and are not produced.

CAPITAL \
AND } are the two great classes of Human Productions.
SELF-MAINTENANCE /

CAPITAL is Human Productions devoted to business, or (more accurately) devoted to reproduction.

I insist on the word *devoted*, because it means both used in business and set apart to be so used. The word *destined* would mean set apart to be used.

BUSINESS.—By used in business I understand used for earning a money-profit, or as in the case of millions of ryots in India, for earning a subsistence. For "business" I afterwards substitute "reproduction."

CAPITAL.—Other definitions of Capital may be given. Capital is savings devoted to business (excluding Gifts of Nature bought with the savings).

Francis Place gave incidentally a similar definition:—"Savings from labour, which again furnish the means of employment." I do not see however, that the savings need arise "from labour:" those from rent or profit may be used as capital. Again, instead of "furnish the means of employment" I prefer "devoted to reproduction." By devoted I mean either in use or set apart to be used. For reproduction see the definition of that word.

Capital then, is "human productions devoted to reproduction."

I exclude Gifts of Nature. Yet land is sometimes classed as capital, and that by learned professors, who thus expose themselves to the censure of Hobbes, as men ignorant of definitions, and who therefore hold "false and senseless tenets."

But, they will object, if a farmer with £20,000 applies part of this sum to buying his farm, the farm becomes part of his capital. For the purposes of Political Economy this is not so. The farmer has withdrawn part of his capital from the business of farming and has bought land with it: this land is part of his assets; it is part of his Principal; but it is no longer Capital.

Similarly, as regards joint-stock companies. A million sterling is raised to construct a branch railway: a considerable part of the million goes for buying the necessary land; and this land appears in the accounts as Capital. Even an Act of Parliament might call the land Capital.

But a political Economist, writing on his science, declines to call it Capital. Land yields an income called rent: capital yields an income called profit. In the case of a railway the rent and the profit are confounded together, but they are really different, and follow different laws.

Take a company of a different kind. Imagine a new one formed with a Principal of £100,000, to buy Dr. Glen's unwieldy farm in the south-west of the United States: the valuation of the 30,000 acres being £20,000, the £20,000 would be reckoned financially as part of the capital.

Imagine the venture so successful as to be carried on for many years. At the end of that time, if the neighbourhood had become populous, the land would probably have risen to a value of £30,000 or £40,000. But the improvements and buildings and implements, if they had merely been kept in working order, would not have increased in value; and the rate of profit would probably have fallen. Since then, the value of land and the value of the means of working it, follow different laws, it is necessary to put them into different classes. While the two together are Principal, the land is a Gift of Nature, the stock and implements are the Human Productions called Capital.

We have a difficulty in realizing the fact that land is a Gift of Nature, because we see it already enclosed, drained, built on; and we cannot easily distinguish between the substance and the accidents. It has been suggested to me that the case would be clearer if we thought of other parts of the world where no improvements have been effected.

Imagine then, a nomade tribe in the centre of Asia, frequently shifting from place to place. The chief, with his sons and daughters and their children, like the patriarch Abraham, fixes on a spot, pitches his tent, and uses the herbage and water in feeding his flocks and herds. Here, not only is the land a Gift of Nature: the herbage and water are the same.

Hereafter, these open plains may be enclosed and farmed, like the soil of India: the land and the streams will still be Gifts of Nature; while the hedges and the implements and the additional crops will be Human Productions.

I repeat the definition I finally approve:—Capital is Human Productions devoted to reproduction.

SELF-MAINTENANCE OR NOT-CAPITAL is the second kind of Human Productions. It is generally what is set apart to be spent: *i.e.*, what is devoted to consumption without reproducing itself: consumption by the owner the wife and the children. Capital on the other hand, though it is expended or laid out, does reproduce itself with a profit.

But what shall we say of wild fruits to be had for the gathering? They do not come within the definitions of Capital or of Self-Maintenance, because they are not human productions. I will offer the wider definition of Self-Maintenance :—Things devoted to gratifications other than that of earning. This definition has the advantage of including money or money's worth devoted to the gratification of our charitable impulses.

In which class shall we place the money a gentleman spends upon his garden? He pays wages, and buys tools and seeds: he gets in return, vegetables and fruits and flowers. Shall we say that the money reproduces itself? Only partially. A man of good fortune may spend £500 a year on his garden, and get in return, vegetables, fruit, flowers, which he might buy for £200 a year: his outlay does not reproduce itself with a profit, but only partly reproduces itself. Some may say that so far as it reproduces itself it is capital.

Self-Maintenance is of two kinds: the one represented by a loaf of bread, a thing which in the hands of the consumer requires no further exchange; the other represented by a sovereign, which is of no use until it is exchanged for commodities or services.

MEDIATE Self-Maintenance consists of things, like a sovereign, set apart to be exchanged, first, for other things which we propose to consume, and secondly for services: it consists generally of money; to which we may add articles we have bought for the support of domestic servants, since these render services in exchange for the purchased articles.

FINAL Self-Maintenance consists of things like bread, clothes, furniture, house-room, to be eaten, drunk, worn, and used by ourselves, our wives, and our children: besides the necessaries of life, it includes superfluities such as beer and tobacco, and luxuries such as champagne and turtle.

CONSUMPTION then, is the using money or money's-worth as Final Self-Maintenance.

SPENDING is generally applied to money: it is the purchase

with money of Final Self-Maintenance. I *may* say that I spend the sovereigns in my cashbox in paying wages: it is better to say, I *expend* it or lay it out.

FIXED CAPITAL is a term used in several senses:

(a) Adam Smith defines it as capital which yields a profit by remaining fixed in the hands of the owner: thus, milch cows are fixed, because they remain in the hands of the farmer while the sale of their milk gives him a profit; a grazier's oxen or cows are not fixed, for they yield no profit till they are sold. Farm-buildings, ploughs, a team of horses, are fixed on the farm.

(b) Ricardo uses the word fixed differently. He applies it to durable capital; to that which is fixed as to time. A strange consequence follows: gold coin is durable, having a life of 30 to 40 years; therefore it is fixed, though in fact it is the circulating medium of trade. To call coin fixed, sins against the maxim of Malthus as to the words in common use.

(c) In commerce, fixed is rather taken to mean fixed as to form, like mills, farm buildings, plantations. It is the reverse of "loanable."

Many things are fixed in all three senses: they are kept in the hands of their owners; they are durable; they are with difficulty converted into money; as mills, factories, improvements of land.

CIRCULATING OR UNFIXED } Capital is all which is not fixed. Unfixed is perhaps the better term, but circulating is rooted in the language.

FIXED PROPERTY has a wider meaning: it includes much property which is not capital: an old country if it is rich, has immense advantages in the possession of mansions, parks, gardens, roads, cathedrals, the accumulations of ages. We may add pictures: these are durable, as we see in the case of the picture lately purchased by the nation from Blenheim, painted by Raphael, who flourished nearly four centuries ago. If the German, Waagen, is right England possesses more fine pictures than all the rest of Europe, and this is an important element in her fixed property and opulence.

PRINCIPAL has a wide signification: it means much more than Capital; everything in fact which yields an income. "The Principal of the National Debt has been reduced since 1815 by more than 100 millions £." It is more commonly said that the Capital has been so reduced; but this is a secondary sense of the word which is better avoided. A lawyer may say the Corpus.

Principal is especially used of money invested on interest. It was said of a certain spendthrift, that he could not understand the distinction between principal and interest, and ignorantly spent his principal.

INCOME
OR
REVENUE. } A man's annual Income is what he can spend year after year without becoming poorer. By spending is meant using Self-Maintenance.

An objection has been made, and an actual case offered as an illustration. A man died, leaving a plot of building-land, valued at £10,000. This was in 1870: thirteen years later it proved worth £50,000; *i.e.* it had advanced in price by about £3,000 a year.

The trustees who held the land for the benefit of the family, could not legally distribute this £3,000 annually among the life-tenants, but had to invest it as Principal. If the man had lived to enjoy this growth of price, he might have spent this £3,000 annually during the *13* years, and still have been in 1883, worth £10,000 as he apparently was in 1870. To him then, the £3,000 a year would have been income.

I feel the force of the objection, and the example. I can only ask the question, whether in 1870 the true value of the plot was £10,000, or whether it was £10,000, plus the then value of an annuity of £3,000 for *13* years. The saleable price in 1870 was only £10,000, but this was because investors and land-valuers were ignorant of the future. If the owner had lived and spent the £3,000 a year, and had been left in 1883 with only his £10,000 he might have been called poorer in 1883 than in 1870; poorer by £3,000 a year for *13* years.

INTEREST is a periodical payment in consideration of Principal advanced previously. This definition includes the half-yearly payment on the National Debt: a payment made in consideration of money advanced to the Government from time to time during the last *200* years: with this peculiarity, that the lenders cannot reclaim their principal, but the Government can repay it at pleasure; and as a consequence, that the lenders cannot raise the rate of interest, but the Government can lower the rate, as they frequently have done.

RENT is a periodical payment by N to M for the possession and use of property assigned to N by M; usually for a term of years, but in some cases for ever. A farmer pays rent for land and building: a townsman pays rent for a house: a hand-loom weaver for his loom.

Sooner or later, in most cases, the owner takes back his property. This distinguishes rent from interest. Money is not "earmarked:" therefore the debtor is not bound to restore the very sovereigns borrowed, but only to pay the same money-value. In the case of rent, on the contrary, the very thing assigned for a time has to be returned.

KINDS OF RENT.—The first kind is the subject of the Theory of Rent: it has to do with the Gifts of Nature, such as land and streams: other kinds have to do with Human Productions, such as houses or hand-looms.

DIFFERENTIAL RENT does not mean rent which on the same land frequently varies: it may be so called because the differences of desirability greatly influence the amount of rents paid for one and another portion of land or water. Not that these differences cause the existence of rent, as some pretend: that existence is caused by scarcity of land, and would arise if all land had the same desirability: what the differences cause is the variation in the amount of rent.

When all the most desirable land that can be got at is occupied, then as population multiplies inferior land will be taken in; rent will be paid on the better land; and the amount of rent will depend on the difference between the desirability of the better and the worse land taken in (better and worse being taken to include situation as well as fertility).

I have used the words "that can be got at:" I have a special meaning in this. The Theory of Rent (*i.e.* of Differential Rent) has been made to rest on the assumption that the land first occupied will be that of the highest desirability as to fertility and nearness to markets: but Mr. Carey and others have shown that frequently the most desirable land lies in the bottom of valleys or hollows covered with water, the sediment from which has enriched the soil; and that the early settlers, not having the means of draining, have occupied land of inferior desirability. The first land occupied then, is that which is at once available and most desirable.

Mr. de Quincey I think it is, who tells us that his mirror of poets, Wordsworth, made a similar objection:—"You say that the best farm-land is occupied first: now we have lately had a common ploughed up, and it turns out to be the best land in the parish."

It has been suggested that if this new land had been left *waste* previously, the objection would have had weight. But it was common land, and the commoners' rights prevented the farmers from enclosing and cultivating it: the rights acted partly like the water in the American valleys; they prevented the land from being available for ordinary farming: they did not, like the water, prevent the use of the land, but they kept it in a state of imperfect cultivation.

I have said that as population multiplies, inferior land is taken into cultivation. Another effect follows: the increase in price of food is an inducement to farmers to apply more labour and to buy bones and artificial manures; *i.e.* to use additional capital. But it does not follow that the farmer will therefore be able to pay a higher rent: the additional crops he gets may be only enough to replace his expenditure with the ordinary rate of farming profit. If he were thoughtlessly to apply still more capital, that might result in loss instead of profit. Each dose of capital (to use a French term) tends to produce less than did the former dose.

IMPROVEMENTS'-RENT.—A large part of the farmer's annual payment to his landlord is not Differential Rent. The land as it exists is only partly a Gift of Nature: man has added walls or hedges, ditches, drains, roads, farm-buildings: these have been produced by capital and the labour it employs. The annual payment for these has been named by Mr. William Mathews, Improvements'-Rent.

In some cases the whole annual payment is of this kind: as for instance where convicts have been set to break up barren moors and sands, to a small extent in England, and to a greater extent in Belgium. In mountainous countries, peasants are found cultivating the hill-sides, by forming terraces and carrying up soil to clothe them: if they let these it would be on an Improvements'-Rent.

CAPITAL-RENT } is a wider term, including many other
OR } things besides Improvements'-Rent, from
PRINCIPAL-RENT } that of a mansion down to that of a stocking-machine: in fact of all Human Productions. Principal-Rent is the true expression; but unfortunately it would be taken incorrectly to mean chief-rent.

MONOPOLY-RENT results from an artificial monopoly of the Gifts of Nature. The govérnments of the United States and of our Australasian colonies require immigrants to buy their land; and the interest on the purchase money is virtually a rent: but this is not more than a few pence per year; and though in form it results from a monopoly, in reality it is in some cases no more than the cost of surveying and selling the land.

Our Indian government collects 20 millions £ a year as land-tax; and this is really a rent, and in form a Monopoly-Rent: but the charge per acre is so moderate, and so much less than that of the native states, that it would probably be much higher if the land, as in Ireland, belonged to private owners, who would take the highest Differential Rents that were offered. This is confirmed by the miserable condition of the ryots in Bengal, where, under the Cornwallis-Settlement, the land is in the hands of the Zemindars.

In the native states, I have said, the land-tax is much higher than in British India: many of the rulers squeeze the last rupee out of their subjects, without caring if they exact more than would be paid as differential-rent.

UNEARNED INCREMENT } seem to be the same thing. John
AND } Stuart Mill describes it as "a kind
SPONTANEOUS-RENT } of income which continually tends to increase, without any exertion or sacrifice on the part of the owners." Mill assumed that the income from land always increases: if he had lived till the present day he would have learnt that it sometimes diminishes: as for example in the case of a neighbour of mine who took a large plot of building land about 1874, at £2,000 a year for 99 years; immediately afterwards there began

a long period of national adversity, and as the land could not be underlet, there was the ruinous loss of nearly £2,000 a year for an indefinite period. Immediately afterwards came the stoppage of the Midland Corporation, with losses counted by scores of thousands of pounds.

If the Government claimed the profits on the increased value in certain cases, ought they not to recoup the losses in other cases?

It has also been asked why the Unearned Increment of land only should go to the Exchequer? Why not that of other property?

For instance :—Lord Beaconsfield, on behalf of the nation, laid out *4* millions £ in the purchase of Suez Canal Shares : these rose in value to 8, 10, 12 millions £. Why should not the Khedive say that the unearned increment of 4, 6, or 8 millions £ should be his? He might urge in his own favour that of the millions which the Canal cost, a large part was given by his father.

SPONTANEOUS ASCENDING } arises spontaneously in a nation
OR } like the British, which is advancing
PROSPERITY-RENT } in well-being.

SPONTANEOUS DESCENDING } arises spontaneously in a nation
OR } like the Irish, which is retro-
ADVERSITY-RENT } grading.

The distinction perhaps is of no great value, and I might have omitted it but that I found it copied from me by Mr. G. B. Dixwell of Boston, who by quoting it as mine showed that he thought it useful.

DISTRIBUTION } Distribution has been used in two distinct
AND } senses : first, it is said that the products of
PARTITION. } labour are distributed to the landlord, the farmer, and the labourer, as rent, profit, and wages. Assuming this statement of fact to be correct, I still object to say here distributed, preferring to limit the word to its second signification. It may be better to say that the products of labour are partitioned among certain classes, just as Poland in the last century was partitioned among Austria, Russia, and Prussia.

DISTRIBUTION.—Secondly, to Distribute means, and is fitly used to mean, to spread over the world. The products of labour are spread or distributed over the world by means of transport, trading, money, and protection by governments.

TRANSPORT means Distribution by roads, canals, railways, sailing and steam vessels.

PARTITION.—It appears inaccurate to say that *all* the products of capital and labour are partitioned ("distributed") among landlords, capitalists, and labourers. None of these products can be securely enjoyed, indeed they could never come into existence, without the protection of government: and this could not exist without taxation. In this kingdom, about a tenth of all the annual produce of capital and labour goes as taxes: as much probably as the rents of land in town and country. Therefore as to the partitioning of the annual produce, the Government must be classed with the landlords as receivers.

It may seem that annuitants are in the same position as the Government. But the annuitants of the National Debt merely receive part of the taxes: mortgagees are for the time part owners of the mortgaged property: annuitants under family settlements are nearly the same. Annuitants therefore, do not form a separate class in partitioning the annual produce, but take a portion of the shares of the other classes.

If it should be objected that what is true of annuitants is true of the receivers of taxes, I reply that annuitants are in many cases accidental and unnecessary, whereas government is absolutely necessary. I should be sorry to suggest that annuitants who are pensioners of government are accidental and unnecessary: a soldier or sailor who has served for a quarter of a century, an Indian civil officer who retires at 50 to 60, takes his pension as "deferred pay" for services.

PARASITES.—There are no doubt, numbers of persons who live upon their neighbours and do nothing in return: habitual criminals and tramps, paupers, become such by wilful idleness and by the illness or death of their husbands and fathers. There are also the idle, vicious, men-about-town; living in clubs and frequenting haunts worse than clubs: performing no duties and corrupting the people about them.

Such men are Parasites of the body politic.

BUSINESS AND TRADE. By Business is meant any occupation in which the income is mostly made by the employment of capital. There are occupations which employ a little capital, and yet are not classed as business or trade: solicitors and accountants require some money, though not much, in carrying on their professions. We talk of the business of a farmer, a dealer, a manufacturer, a carrier, a banker. Farming is a business but not a trade.

A trader is properly one who buys and sells: "one engaged in merchandise or commerce," says Johnson: but we now extend the term to most men of business, except farmers.

In several of these Definitions, I am guided by the maxim of Malthus, that we should use words as educated men generally use them.

UNDERTAKER means in ordinary discourse, one who undertakes funerals. John Stuart Mill regretted that it was not used as the French economists use *entrepreneur*:—a projector, a promoter of schemes. Mill might have known that Adam Smith does use it in speaking of the improvements of Scotch estates.

PROFIT is income earned by carrying on a business.

EXCHANGE } Dealing is in its simplest form, Barter. When
BARTER. } civilized men go among savages, they barter with them: they exchange a hatchet for a skin; or a string of beads for the carcase of a deer. On the west coast of Africa, the negroes bring down hogsheads of palm oil, for which they take rum or "bars:" the bar consisting of a flint gun, some matchets (macheta or cutlass), some beads or cowries; the bar itself varying in value with the state of oil as to supply and effective demand, and with the number of European vessels competing with each other.

INVESTMENT. } *Investment* is buying or lending with the
SPECULATION. } intention of earning money. If I buy iron
GAMBLING. } I do this hoping to sell it again at a profit. If I lend £1,000 to a railway I hope to receive 3 or 4 per cent. per annum upon that sum. These are investments.

If I lend £1,000 to a friend without any charge for interest, that is not an investment: if I stipulate for payment of interest, that makes it an investment.

SPECULATION is investment at a considerable risk with the expectation of unusual profit. High interest means bad security, said the Duke of Wellington. Time-bargains require no actual investment but only create a liability: these certainly are speculative.

GAMBLING is playing extravagantly for money, or speculating extravagantly.

MONEY. ⎱ It is unnecessary to describe money, with which
COIN. ⎰ everyone is familiar from infancy. Nor is any careful definition required: Johnson says it is "metal coined for the purposes of commerce;" but it is now used in a wider sense, since we say that the pretty little shell, the cowrie, is the money of African tribes.

Coin is "money stamped with a legal impression." We Englishmen knew formerly that $44\frac{1}{2}$ guineas fresh from the mint contained a pound troy of gold, of standard fineness (11 of pure gold to 1 of alloy): since guineas have ceased to be coined, we know that 46 sovereigns and 14s. 6d. contain the same pound troy. This saves us from the trouble imposed upon the Romans, who had to send for the *libripens* with his scales to weigh the copper tendered to a creditor.

Some authors, in search of a generalization, affirm that money is a commodity, like wheat or calico. This is going too far: gold-dust or a nugget is a commodity like wheat or calico; but when it is refined, mixed with alloy, stamped, milled, it is not used as a commodity, but as a means of paying for commodities: just as a bushel of wheat would be something more than an ordinary bushel, if a government department cleaned it, weighed and measured it, and tested its exact quality.

This suggests an answer to a question often asked:—What is meant by the "Price of Gold?" It means the price of uncoined gold (dust or nuggets) in coined gold. It happens that the coined gold given at the Mint for uncoined gold is identical in fineness and weight: $44\frac{1}{2}$ fresh guineas weighed a pound troy, and these guineas are given for a pound troy of gold-dust or nuggets of standard fineness; but this is because the Mint charges nothing for its trouble in coining. Lord Sherbrooke when he was Chancellor of the Exchequer as Mr. Robert Lowe, proposed that the Mint should charge a seignorage for coining: if that unwise project had been adopted, a pound troy of gold-dust would still have been paid for with $44\frac{1}{2}$ guineas, but those guineas would have contained less than a pound troy. The price of a pound of unrefined gold at present is a pound of coined gold: it would then have been less than a pound of coined gold.

Though coin is not a mere commodity at home, it is such as between one nation and another. If we sent 44½ guineas to Paris, these were accepted only as a troy pound of standard gold: if by means of a seignorage at the Mint, the 44½ guineas had had only 11 oz. and 15 dwt. they would have been accepted only as that weight of gold.

From this notion that gold coined into money is a commodity, arises a second notion: that if we find commodities generally cheap, it follows that gold, coined gold, is dear; and vice versâ. Now in 1885 commodities generally were very cheap: wheat had fallen to the low rate of the middle of last century; iron and coal were at their lowest; calico and woollens were the same: the farmers, the landlords, the manufacturers, were much distressed.

In 1885 then, commodities being unusually cheap, gold money ought to have been unusually dear.

Now, when things are dear they are generally scarce. But in 1885, gold was not scarce: on the contrary, it was abundant; the national banks of England, France, and New York, held among them nearly 100 millions £, a sum greatly in excess of what they required.

Again, when things are dear borrowers pay at a high rate for the use of them: when houses sell at a high price they let at high rents; when hunters go up in price a hirer pays much for a day's sport. If then in 1885 gold were dear, a high rate would be paid for the use of it: but in 1885 a low rate was paid: good 3 months' bills were discounted about Midsummer at less than 1 per cent. *per annum*, and in some cases at ½ per cent. *per annum*, instead of the ordinary 2 or 3 or 4 per cent.

Apparently then, gold coin was at once abundant and dear: was at once lent at a low rate and yet dear. Imagine anyone saying that about the year 1800 wheat was abundant though it was selling at a famine price, and that in 1885 it was scarce though the price was the lowest of the century!

Cheapness of gold coin and dearness of merchandise are not convertible terms.

The case was different at the gold-fields when they were first discovered: gold was abundant; commodities for a time were scarce: prices rose vastly; and cheap gold-dust did mean dear commodities.

RISE AND FALL IN VALUE OF GOLD,⎫ When gold falls in
ENHANCEMENT AND DEPRECIATION. ⎭ value it is said to be depreciated. When it rises in value, it *may* be said to be enhanced. Depreciation and Enhancement are correlative.

An attempt has been made, and unfortunately with success, to use the word *ap*preciation instead of enhancement. To me this seems a mistake. I might object on the ground that the new term has another and familiar meaning; as when we say that we have a high appreciation of laborious attempts to give clear definitions. Putting this objection aside, I dislike the term because it tends to confuse a reader and still more a listener. A professor lecturing on money, and mentioning the appreciation of gold, would be often misunderstood to say *de*preciation, to the ruin of his argument. The case is like that of the words starboard and larboard applied to the right-hand side and left-hand side of a ship: the words were in practice so often confounded by steersmen, with ill results, that larboard was abolished, in favour of port; so that now instead of starboard and larboard we have port and larboard. For similar reasons I prefer depreciation and enhancement to depreciation and appreciation.

The French carry this objection very far: under the head *assonance* they forbid the use in one sentence of words of such general resemblance as *autel* and *orteil*.

For the same reason it is better not to compare "the United States" with "the United Kingdom," but rather to compare them with "Great Britain and Ireland.

Here is another example. Railway and other companies have stocks or shares of various characters. There are ordinary stocks and preferred stocks. The preferred stocks pay a certain dividend before the ordinary stocks pay anything. Besides these there are deferred stocks which by agreement pay nothing for a certain term of years. Brokers and newspapers delight in the antithesis "preferred and deferred:" I object to it because though it is quite precise it is confusing to the comparatively uninformed investor, who will be likely to say or even write preferred when he means deferred. It is better to say preferred and postponed.

WHAT IS A POUND? is a question inevitably suggested by the "Price of Gold." On no definition has more nonsense been talked. Yet it is not for us to boast of superiority, when we know that so sound a thinker as John Locke was unable to satisfy himself with a reply; and that it was the genius of Sir Isaac Newton which determined that a pound is a certain weight of gold or silver: we may be sure that we minor lights should not have outshone Locke; and we may concede that probably we should have adopted Mr. Bosanquet's definition at a later date:— a pound is "a sense of value with reference to commodities;" or the amusing *petitio principii*:—"a pound is the interest of £33. 6s. 8d. at 3 per cent.:" *i.e.* a pound is $\frac{3}{100}$th of 33 pounds and $\frac{1}{3}$d.: *i.e.* a pound is a pound. At present we may say that a pound is a little more than a quarter of an ounce of gold of standard fineness (123·274 grains out of 480 grains contained in an ounce).

BANK-NOTES AND CHEQUES. } Are Bank-Notes money? During a Panic, if a trader complains that no money is to be had though he has thousands owing to him, he does not mean that coin is scarce: he is commonly paid in bank-notes and he prefers these to sovereigns as being more portable: to him bank-notes are money.

But the trader may also regard a cheque as money. Yet not exactly: for during a Panic, when credit is precarious, the receiver of a cheque goes straight to the bank and cashes it: the cheque is not on the level of notes and coin.

In a country district no doubt, a cheque received is sometimes passed from hand to hand in payment of accounts, and does not reach the drawer's bank for weeks or months. The cheque performs some of the functions of a bank-note, but it is not called money.

VALUE, says Adam Smith, has two meanings: value-in-use, and value-in-exchange.

VALUE-IN-USE.—Air is of the highest value-in-use, since without it we cannot live: yet as it cannot be appropriated it has no value-in-exchange. Value-in-use however, is not a term adopted in ordinary life.

Bentham founded his system of morals on utility: honesty, he maintained, was a virtue because it promoted the greatest happiness of the greatest number: this was its utility, he said; he did not say this was its value-in-use.

DESIRABILITY. ⎱ It has been proposed therefore, to substitute
UTILITY. ⎰ utility for value-in-use. But the word utility
is ambiguous. Nothing, it is said, can have a price, unless it
possesses utility. Now there are two ornaments in the world of
which the price is reckoned by hundreds of thousands of pounds
sterling: I mean the Pitt diamond the property of the crown of
France from the days of St. Simon and the Regent Orleans, and
the Koh-i-noor (the Mountain of Light) a recent acquisition of
the British crown. Shall we say that these are useful? that they
have utility? Shall we not rather say that they are objects of
desire, because, having much beauty, they are very rare. For the
word utility let us substitute desirability.

Extraordinary prices have been given of late for objects of
virtu. The late Lord Dudley gave ten thousand guineas for the
Coventry *garniture*-de-cheminée: "it has two great qualities, excessive rarity and absolute beauty and perfection." On the 19th
December, 1884, Mr. Quaritch bought to sell again, a *Psalmodum
Codex*, printed in 1549, on vellum; he gave £4,950 for it: "this
is the second book with a date, and contains the Athanasian
Creed printed for the first time." In 1883, the executors of the late
Warden of Wadham College, sold "a first state of Rembrandt's
etching of the advocate van Tol," for £1,510. The armour of
Francis I. of France, who died in 1547, was bought some years
ago for £100, was resold for £1,000, then for £4,000, and
within 24 hours for £17,000: afterwards, dug out of the ruins
after the burning of the London Pantechnicon, it went as old
iron, but being pieced together actually realized £12,000.

Shall we say that these costly toys were useful? that they
possessed utility? or rather that they were desirable, and possessed
desirability?

VALUE ⎱ Then as to value-in-exchange: this is not a
IN ⎰ term used in the world: we do not ask, what is
EXCHANGE. ⎰ the present value-in-exchange of bread, calico
copper; we ask what is the price of the things. Price is the
money for which an article will exchange: it is the value-in-
exchange reckoned in money. A certain sideboard sells for
£46. 14s. 6d.; *i.e.* it exchanges for the gold contained in 44½
guineas, or a pound troy of gold of standard fineness.

Value therefore, has two meanings :—desirability, and price.

VALUE OF MONEY.—We constantly find this term used in the money-articles of newspapers :—" The value of money has risen so much, that bills discounted last week at 2 per cent. cannot now be done under 3 per cent. :" the value of money is here judged by the rate of interest. Purists say that this is inaccurate, since the value of a thing (*i.e.* the value-in-exchange) is what it will exchange for. No doubt this is the primary meaning of value or price. After the discovery of Potosi and other mines, the English prices of wheat gradually rose greatly. Our average price of wheat (reckoned in our present weight of coin) was,

From 1453 to 1497 . £0 14 1 the quarter.
From 1561 to 1601 . . 2 7 5 ,,
From 1621 to 1636 . . 2 10 0 ,,

Everyone says that this great rise was really a fall in the value of gold and silver: wheat exchanged for more gold or silver; silver or gold exchanged for less wheat. Now it is said, when a money-article asserts that money has risen in value, it ought to mean that a sovereign will exchange for more commodities: but it does not mean this; it means that more interest will be given for the temporary use of it.

We must concede that in these money-articles the word value is not used in its primary sense. It is used in a secondary sense. Such is the inevitable fate of words in frequent employment. Suppose you apply to an agent about a certain house, and he tells you that its value has risen greatly: you reply that you remember its being sold twenty years ago for £2,000 and you ask what is the price; is it £2,500 or £3,000? The agent answers that the house is not on sale, and that when he said that its value had risen he meant that its rent had risen. The value of the house is estimated in two different modes: first by its saleable value, and secondly by its letting value (or rent).

So the value of money is estimated in two different modes: first by the commodities it will purchase, and secondly by the interest it will bring.

PRICE.—I say that price is the money for which a commodity will exchange. During the season of 1884-5 the price of potatoes was 3s. the cwt.; *i.e.* a cwt. of potatoes exchanged for 3s.

Among the various commodities, there are three classes, which follow respectively different laws as to price. (1) Manufactures are sold on the average according to their cost; which consists mainly of the wages paid in producing them, and of the profit on the capital employed. This cost is much reduced as population, skill, and capital increase; these causing greater division of labour and a growth of machinery. I have said *mainly* of wages and profit, because there is the element, sometimes considerable, of the Gifts of Nature, as in a cowshed where the boards, cut from a natural forest, are a considerable element.

(2) Then comes agricultural produce. We are often told that wheat is a manufacture as calico is. No doubt, wheat like calico is a result of labour and capital. But the price of wheat is not determined, like the price of calico, by its cost in wages and profit: the price of wheat rises as population increases because fertile land becomes scarce; and rises also in new colonies as the means of transport to markets become more plentiful and cheaper.

The average price of wheat in England was—

From 1666 to 1706	£2	1	0
From 1766 to 1786	2	9	0
For many years before 1846	2	15	0
War prices much higher: 1796 to 1815	4	9	0

But from this £4. 9s. 0d. some deduction has to be made for the depreciation of the currency during the years 1802 to 1815, bringing down the price perhaps to under £4.

Milk, eggs, dairy produce, have risen greatly since the last century.

On the other hand, hardware, clothes, furniture, have fallen greatly.

During the last few years wheat has fallen again to the prices of last century. This has been caused by the removal of restrictions on importation and the cheapness of transport.

We see the distinction then:—manufactures are on the average sold according to their cost: agricultural products rise in price as land gets scarce. This is because the supply is less than the effectual demand. When the supply is increased by additional importation, the price falls again.

Commodities of the third class are those which cannot be

increased at all. Aërolites furnish an example: no man can attract them from the sky to the earth. Though aërolite dust reaches us by tons every year, or perhaps every week, yet it is not often that we meet with a portion large enough to use as an amulet. Now suppose that in 1832, when the cholera was first heard of in Eastern Europe, and men held their breath as they read from day to day how it was creeping westward, it had been announced and believed that a portion of aërolite used as an amulet, was an absolute safeguard from contagion: the price might have risen to £1 an ounce, or £100 an ounce: it would have been determined solely by the relation of the absolutely limited supply to the effectual demand.

Supply and Effectual Demand. } The phrase commonly used is Supply and Demand. But a learner is apt to confound demand with desire; as there are always hungry families, there is always a desire for food; but this desire is not an effectual demand, since many of the hungry families have not the means of payment. Adam Smith says:—
"A very poor man may be said in some sense to have a demand for a coach and six; he might like to have it; but his demand is not an effectual demand." It is safer I say, to use the phrase, Supply and Effectual Demand.

The results of this relation are often misunderstood. It makes all the difference, we are told (and this is the opinion of Malthus), whether workmen are seeking a master, or a master is seeking workmen: this determines the rate of wages. Not so. It is true that the condition of the Labour-Market makes a difference and a considerable one; but it is untrue that it principally determines the rate. Yet we find excellent economists besides Malthus maintaining the doctrine that the ratio of supply to effectual demand is the determining cause: *e.g.*, J. B. Say maintained it; so did Professor Richard Jones.

Suppose that in consequence of emigration, and migration to English towns, the farmers are short of hands; they have to raise wages from 12s. up to 14s. a week.

At the same time, trade being bad, numbers of mechanics want work: the employer may lower wages from 35s. to 28s. a week.

The rate of wages of the ill-employed mechanics is still twice as high as that of the fully employed farm-labourers. The relation of Supply to Effectual Demand has raised farm wages and has lowered artizans' wages: but it is not this relation which has made the standard or ordinary wages higher in the case of the artizans.

The same erroneous opinion has prevailed with regard to commodities. So high an authority as John Locke, wrote:— "that which regulates the price, is nothing else but their quantity in proportion to their vent." Malthus agreed with this dictum. Ricardo, on the other hand, disputed it.

Suppose that, on a market-day, all the hurdles are cleared off, and that the afternoon buyers may even have had to pay an extra 10 per cent. At the same time few ploughs having been sold, the price may have fallen 10 per cent. Yet a good plough may still bear a price equal to that of a load of hurdles. The relation of Supply to Effectual Demand has raised the price of hurdles and has lowered the price of ploughs: it has disturbed prices, but it has not determined the standard or ordinary prices.

It has not determined the actual prices for a single day: much less will it do so permanently; for the rise in price of hurdles will increase the supply, and the fall in price of ploughs will diminish the supply, so that possibly on the next market-day, the hurdles offered may rise beyond the effectual demand, and the ploughs offered may be short of it. In the long run, the supply of both will be about equal to the effectual demand; and therefore it *cannot be* that relation which makes a hurdle sell for less than a plough.

I must defer the further discussion of this question.

WAGES, or Wage: may be defined, according to Johnson, payment for service.

This includes the salary of a clerk, the pay of a soldier, the stipend of a clergyman; though it must be conceded that in the conversation of educated people a clergyman is not said to earn wages.

REAL WAGES. } Wages are usually reckoned in money.
TRUCK. } Real Wages are wages paid in kind, *i.e.* in commodities. Domestic servants are paid partly in money and partly in kind. When manufacturers pay their hands in kind, that is called Truck. The practice of Truck is justly forbidden

by law, on account of the abuses to which it leads when the employers are unscrupulous.

Economists like to know the real wages at different periods.

Early in the last century wheat was as low as 1s. a peck, and therefore a labourer, with wages at 6s., earned . 6 pecks a week.
Later in the century wheat was dearer, even during peace, by one-half, and where wages remained at 6s., the labourer earned only . 4 ,, ,,
From 1800 to 1815, during the war, wheat was so high, that if the labourer had had but 6s. a week to live on, he would have had only . 2 ,, ,,
In 1885 wheat was as cheap as early in last century, and with 12s. a week the labourer earned . . . . 12 ,, ,,

This comparison is more instructive than one of money-wages.

NECESSARIES OF LIFE. ⎫ The Necessaries of Life ought to
   SUPERFLUITIES. ⎬ be supplied by the lowest wages
     LUXURIES. ⎭ earned. But what are Necessaries?
It has commonly been said that they are all things necessary to support life and keep up the population. If this be a correct definition, then the Irish, before the famine of 1845—52, had the necessaries of life; for they lived and far more than kept up their numbers. The term I think, may be taken to mean much more: *viz.*, all things necessary to maintain health and vigour.

Economists generally have recognized only necessaries and luxuries: I add superfluities: for it can hardly be said that beer and tobacco are to most persons necessary: yet they can hardly be regarded as luxuries: they are at most superfluities.

To PRODUCE has two meanings; to bring forward and to call into being. (1) "The policeman produced the purse:" *i.e.* he brought it forward. (2) "The farmer in his great field produced 100 quarters of wheat:" *i.e.* he called the wheat into being.

LABOUR means human effort generally, but bodily effort especially.

By the Labours of Hercules we mean the laborious tasks he performed: the slaying of the Lernaean hydra; the cleansing of the Augean stables.

In the expression Labour against Capital, we understand

Labourers against Capitalists. Labour-Market means the collective body of employers and labourers.

Is Labour, Capital? Many intelligent labourers wish to say yes, fancying that they thus add to its dignity. Now take the case of a slave employed on a plantation: he is on the same footing with a horse; reared or bought, fed, and compelled to work: he is capital. His bodily exertion is not capital but produces it. The free workman is not the property of anyone and is not capital: his bodily exertion, like that of the slave, is not capital but produces it.

What then, is his labour? It is a productive force, like the active qualities of the soil, the air, the rain.

We shall see elsewhere that land is not capital, and for this reason among others, that it follows a different economic law: the income from land is rent, that from capital is profit; and we know that rent and profit follow different laws, rent *e.g.* generally rising as profit falls. Similarly, capital and labour follow different laws, and so different that in the eyes of many persons capital and labour are antagonistic. Certainly, they cannot be the same thing.

PRODUCTIVE LABOUR may be defined: all labour which accomplishes a desirable end. The labour of farmers and their men are productive of crops: that of manufacturers and their men are productive of goods. The labour of a domestic servant is productive of services.

Economists have strangely refused the epithet productive to labour which renders only services: the skill and attentions of a physician they call unproductive, although they recruit the vigour and save the life of producers of commodities.

PRODUCTIVE COST is a term improperly substituted for cost of production.

UNPRODUCTIVE LABOUR is labour which fails to accomplish a desirable end. Unproductive persons are those who neither produce commodities nor render services: *fruges consumere nati*.

REPRODUCTIVE, so far as I know, is not as yet applied to this subject. We see the meaning of it if we say that the horse and the mule are both of them productive in drawing loads and carrying burdens; but that the horse also reproduces his race, whereas the mule is barren and not reproductive of his race.

All labour which accomplishes a desirable purpose is productive.

But reproductive is another thing. It is better applied to capital than to labour. If you employ a man for a year, at a cost of £80, in mowing your lawns, rolling your walks, and tending your flowers, you have had during the year great satisfaction in the sights and odour of your flower-garden. But this does not give you the means of employing the man the next year: you have used the £80 productively only; you have got from it pleasant sights and odours.

If at the same time you have employed a number of labourers for a year in raising potatoes for sale, and having expended £300 upon them you get a return of £350, you earn a profit of £50; and besides this you have your £300 ready for the same farming next year. The capital has reproduced itself.

If J. B. Say had understood this, he would have defined capital, not as everything which produces, but as everything which reproduces itself: he would have avoided the mistake of saying that your easy chair is capital because it gives you rest; and that champagne is capital because it gives you pleasure: he would have called the easy chair capital to the upholsterer, because when it is sold it reproduces itself with a profit; he would have called champagne capital to the wine merchant, because when it is sold it reproduces itself with a profit.

If your gardener were employed in raising vegetables and fruit, he would partly reproduce the sum spent on him: he would save you part of your income you spent in the market; and that part you might use in partially supporting the gardener next year. Such a gardener's labourer and wages are partly reproductive.

DIVISION OF LABOUR.—This term has been objected to as ambiguous or even misleading. It might be so if it were new; but in fact it is old and well understood. If for example, talking of retail dealers, you say that formerly in a small town the same man sold calico and tea and earthenware: that later on, and especially in large towns, one man sold only draperies, another groceries, and another earthenware: that to the surprise of the world shops are now found in London where you may buy everything from a needle to an elephant, you denounce this latest development as inconsistent with the principle of the Division of Labour. Everyone knows what you mean.

Even if we could find a better term it would be difficult, if not impossible to get it substituted: we should not get men to say as Gibbon Wakefield would have them say:—the division of lawyers into solicitors and barristers is a good example of "the Distribution of Employments:" we might perhaps get a few men to say, a good example of the Division of Labour*s* (in the plural): taking the word in the sense of the Labours of Hercules (his laborious tasks).

LAISSEZ-FAIRE. Objections are raised to the use of this French expression.

We are asked why we do not say Let-alone. We reply that we use this French expression just as we use the terms Political Economy or Division of Labour: they are naturalized in the language, and cannot be treated as aliens. Auguste Comte says that the people make the language: if so it is a hopeless task to alter it.

During the centuries of hostility to France from our Edwards to our Georges, our soldiers would no doubt have been glad to shake off the French terms of their profession: portcullis (porte-coulisse, a groove door), dungeon (donjon), serjeant (sergent, serjent, serriant, one who locks or serries the rank and file), bastion, glacis, esplanade. French patriotism too, must revolt against the adoption of English sea-terms: quille (keel), brique (brig); and must be wounded on board a French steamer by the cries, easère, stopère.

As we cannot make or unmake the language, we must submit to what is impressed upon us by the people, who, as Auguste Comte says, make the language. Laissez-faire is so imposed upon us.

ERRATA.

PAGE	LINE	
41	—	Heading: "Lesson" should be "Lessen."
47	30	For "immigration" read "immigrating."
74	15	Omit "also."
99	13	Omit "who."
105	25	For "disciplined" read "discipline."
120—199		The heading should be "Mr. Spencer's Barbarism."
185	27	For "was unmarried" read "had no family."
213	8	For "1813" read "1873."
220	21	Omit "for it."
226	14	For "including" read "excluding."
276	—	A treaty ratified since this was printed, has partly rectified the injustice.

Chapter I.

INTRODUCTION.

FIRST PART.

I.

THE DISMAL SCIENCE.

POLITICAL Economy! says the man of sense and humanity:—"the Philosophy of Selfishness!" I fear that he is right.

Not that Adam Smith or Jeremy Bentham taught such an odious philosophy: the opprobrium falls on Malthus, Ricardo, the elder Mill, the early Westminster Reviewers. I was sorry lately to see a small treatise for beginners laying down the same hateful doctrine, condemning the exercise of charity, and instilling the philosophy of selfishness into the minds of youth. As to Mr. Herbert Spencer, his sins in that way are past redemption.

Political Economy! says the humourist:—"the Dismal Science!"

Carlyle has been blamed for having christened political economy the Dismal Science: it has been thought that he should have shown more respect for a favourite subject of his friend John Stuart Mill: but the rugged egotistical Scotch peasant, despite his genius, must have changed his nature before he could learn to spare the feelings of an associate or even of a wife. Indeed if he had done nothing worse than this witty depreciation of social science, he might receive a free pardon. For us the question is, whether political economy has been and must be a dismal science.

In the hands of some writers it has been dismal, because it has been treated in a formal and dry fashion. To say nothing of Gournay, of whom we know little, the French Économistes, and Quesnay especially just before Adam Smith, while founding their system on the interesting problem whether all taxes fall on rent, discussed the matter in so scholastic and formal a mode as to make their treatises unreadable.

On the other hand, Adam Smith is interesting even after a lapse of a hundred years. It is true that he is sometimes diffuse and discursive; so that we may partly apply to him what Johnson said of Warburton: "he goes round and round his subject and seldom reaches it; but then we like to go round and round with him." Adam Smith also goes round and round, but unlike Warburton he often reaches his subject; and whether he wheels in mid-air or settles on solid ground, he carries his readers with him. J. B. Say also is quite readable:

and though his system is damaged by his loose and unphilosophical notions of capital, he is interesting as well as useful, because he writes on "*Practical* Political Economy," and abounds in facts.

II.

ADAM SMITH'S SUCCESSORS: DULNESS, SELFISHNESS.

ADAM Smith's eminent successors were dull, very dull. A student may labour through Ricardo and believe that he understands him; but he asks why his doctrine should not have been explained with the clearness of the Wealth of Nations.

It was quite open to Ricardo to confine his attention to a few leading topics, such as rent, profit, wages, taxation: but he ought to have had more regard to facts; he should either have reached his conclusions by induction, or verified them by observation and reading. The absence of this appeal to things as they are, makes his system inconclusive as well as dull and dismal. His contemporary, admirer, and friend, James Mill is open in a lower degree to the same charges.

But the name, Dismal Science, may be justified by the charge I have mentioned, that Political Economy is the philosophy of selfishness.

The answer, the plausible answer, commonly given is, that political economy does not profess to teach morals, but only to discuss the national means of living; and that to condemn it because it does not advise men to be kindly and generous, is as uncalled for as it would be to disparage Loudon's Encyclopædia of Agriculture, because it fails to exhort farmers to go to church on Sundays.

This apology I say is plausible, though I think it is false: false because many economists do not merely fail to recognise charity as a necessary part of the social system, but go much farther, and denounce all charity. They take their stand on justice alone, overlooking the two other foundations of society, benevolence and expediency. When they tell us to give nothing in charity, it is as if Loudon had advised farmers never to go to church.

Malthus was in private kindhearted: yet he denounced poor-laws, because as he thought the good they did was far overbalanced by their mischief in promoting improvident marriages. It is true however, that he was wise enough to learn: and confessed before he died in 1834, that the evils of our poor-laws were far less than he had supposed, because their tendency was much counteracted by the Law of Settlement, which caused the landlords to keep down population by limiting the number of cottages.

Adam Smith, as all his readers know, was friendly to poor-laws. It is strange that the branch of them which he condemns is the Law of Settlement, the very branch which almost reconciled Malthus to the laws. The explanation is simple: Malthus discovered that in modern times population multiplied faster than food: Adam Smith said that an old nation does not double its numbers in less than 500 years; he would have been astonished if a trustworthy prophet had foretold that England and Wales would double in 50 years; viz., from 9 millions in 1801 to 18 millions in 1851: such a prediction might have reconciled him to the law of settlement with its retarding force.

Jeremy Bentham agreed with Adam Smith in the support of poor-laws: he regarded them as absolutely necessary. Yet his followers took the other side in their especial organ, the Westminster Review, established during his lifetime: their thoughtless cry was free-trade in everything; *laissez faire, laissez passer;* let every family take care of itself. "Which is the best?" they said; "to relieve the destitute or to get rid of destitution?" Assuming with a childish and shameful levity, that if we left the improvident, the widows, the orphans, to pine and slowly die, there would in another generation be no improvident, no helpless widows, no destitute orphans. Yet if these shallow and glib economists would but have used their eyes, they would have seen that notorious facts gave the lie to their platitudes : they would have seen Ireland till then without a poor-law, yet with a destitution, a mendicancy, an improvidence, a raggedness, such as to astonish an English visitor: they would have seen the peasant-cultivators of Hindostan without a poor-law, yet always on the verge of absolute want, and so improvident as to require their offspring to marry while still children. Ireland and India without poor-laws, ought to have stopped the mouths of men of education and influence, when they dared to assert that the pauperism of England was caused by her poor-laws.

III.

THE ALMSGIVER CLASSED WITH THE SPENDTHRIFT.

EVEN now, this pestilent heresy of unlimited *laissez-faire* has not died out. A recent abridgment, "Political Economy for Beginners," speaks slightingly of all charity, and not merely of public charity. It preaches the philosophy of selfishness.

It tries to harden the hearts of the young, by teaching them that the true benefactor of society is not the *spendthrift* or the *almsgiver*, but the capitalist. It places in the same category the reckless and the benevolent. It tells its young readers that if they have a little money at command, they should no more spend it on rescuing a starving family than they should spend it on sweetmeats and follies: that if they want to do real good they should invest it so as to bring in an income to themselves.

The writer of such odious doctrine holds, that when Sir Josiah Mason laid out a quarter of a million in founding an orphanage, he deprived the working classes of the benefits they would have enjoyed from having the money used in business.

The writer, I imagine, jumbled together a number of notions true and false.

1. Alms to unknown beggars are not kindness but vicious thoughtlessness.

2. If you want to give an able-bodied man half-a-crown, make him earn it by work.

3. Do the same on a larger scale if you aim at saving a village in decay. Establish a factory if it can be made to pay. This is far better than employing the people in making and maintaining pleasure-grounds, because the capital used in the factory is constantly returning as the goods made are sold, and continues to give employment; whereas the wages paid for the pleasure-grounds must come from some other source, which will perhaps be dried up at your death, or by your caprice.

So far we are all agreed.

But here comes our difference of opinion. The abridgment says that the almsgiver, like the spendthrift, is not a benefactor to society, while the capitalist is a benefactor. Now take the real case of a young widow with an infant and other children, and manifestly unable to support them; a few shillings a week for a year, and still fewer for another or two, will enable her to tide over her difficulties. A kindhearted young lady of some means supplies the want: is she to be classed with spendthrifts? Is she to be told that she is no benefactor of society? I speak of facts within my knowledge. Forty years ago a blight fell on the potato-plant, and the Irish were reduced to the extremity of want: such landlords as continued to receive their rents, did much to relieve the starving: ought they to be classed with spendthrifts? The English public subscribed large sums: were they worthy to be denounced as vicious? The British Government advanced 8 millions £, as a loan, afterwards converted into a gift. Oh spendthrift and disgraceful administration! In Hindostan, famines are so frequent and so widespread, that the central power has arranged for an average charge on the revenues of India, and that to the extent of several millions sterling a year. Inexcusable improvidence and abuse of power, to stand between the cruel eastern droughts and the pauper ryots!

The writer of the abridgment cannot have reflected on the meaning of those foolish and hateful words which class the benevolent with the spendthrift.

IV.

POOR LAW RELIEF NECESSARY THOUGH ABUSED.

BUT objectors will contend, that in vindicating *true* political economy from the imputation of being the dismal philosophy of selfishness, I run into extremes: "you support a system which will relax the self-reliance of Englishmen, already weakened by that pauperizing poor-law you commend: you are no better than a socialist."

As to the poor-law now at work, freed by various statutes and careful administration from the abuses before 1834, I will strenuously defend it at length in the proper place: for the present I will only say, that by induction from facts publicly established, I infer that the recklessness and occasional squalor which we lament, are not peculiar to England but exist everywhere: in France, Germany, Italy, the great cities of the United States.

Look at the Austrians as lately described in a Return of the Inspector appointed by their Government. "Every one has heard of the crushing toil and scanty pay of the Staffordshire nail-makers; but has any one ever heard of anything like the state of affairs reported from Carinthia? The nailsmith works hard, fourteen hours in the day;

his toil commences at three o'clock in the morning, sometimes even earlier. Children from eight to ten years work three hours, from ten to twelve years six hours, those from twelve to fourteen years nine hours. The total earnings at Steinbüchel amount to from 4s. to 8s. per week, at Kropp from 6s. to 10s. per week. He eats three meals a day; but what food is it that is placed upon his table? A dough made of flour and water, swimming in grease; meat only on holidays. There were many years when wages were even lower than they are to-day."

"The factories may be bad, but the mines are ten times worse. From the petroleum mines of Galicia comes a description of a state of things such as we may confidently assert has never existed in Great Britain since Adam Smith helped to stamp out the last traces of slavery in the coal mines and salt pans of the Scottish Lowlands. The workmen, some 12,000 in number, are treated by the cashier like cart horses. The cashier boards and lodges and employs them. For the favour of employment alone the labourer pays the cashier a commission of 10 per cent. of his wages, 10d. to 1s. 8d. for twelve hours' work. The balance of 90 per cent. of his earnings he is compelled to pay to the cashier or his wife for board and lodging and drink. He is always in debt when the balance is struck; so that he neither has the means to clothe himself nor to escape from this truly pitiful slavery. These petroleum slaves, clad in miserable rags, may be seen in droves any day. In order to obtain a correct opinion of the physical and moral degradation of the labourers of Boryslaw, it is quite sufficient to cast a glance into one of the labouring men's quarters, where in one narrow room sixty or seventy persons of both sexes, clad in filthy rags, are lying together so closely that they cannot turn from one side to the other. Whether a labourer breaks his neck or dies miserably matters not; there are always unfortunates ready to step into his place."

I even find that these miseries are not peculiar to Europe and its American issue; for we are told by a Chinese who wrote in 1884, that in his native country the two scourges of society are war *and pauperism.* We are told that in that ancient land you now see bands of blind beggars, many of them lepers, wandering hungry and almost unclothed, seeking for a refuge and finding none. How thoughtless it is then, to say that it is our poor-law which causes our pauperism, when the same condition is found among nations which have no poor-law! But I go much further: I hold that our poor-law much reduces pauperism, a fertile cause of which is dejection and hopelessness: I am convinced that two maxims are unquestionably true :—1. help the poor and they will help themselves; 2. so help the poor that they shall help themselves.

It was the abuses before 1834 which disparaged all poor-laws. No doubt these laws were attacked before the worst evils were general. Witness Arthur Young, a gentleman-farmer, who wrote vigorously against them a hundred years ago. But it was at the end of the last century and at the beginning of the present, that the greatest mischief was done: for at that time, the quartern loaf having risen through the war from 5d. to 10d. and then even above 1s. 3d., the labourers fell into a deplorable state: the farmers and landlords, fearing to raise wages lest they should not fall again when peace was restored, adopted what we now call socialism: *i.e.*, they paid all their men according to their needs, not in proportion to their work; a man had his wages made up out of the rates to a fixed sum for himself, for his wife, and for each of his children.

The labourers claimed this payment as a right. A young couple married on Tuesday, applied for assistance on Friday. This is a case in which the present test of "the house" and separation of married couples would be a cure.

Other abuses and gross ones continued, until the new poor-law of 1834 put an end to them. It was shortly before that time that in the notorious case of Cholesbury in Bucks, the rates so grew as to swallow up the rents, the rector's income, and even the farmers' profits, so that the parish was in danger of becoming a wilderness.

The poor-law Commissioners reported that in this unfortunate parish, the collection of the rate had suddenly ceased, because there were no rate-payers; "the landlords having given up their rents, the farmers their tenancies, and the clergyman his glebe and his tithes."

The impoverished rector, Mr. Jeston, had heard that sixty years earlier there had been only one person in receipt of parish relief: that was twenty years before the rise of prices, the great war, and the systematic payment of wages out of the rates. But "about October last (1833-4) the parish officers threw up their books: . . . . the poor left without any means of maintenance, applied to me for advice and food." Mr. Jeston's income was under £140 a year, but he kept the people alive until he could get for them a rate in aid from an adjoining parish. A great part of the evils were caused by the want of firm administration. The Rev. J. C. Egerton in his *Sussex Folk* lately published, gives a singular example of anarchy about the same time (1833-4). "We had a labour farm, called the "Bough Farm," on which were employed at the *expense of the parish*, 50 or 60 unemployed persons. A labourer on the farm happening one day to pick up a dead robin, was struck with the sudden humour of giving the robin a public funeral; and such was the *powerlessness* of authority at the time, that *two days* were *actually wasted* by all the hands on the farm in carrying out this curious freak."

V.

CHARITY IS NOT SOCIALISM.

WE are told that our poor-law is socialism. What is meant by this charge is that a poor-law is a socialistic measure, and that the supporters of the law act as socialists would act. I reply that "there is a soul of good in things evil," and that the evil thing socialism has in the poor-law a soul of good.

If anyone seriously maintains that in favouring a poor-law I become a socialist, he talks in absurd ignorance or perverse folly. What is Socialism? M. Louis Reybaud claims the invention of the name, but so far as I know he has not defined it. I understand by it the performance by *society* of the functions now performed by the individual: but society is superseded or represented by Government; therefore socialism is the performance by Government of the functions now performed by the individual. At present men and women choose their own employments, but in the golden future they will have this done for them, like slaves or serfs, and like the miserable lower Peruvians before Columbus and Pizarro: at present private capitalists deal with the workmen; in the future private capitalists are to be done away with, and the

Government alone are to find capital and are to employ and pay workmen. Liberty, equality, fraternity, are to reign undisturbed: capitalists are to be extirpated as enemies of working men.

Such are the aims of socialists: we condemn and disclaim these aims: are we socialists then, because we agree with them that it is the duty of Government to alleviate distress and if possible prevent it?

We should not shrink from any measures because socialists approve of them: on the contrary, we should rejoice to find measures which gratify them while they commend themselves to us as at once merciful and just. Such approval redeems political economy from the charge of being the dismal science of philosophical selfishness.

Happily for us, our Parliament has not waited for the reform or reconstruction of the science: with its 670 members, of whom we may say that 70 are pleaders and 600 constitute a jury, or that 70 are orators like Pericles, Lysias, Isæus, Æschines, and their inferiors, while the 600 play the crowd in the Pnyx (a loquacious crowd), our Parliament has never been the servant of pedantic, so-called philosophy: it has always represented the ordinary sense of the nation.

The result has been a Government more or less Paternal; a thing hated by philosophical liberalism and false political economy. No doubt paternal government may be good or bad; it may be the absolute power, a little tempered by good intentions, of a Great Mogul, of a Sultan, of a Philip II., of a Louis XIV., of a Czar. But it may be the really beneficent despotism of our Indian administration, which gives 200 millions of people the Pax Britannica, and which compels Hindoos (Brahmins and Parias), Mahommedans (Sunni, Shia, and Wahabee), Parsees, Sikhs, Rajpoots, and Mahrattas to live peacefully and sit side by side in railways: we may hope that in a few generations, local self-government and even representative general government may arise.

It is through paternal government that India is emerging from barbarism: it is through such a government, gradually liberalized, that we have ourselves arrived at our free and orderly political state. Our Parliament is still more or less Paternal: it imposes many regulations which hereafter may be dispensed with. But moral progress is slow: just as we cannot conceive a time when we shall have no rogues to repress and punish, and no foreign enemies to withstand, so we cannot conceive a time when there shall be no lunatics to restrain, no fools to guide, no spendthrifts and drunkards to rescue from starvation, no deserted wives, no widows and children to assist; a time when no central power will be necessary to limit the retail sale of intoxicating liquors, to regulate common lodging-houses, to raise funds from all for drainage and maintenance of roads, to protect the young from overwork, to force instruction on the ignorant, and authorize public free libraries. All these functions are performed by our Parliament and its executive. We live under a Government still paternal: and advancing democracy calls for more and more of intervention.

VI.

CENSURES EVEN ON FACTORY AND MINES ACTS.

NOW this intervention is just what is condemned by laissez-faire and philosophical Radicalism (though not that of Bentham). The head of these schools is an able and eminent man: Mr. Herbert Spencer. I cannot say what his opinions are at this moment, because through a candour which runs into excess, those opinions are unfixed and in a state of flux. But we know what they were so late as 1884, when he wrote "The Man against the State."

He begins by conceding ironically, that our motives in legislation are as good as those of our ancestors, when they passed laws now generally condemned: our good intentions he puts on a level with theirs, when they tried to check luxury by forbidding certain fashions of dress: when in Scotland they restrained masters of vessels from leaving harbour during winter: when they required all English manufactures to be carried on within ten miles of the Royal Exchange.

From the best of motives we have rushed into foolish enactments without end. We have passed an Act to regulate baby-farming (or as plain people say to check baby-murder): other Acts to make a common lodging-house a decent abode instead of a pandemonium; to prevent certain people from poisoning themselves by taking their meals in match-factories; to shut up public-houses every night and part of Sunday; to hinder the spread of cattle-disease by isolating the beasts already attacked; by regulating the fares of cabs, so that a driver shall not, as in New York, take advantage of a shower to ask 5s. a mile; to determine the quality and price of gas supplied under a monopoly; to confer on local boards the power of raising taxes for the construction of sewers; to assist and restrain tramps. All these *follies* Mr. Spencer ranks with the acknowledged follies of our progenitors.

Factory-Acts generally, he condemns. I wish that those who are likely to be misled by his authority, would read an account of what happened before the first Act was passed. It is remarkable that the earliest and most strenuous supporters of parliamentary interference, were two great manufacturers who had daily experience of the cruelties they deplored: I mean the first Sir Robert Peel and Robert Owen.

Owen asserted that in 1815, the white slavery of British factories was far worse "as regards health, food, and clothing," than negro slavery itself. He said that at New Lanark, orphan children were sent by the overseers of parishes by hundreds, to be worked and maintained by an irresponsible manufacturer and his illiterate subordinates. Children of six years old were condemned to labour ten, twelve, or fourteen hours a day.

Sleepiness and inattention were cruelly punished. At a much earlier period, about 1730, we find a boy, William Hutton, afterwards a well known antiquary and local historian, set to work in a silk-mill at Derby, when he was so short that he had to stand upon stilts: for flagging attention during the tedious hours, he was so inhumanly thrashed that his life was in danger from the gangrened wounds which resulted. Hutton could leave a narrative of his miseries: he was not an orphan: how many unprotected children must have died victims to greed and cruelty!

Owen again, tells us that in his time children were admitted into some mills at five years old: that the time of working, winter and summer, was commonly fourteen hours a day; in some mills fifteen; and in a few hateful instances sixteen.

Factory-Acts have been passed to prevent such

enormities: repeal these and competition would restore the iniquities, or at any rate would partly restore them. We know that even fathers at the present day, in trades to which the factory-acts do not apply, are guilty of much overworking their own children.

Yet Mr. Spencer sneers at these Acts as sentimental fatuities. He maintains in another book, that if the weakly members of the race were killed off, the survival of the fittest would more than compensate us for these tortures of young children, and for the horrible sufferings of the slow death by cold and hunger of unfortunate widows and orphans. So much for the fanaticism of a so-called philosophy!

Other beneficent *follies* have been committed. Acts have been passed to forbid the employment of girls underground, among miners more than half naked: to correct the abuses in lacemaking and bleaching: to rescue young boys from being driven up narrow and sooty chimneys.

Public Health has been cared for by the appointment of inspectors and analysts of food and drink offered for sale, with powers conferred upon magistrates to destroy stinking fish, tainted meat, rotten fruit, and to punish the sellers; powers frequently exercised. Then came *despotic* interference with bakers, forbidding them to store their flour and knead their bread in foul cellars; and going to such arbitrary extremes as to require them to wash walls with soap and water *once in six months*, besides periodical whitewashing and painting. If however, all these precautions add to the cost of baking, the price of the loaf may be raised, since an "assize of bread" has been long ago disused.

To relieve the crowding of towns, railways have been required, in consideration of the monopoly they enjoy, to run trains into the environs at low fares. Public baths and wash-houses have been set up at the expense of the ratepayers. Public parks have been widely opened; many of them gifts of rich men and rich ladies, others bought or laid out with municipal funds.

The philosophical fanatics say:—let us repeal these Acts of Parliament under which are done all these things, apparently good but really pernicious: let us go back to our original liberty which some persons ignorantly call license: let us have dirt, oppression of the young, gross immorality in lodging-houses and mines, rather than lose unfettered freedom of action: Paternal Government is worse than semi-barbarism.

VII.

EDUCATION REQUIRES GOVERNMENT AID.

BUT the vicious eccentricities of legislation do not end here. Education has been seized on as an object of public interest and of great public expenditure. Formerly it was thought that to tax the nation for the building of schools was inexpedient and unjust, like taxing it for the building of churches.

No doubt a father is bound not only to maintain his children but also to educate them: or at any rate a father has no claim of mere justice to have his children educated by others. Unhappily, if no interference takes place, progress is impossible: for the illiterate father does not appreciate book-learning, and he knows that reading and writing are no aids to ploughing or filing: the employer also likes to get his boys young, while they are flexible in mind and body; "just as the twig is bent the tree's inclined." The father naturally prefers the field or factory to the school-house: the means of gain to the demand for payment. He must support his offspring; but education seems to him a duty of imperfect obligation. He may have a dim notion that those who prevent his children from getting wages may justly pay for their school-instruction.

But justice is not the only consideration in this question. Government ought to rest on three principles: firstly justice, secondly mercy, and thirdly expediency so far as it does not clash with the other two.

Even if we reject the poor man's plea, that if Parliament and the School-Board deprive him of his children's wages they may justly be called on to contribute towards their education, there remain the principles of mercy and expediency.

Mercy says that even if justice does not require gratuitous school instruction, yet kindly sympathy may reasonably go far in that direction. The expense in question is a heavy one. A good elementary school cannot be carried on for less than 9d. a week for each child, excluding the holidays. Many cottagers have four children of school age: *i.e.* they would have to pay 3s. a week if all the cost fell on them: but 3s. a week would be a fourth of the ordinary wages of farm-labourers, and nearly as much as the rent paid by many artizans: such a charge mercy forbids.

Experience says that it would make regular school-instruction impossible. Attempts to enforce it at Petty Sessions by fine and imprisonment, would be met with such appeals to the bench and indignant remonstrances by the press, that there would soon be an end of the system. It is difficult now to get the lowest children to attend school regularly: it would then be impossible to get even the better class to do this.

Justice perhaps, mercy and expediency certainly, justify our present system, established under Mr. W. E. Forster's admirable Act of 1870.

Mr. Herbert Spencer classes Mr. Forster's scheme with all those other Acts which he condemns, as the meddlesome silliness of Paternal Government or of Socialism. He even denounces the milder Act of 1860, which provides that factory-boys under 12 who cannot read or write, shall be compelled to go to school: this is disparaged as on a level with the Acts for appointing analysts and inspectors of food and drink.

It is almost as surprising to find a denunciation of the "Public Libraries Act, giving local powers by which a majority can tax a minority for their books."

To me it seems shocking as well as astonishing that such a condemnation should be uttered. Mr. Spencer, a recluse, probably knows nothing of the working of Free Libraries: he does not enjoy the pleasant sight of artizans flocking to read the morning papers in a lofty and well-lighted room, which as they help to pay for it they feel to be partly their own; the pleasant sight of men and youths constantly fetching and returning volumes of the lending-library: he is perhaps ignorant of the fact that in the reference-library, containing books to be read on the spot and not to be taken home, there are the means of high literary culture; that there are on the shelves such works as Dugdale's Monasticon, various editions of Shakespear, the Acta Sanctorum: if he had known all this he would have seen that these libraries, as they are paid for by all classes, so are they for the benefit of all classes.

Then the cost is not much. Out of the 6s. or 7s. in the £. paid by great towns for the whole local rates, one-fortieth part may go to maintain the free libraries. Besides; so careful was Parliament in the Act establishing them, that it did not entrust the power of raising the small necessary funds even to the popularly elected town-councils, but required a plebiscitum (a voting of ratepayers) to confirm or reject a resolution of the Council.

Mr. Spencer, a cordial friend of education, writes like its bitter enemy. The explanation is, that there is a thing he values still more highly, and that is political principle. He belongs to a small class who are troubled with such squeamish consciences, that to be consistent they would cancel the appointments of all chaplains to the army, the navy, the gaols and workhouses, the district pauper schools, because these clergymen are paid out of the taxes, and if they are Protestant, part of their stipend is paid by Roman Catholics, and if they are Roman Catholic, part is paid by Protestants; and again, whether they are Protestant or Roman

Catholic, part of their stipend is paid by Quakers who abhor all paid ministers. The careless world brushes aside these cobwebs of the brain, and thanks heaven that it has not a Parliament of such intractable philosophers, who would make nearly all government impossible, or reduce it to army, navy, police and courts of justice. There has of late been an absurd phrase current :—force is no remedy. Mr. Spencer will have it that force is the only remedy for our ills.

VIII.

MR. SPENCER CONSISTENT. PHILOSOPHICAL VANITY.

MR. Spencer however, has for once been consistent: for so long ago as 1841, when the *Nonconformist* periodical was begun, he successfully used his influence with the dissenters to induce them to refuse a share in the government grant to schools; the result being that the dissenters lost the education of the people, and the church gained the greater part of it.

Such a political conscience is irritated by Mr. Forster's Act of 1870, "which enables the Education Department to form School-Boards, which shall purchase sites for schools, and may provide free schools."

This grand Act, as I think it to be, having the full sanction of the nation, which it would not have had formerly, started an educational and social revolution: a revolution safe because it has come from above, by constitutional means, without the least popular excitement. During the seventeen years since the Act was passed, it has been strenuously and steadily filling up the wide and deep gulf of ignorance: it is raising the mechanic towards the former level of his employer; it is lifting the families of the hodman and the boatman out of the slough of half-barbarism; giving us hopes that as the present children grow into men and women, they will be civilized and orderly persons, instead of being the disgrace of the nation.

The insuperable difficulty before 1870, was to keep pace with the growing population; the school accommodation was always in arrear. Then again, when more school accommodation was provided, the worst of the people were the most backward in using it, though it was their children who especially required culture. Under Mr. Forster's Act, sufficient schools are built from year to year; and under the compulsory clauses generally adopted and enforced, most children are swept in: if some of them learn little, they acquire at least some notions of regularity and decorum.

Not without hardship and injustice, though much less than accompany most revolutions: hardship in preventing the children from earning their customary wages: injustice in calling upon the poorer professional men and the widows and spinsters, to contribute to the instruction of children of artizans earning ample wages; injustice in taxing Roman Catholics, Wesleyans and others, for the support of the Board-Schools, while they also provide schools for the children of their own faith.

Such injustice ought to be corrected; so far as that is impossible, the sufferers must submit to the inevitable cost of promoting the civilization of their nation, which supplies them on the whole, at no ruinous price, with protection and all the other advantages of a thoroughly good government.

To this promotion of civilization, and to the supply of many of these advantages, Mr. Herbert Spencer objects: not because he is hostile or indifferent to them, but because he believes that we pay too high a price, in yielding our individual action to imperial or local authorities.

Let us sum up this long account He condemns wholesale all our Acts of Parliament in favour of the poor, the weak, the oppressed: the Act to save infants from being farmed, neglected, famished, drugged, slowly murdered: that for rescuing young children from working in factories 12 to 15 hours a day, exposed to unfenced machinery, and without education: that for the regulation of mines, requiring sufficient ventilation and means of escape from fire, and forbidding the employment of girls in subterranean darkness among half-clothed men: that for the appointment of analyists and inspectors to check the adulteration of food and medicine, and to punish the use of false measures; that requiring bakers to knead and bake in places superior to hogstyes: that for imposing upon railways as a price for their monopoly, the practice of running cheap workmen's trains: that above all for furnishing (since 1870) good and cheap education and compelling negligent parents to avail themselves of it: that for giving to those persons who can read, the use of newspapers and books as antidotes to the beerhouse and the concert hall.

That all these ends are very good is conceded; but then they are purchased by a sacrifice of liberty. "Liberty, Sir, is the Briton's boast," says the masquerading butler in the Vicar of Wakefield; "it is at once my boast and my terror." But what if liberty degenerate into license? "O Liberté qu'on se moque de toi!" (O Liberty how art thou befooled!) was the despairing cry of the flighty Madame Roland, as she glanced at the hideous statue on her way to the guillotine.

IX.

MR. SPENCER A VISIONARY.

MR. Spencer's state of mind is, to one moving in the ordinary world, unintelligible, and of a morbid if not maniacal eccentricity. But if it cannot be understood it may be accounted for. Mr. Spencer lives in a land of dreams: he has not condescended to the business of life: he has not bought and sold: he has had no clients to advise: he has not taken a brief in a court of law or equity: he has not watched as a clergyman or a medical man by the bedside of the sick or dying: he has not acted as a poor-law guardian, or a municipal councillor, or a justice of the peace, or a chairman of a school-board: he knows little more of men in action than he knows of beavers, apes, or elephants.

If he had been familiar with men and women as they really live, he would have scorned to hint at the money-cost of efforts and institutions intended to raise the standard of well-being, of intelligence, of morality, among his countrymen, and especially among the most miserable and degraded of them. The money-cost to the richest of European nations! to a nation in which one suit of armour was lately sold and re-sold at prices rising gradually to 20,000 £. because it had belonged to Francis I. three or four centuries ago; in which one nobleman gave 10,000 guineas for "the Coventry *garniture de cheminée*;" in which the Gladstone Ministry liberally if wisely gave, on behalf of the nation, £70,000 for a Raphael from Blenheim; in which a noted race-horse, Blair-Athol, sold for £12,500; in which there are men enjoying annual incomes of £100,000 a year; in which an income-tax of six-pence in the £, produced (exceptionally however) in 1884, 12 millions £, while in 1847 it would not have produced half that amount.

Yet Mr. Spencer stoops to count the money-cost. " Partly for defraying the costs of carrying out those ever-multiplying coercive measures, each of which requires an additional staff of officers, and partly to meet the outlay for new public institutions, such as board-schools, free libraries, public museums, baths and wash-houses, recreation grounds &c. &c., local rates are year after year increased; as the general taxation is increased by grants for education and to the Departments of Science and Art &c. Every one of these involves farther coercion—restricts still more the freedom of the subject to spend his income as he pleases."

As if the evil of paying these taxes were comparable to the services rendered! Let us see what we do pay. This is commonly much exaggerated; for most readers of an annual budget-speech misunderstand it. For example, it was stated that in 1884 the Government had to account for 85 millions £. which had passed through its hands; it was ignorantly concluded that all this large sum was raised by taxation: the truth is that the taxes yielded, not 85 but only 72 millions £., and that the remaining 13 millions £. came from other sources. We must add however, the heavy local rates, which bring the total to over 100 millions £. of taxes..

Say that a tenth of each man's income goes to the support of government general and local, and that a tenth of this tenth goes for the paternal part: then the man with 200 £. a year pays for the paternal part 2 £. a year, and the man with 1000 £. a year, 10 £. And for what? To save the destitute from starvation; to keep down begging; to give to the poor and ignorant, protection, instruction, recreation.

Independently of considerations of humanity and brotherly kindness, there is a powerful and unanswerable apology for such paternal Government: it is that without it, the institution of private property, with its gross inequalities, would be in danger: under our kindly institutions, a small portion of the manifest riches of the governing classes overflowing into the abodes of the poor, reconciles them partially to the caprices of fortune.

If political economy will teach the propriety of a reasonably paternal government, giving the needy and ignorant those gratuitous benefits Mr. Spencer condemns, it will cease to be a philosophy of selfishness and a dismal science.

X.

"*NOT SOCIALISM*" *RESUMED.*

I HAVE said that a poor-law was denounced by the political economy of the first half of this century; by the system still taught in most schools and universities as the orthodox creed; though the earlier system, that of Adam Smith and Bentham took the opposite side without hesitation. It is a case of a host of ordinary writers against two great original thinkers.

According to inferior writers, Adam Smith and Bentham were socialists in the century before that name had been invented. No doubt, a poor-law does what socialism desires: it gives maintenance according to the need of the receiver and not as the reward of labour. We followers of the two great writers march so far side by side with Louis Blanc and his admirers.

But only for a certain distance and that a short one. Fifty years ago Joseph Hume, an admirable financial reformer and a Radical, was constantly found voting in the House of Commons with the Whig majorities of Earl Grey and Lord Melbourne. When he was twitted with supporting ministries which treated his own nostrums with disdain, he replied conclusively that as the Whig measures were in the right direction though they did not go far enough, as far as they did go he would bear them company. It is the same with us: the socialists will go along with us in relieving the destitute even though they are undeserving: we are willing on our part to spend annually eight millions of taxes in this way, provided that the remaining hundred millions a year shall be laid out on other principles. We are not socialists because we travel a few miles in their strange company.

Here we come into conflict with Mr. Herbert Spencer, who represents the entire party of individualism: who holds that what a man makes, saves, or inherits, is his own absolutely: who disregards the maxim that property has its duties as well as its rights; or at least confines the duties within the narrowest limits: who holds that it is not incumbent on the possessor of property to rescue the destitute from the bitterest distress: who says to Dives, eat, drink, and be merry; and as to Lazarus lying at your gate full of sores, let him die: nay, the more surely he dies the better for the world: since on the grand principle of the survival of the fittest it is well that the weak and unfortunate should disappear; and this is in accordance with the doom of beneficent nature, cruel to the individual but kindly to the race.

Fear not Dives! The millions will condemn you: but you will have ample compensation in the approbation of a score of philosophers: to be hissed by the ignorant is nothing, to be applauded by wise men is delightful, and especially charming when it encourages your self-regarding thrift, called by the world meanness and hardness of heart.

The dismal philosophy of selfishness!

Thus we stand between the Socialists who would overturn the existing order of society, and a rigid school which would render society valueless and probably impossible; we stand between socialists, communists, nihilists, Wat Tylers, Jack Cades, and the French Jacquerie, on the one hand, and on the other hand the Malthusians, the Westminster Reviewers, the blind followers of Mr. Spencer.

XI.

SUMMARY OF INDICTMENT AGAINST MR. SPENCER.

WE present this indictment against Mr. Spencer and his school:—We say that they harden the hearts of the rich and embitter the pangs of the suffering, while they look complacently on the luxury of Dives and approve his neglect of Lazarus: we say that they aggravate the discontent of the many and widen the deep gulf between them and the prosperous few: that they relax the bonds of society by discouraging active sympathy, and by approving those hypocrites who whine out, be ye clothed and be ye fed, but who will not sacrifice a glass of wine towards the price of the necessary food and clothing: we say that they would retard our progress in civilization, and even carry us back towards barbarism, by weakening our efforts to rescue the half-savages of our slums: that they appeal to the cupidity of the rate-payers by suggesting that every shilling taken from them is an infringement on their liberty; the liberty to wit, of present enjoyment or of saving for the future.

And what is the motive of these pseudo-philosophers? The gratification of a philosophical vanity, such as that of Madame Roland, when she coldly informed her attached husband that she had thrown herself into the arms of the Girondin, M. Buzot; or when she wrote in her memoirs passages which no decent Englishman would publish. These eccentric thinkers fancy as she did, that they rise above vulgar prejudice and exhibit their superiority when they flout the opinions and sentiments of the wise and good of all nations and ages.

SECOND PART.

XII.

A FREE GOVERNMENT: JOHN LOCKE: RELIEF-WORKS AT ALL TIMES.

IT would simplify this question if we could determine what the functions of a free government are; meaning by a free government one that is restrained by laws, and is not the undisputed prerogative of the Executive power. Much has been written on this question, and no opinion perhaps, has in modern times been better received than that of Locke, whose functions of Government are

1. To resist foreign aggression.
2. To secure at home the protection of person property and character : *i.e.* to administer justice.
3. To do all other good that is possible.

But the experience of two centuries since Locke flourished, may enable us to analyse the third head, and to determine what other good a government is capable of. I think we may expand Locke's functions from three heads into five:

1. To resist foreign aggression.
2. To administer justice.
3. To relieve distress.
4. To raise the character of the people.
5. To do all other good that is possible.

Let an administration be so conducted, and we shall hear little of Wat Tylers and Jack Cades, of Communism and Nihilism, of Revolution and Anarchy: and for the best of reasons; that all classes from the highest to the lowest, from the peer to the pauper, from the palace to the cabin, would benefit by the existing order and shrink from disturbing it.

I repeat what I learn from "Colonel Tcheng-Ki Tong," one of the embassy in Paris, that the two great scourges of China are war *and pauperism.* Such a classification of pauperism with war proves the intensity of the evil. I need hardly say that a system of poor-laws is unknown in that country. The only resource in old age is filial affection: therefore it is declared there, that the three great misfortunes in life are, to lose your father in your youth, your wife in your middle age, and your son in your old age. Wanting a son you may die on a dunghill, though your manliness has not been sapped by poor-laws.

"But," say objectors, "what lavishness of expenditure do poor-laws bring! How inconsistent are they with the maxim of the experienced M. Thiers, that a finance minister should be ferociously frugal!"

But M. Thiers was orator and politician more than legislator, and had before his eyes a ministerial dread of a deficit in the annual budget. A true statesman regards efficiency as well as thrift, and when he reads the Report of a Local Government Board, containing congratulations on a diminution of cost of out-door relief, he asks whether this saving has unduly pinched the destitute; he inquires how many premature deaths it has caused, and how many hearts it has broken. A wise frugality is consistent with liberality: "only frugal men are truly liberal," says Sir Henry Taylor.

We do not ask for the adoption of any new principle: we only desire some extension of practice. The English government, general and local, does much to relieve distress, the general government by such liberality as that of granting 8 millions £. to Ireland during the famine, and the local government by the everyday administration of poor-laws. We desire to extend this practice so far that whenever and wherever there is general distress, it should be the acknowledged duty of some Department such as the Local Government Board to intervene at once, and subject to the control of the Cabinet, to grant relief, in conjunction if possible with voluntary associations.

We ought further to inquire whether it would be possible to offer to unemployed persons at all times work fitted for them, but at low wages. At first sight it seems impossible to devise the means of doing this, yet many tasks of greater difficulty have been accomplished.

For example: before 1832 the poor-laws as they were administered were so corrupt and pernicious that at first sight to reform them seemed impossible, and the cry naturally arose that they should be abolished: men pointed to Cholesbury in Bucks, where the cost of pauperism had grown until it had swallowed up the rent of the land, the farmers' profits, and the vicar's stipend; they pointed to the case of the young man and woman who married on Tuesday and demanded relief on Friday.

Yet the poor-laws were not abolished but reformed. We hear no more of parishes thrown out of cultivation as Cholesbury was: a reckless young couple applying for relief would be told to come into the House, and would there be required to live apart. The reformation was accomplished. Let it also be agreed that work of some kind ought to be always available, at low wages, and then by meditation and experiment a scheme might be framed. Again, during the Irish famine, if charity or wages were dispensed in money, the receivers too often bought whiskey instead of food for their families: nay, if meal were given, that also went to the whiskey-shop. Yet even this difficulty was overcome: the charity and wages were furnished in stir-about, which turned sour in a few hours, and which therefore was unsaleable. So, let it be agreed that ill paid work ought to be always available, and quick wits controlled by good sense would find the means.

Thus much for that function of government which consists in the relief of distress; that distress which the Chinese minister classes with war as one of the scourges of a nation. I will add in a fitter place another extension: provision for the poorest of all classes; that of decayed gentry, of those who themselves or whose families have contributed largely to the rates and are therefore entitled to a share of them. Among aged governesses and the sempstresses of London are hundreds who are more in need of assistance than perhaps any other class.

XIII.

COULD WE LESSEN THE INEQUALITIES OF FORTUNE?

BUT can nothing be done to lessen the inequalities of fortune? Nothing I fear in many cases, and especially in the case where one would desire it most; I mean in that of men of emotional genius; in that of such men as Goldsmith who bestowed on the world the Vicar of Wakefield and She Stoops to Conquer; or Sheridan in return for his brilliant School for Scandal and The Rivals; or Coleridge who endowed us with his Ancient Mariner and Christabel. The poetical temperament, divided by so thin a partition from madness, must needs pay the penalty of its greatness.

But genius is rare. Can we in the ordinary case of commonplace persons do anything to equalize the enjoyments of men? It is said that there are three principal sources of importance in ordinary society: birth, rank, wealth. Of these, birth (or family) is decided for us: rank is open to a few ambitious, able, and fortunate men. Wealth is often inherited but often gained. The result of the whole is that as men cannot earn birth and can seldom earn rank, they devote themselves to money-getting. If they did this for the sake of a competency now and a sense of security for the future, they would be simply fulfilling their duty as good citizens. Unfortunately they do not stop at that point: they long to be distinguished in the only way open to them, that of accumulating a vast fortune: having done this they bring up their sons if they can to the same career: Richard Arkwright, the barber and inventor of the spinning-jenny, patented in 1769, left a son who died so lately as 1843, at the age of 88, leaving we are told a fortune of 8 millions £. It happens too often that such great capitalists crush their weaker brethren.

Something is wanted to divert rich men from the pursuit of more wealth, or to direct their sons' energies into other channels. But since of the three sources of importance, birth is decided for us, and we wish to discredit purse pride, there remains only rank. Now among the middle classes this commonly is not to be obtained without riches: in the absence of these a man can hardly be a justice of the peace and with still more difficulty does he become a Member of Parliament, a knight-bachelor or a baronet. Novelists of course, disparage or deride the desire of such honours. But there are other honours that even they acknowledge to be desirable: such as are to be obtained, not by court favour or parliamentary influence, but by the strenuous pursuit of liberal studies. I have developed this notion in an essay, "The New Academy" (1871) in which I proposed that there should be an Order of Merit, such as is found in other countries, the entrance to our Order being obtainable only by the superiority of published works, and this by the verdict of competent jurors. If the cultivated man, however poor, had social precedence of the millionaire, as the M.P. has now, purse-pride would be discouraged and rich men would urge their sons to mental superiority as a means to social distinction.

There is another possible mitigation of gross inequality of fortune. We find two widow ladies, equals in birth, education, and personal excellence: the one with £4,000 or £5,000 a year, the other unable to keep a servant, or driven to slave as a sempstress or take refuge in a workhouse. This is not only lamentable; it is unjust. It is not unjust that the rich widow should have the possessions bequeathed by her husband or father, but that the unfortunate one should be so neglected. The poor widow's father and husband paid considerable poor-rates during a long period, and took nothing in return: she now gets no more consideration than the widow of the labourer, whose family contributed little during the same period. If the labourer's widow has a claim to necessary subsistence, the lady has an equal claim to much more: to those things namely, which have become to her the necessaries of life. To grant small pensions would not be ruinous, and if they could not be supplied from the poor-rates let them be raised by a special tax on the richer classes: a fraction of a penny in the £. of income-tax even exempting the lower incomes would yield a sufficiency.

XIV.

DISCUSSION AS TO DIRECT ACTION.

As to improving the means of living among the working classes, I fear that little can be done directly. I have heard the contrary maintained, and that by a gentleman of much reading, intelligence, and familiarity with political economists.

In substance, his argument was this:—We import and retain commodities *every day* of nearly a million £. in value: a good deal of these consists of luxuries and still more of superfluities: surely a part of these might be spared, and the price might be applied to buyiug wheat abroad for our use. How much wheat do we consume annually?—About twenty-four million quarters, I replied; of which we now import more than half.—And we could increase our imports by one half?— No doubt, and especially if our demand were regular, according to your manifest intention.—And the cost?—From 10 to 15 millions £.—Yes! out of 350 millions £. which we pay abroad. Why then, should we not do it, knowing that this trifling sacrifice or a much smaller one would satisfy the hunger of all the needy people?

Let us, I rejoined, imagine the importation accomplished, and the six million quarters housed in London, Liverpool, and Hull: what is the next step?— Evidently, said he, to distribute it to the hungry all over the kingdom.—And by what means? Shall it be given to the affluent to hand over to their poor neighbours? Or shall every citizen, every voter, have his share? I presume rather that you would wish to give it directly to the hungry and ragged, *i.e.* to families, and to widows and orphans, incapacitated as voters, and claiming only as being needy.— That is certainly, said my friend, the aim I propose. Then, said I, these 6 million quarters of wheat, costing us nearly as much as our navy, and twice as much as the actual relief under our poor-law, would be given away as a form of charity now generally condemned as causing more pauperism than it relieves.

This question of distribution was embarrassing: we agreed however, that able bodied men ought to be required to earn their wheat, and that women and children should be dealt with as at present by the guardians of the poor. But what work could the men perform? I suggested my notion, perhaps a utopian one, that by search and discussion we might find the means of relief-works always ready, and with low wages.

But then I asked another question. If the men earned wages, why should not they get their bread from the baker, who would buy his flour from the miller, who would order his wheat from the foreign merchant? The six million quarters would come in and get distributed through the ordinary channels of trade, without our intervention. All that you want is the means of payment, and this would follow from the provision of work and wages. Work and wages, these are the needs.

XV.

HIGHER WAGES WANTED: CHINESE IMMIGRANTS.

PUTTING aside hypothesis and conjecture, I am seriously of opinion that the great want in our social organisation is an improvement in the earnings of bodily labour: greater regularity, and if possible a higher scale.

This truth seems unknown or disregarded. Politicians of mark, and writers on finance, belong to the middle or higher classes, and do not understand the wants of those below them. In the year 1884, a deputation of sugar-refiners had an interview with the President of the Board of Trade to complain of foreign bounties and consequent depression of prices: the President, a Radical of the Radicals, asked them whether they could not lower the cost of their refining by *reducing the wages* of their men. What a suggestion by a Minister of State and a leader of the Caucus! A suggestion that inadequate profit to the comparatively rich class should be supplemented by the reduction of the gains of the poorer class! That one evil should be corrected by another and far greater one! Manufacturers, no doubt, must regulate the wages they pay according to the prices they can get, but they want no ghost or Radical politician to tell them this.

I see the same middle-class selfish ignorance in the discussion of another problem; the propriety of admitting the unlimited immigration of Chinese labourers into California and Australia. For myself I am on the side of carefully limiting the immigration: the Chinese should come in if they pleased, for temporary work such as making a railway; but they should not come in to compete with Englishmen or Americans in ordinary permanent occupations. The United States have many troubles in prospect. To say nothing of the Indians, who as it is painful to think, are doomed to disappear as their hunting-grounds are taken from them, there are the negroes in the South. It is said that these multiply faster than the whites, and may become numerous enough to be very troublesome, and the more so as they rise in education and intelligence. It would be an additional calamity if the yellow race of China grew into multitudes. Immigration without women, and living therefore without the restraining influences of wives and families, they introduce shocking Eastern corruptions into the nation.

The extravagant partizans of laissez-faire would leave things alone, with the expectation that they would right themselves; just, I suppose, as the Irish left alone without a poor-law righted themselves, by falling from potatoes and milk to potatoes and water, and from such abundance of potatoes a hundred years ago, that there was enough in every cabin for the children, the fowls and the beggars, to such scarcity for years before the famine that strong men lay in bed all day "for the hunger." When men fold their hands as we did in the case of Ireland, and wait upon providence, they find at last that providence helps only those who help themselves. If the Americans and the Australians leave the Chinese to multiply by immigration into multitudes, they may have to regret their own inertness.

But apologists go much farther: they say that the yellow immigrants bring a great profit to the United States; for suppose a million of them there, doing a good week's work for 15s. instead of 30s., there is a saving of 40 millions £. a year in wages: a saving? not at all; it is only a transfer from workmen to employers: the million of workmen earn 40 millions £. less, and their employers add that sum to their gains. The national income, per head of population, would not be increased, but it would be differently shared: there would be a wider gulf than before between one class and another.

Worse than this: as the Chinese competition would lower the general rate of wages, the white labourers would have their means of living reduced: a real misfortune to the community, the prosperity of which requires a well-paid and contented people. I approve of the resolution of the native Americans and of the Australians, to limit the immigration. I rejoice that the yellow men can be at any time got rid of, because there is no need of decrees of banishment such as the Spaniards centuries ago issued against the Moors, and no need of dragonnades such as those of Louis XIV. and Louvois to drive men, women and children into exile, The Chinese spontaneously return to their country to die, and if immigration of new men ceased America would soon be rid of the race.

XVI.

HIGHER WAGES INSUFFICIENT ALONE. MORAL QUALITIES.

IT is much to be desired then, that a high rate of wages should prevail: because it is a lamentable thing that while the annual productions of a country are abundant, a few men should consume a hundred times as much as nature requires, a considerable class should enjoy more than the inestimable advantage of a competency without anxiety, while seven-eighths of the people are living from hand to mouth, exposed to utter want if the head of the family dies or even sickens.

But, say objectors, the precarious state of workmen is caused by their want of foresight and thrift: if they would but save from youth upwards, there would be few paupers and these might be easily relieved. If then, a workman is improvident it is just that he should pay the penalty: just certainly, I reply: but government must temper justice with mercy and expediency; it is not merciful that the improvident man's family should die of hunger, and it is inexpedient that the man himself should be driven to despair, crime, rags, and squalor.

Another objector says that liberal assistance is thrown away, because present relief will be followed by recurring poverty. This is too true. We must have seen that if an artizan inherit £100, he probably becomes unfit for steady work: if he is a drunkard he soon spends his bequest in taverns; if he is a quiet, inoffensive person he muddles it away.

Even an annuity, or unusually high earnings, will benefit a man little if he does not rise above the habits of his class; a superiority which is improbable.

An example is to be found in England. During the years 1872 to 1874, a railway-mania in the

United States caused, for the time, an unlimited demand in England for iron and therefore for coal: in the Midland Counties we found our coal-bills doubled; old pits were re-opened to get the rubbish that had been left behind; coalowners almost insolvent found themselves suddenly rich.

Wages of course rose greatly: miners and puddlers got the incomes of professional men. Most of them might have bought themselves a house, so as to be free for life from the teasing visits of the rent collector. Some no doubt did this or more: I have known artizans who during a wave of high wages have saved £500 or £1,000, and have become capitalists. But the greater part of the miners and puddlers, like the greater part of artizans, spend what they earn, be it much or little: the miners and puddlers bought heavy dinners and bad champagne. One fancy however, was more than innocent; the men freely bought or hired pianos. On the whole they wasted their opportunities.

And this brings us to the great principle, that the well-being of a nation depends mainly on the good qualities of the people; a principle well expressed by M. Bastiat in his *Harmonies Économiques.*

"In beginning this book I said that political economy had for its object man, considered with reference to his wants and the means of supplying them.

"M. Dunoyer, in his fine work on *Freedom of Labour*, has introduced, and that with perfect scientific rigour, our moral faculties into the list of elements to which we owe our wealth. This is a new idea, as fruitful as it is exact; it is destined to enlarge and ennoble the field of political economy."

I may add that it is just what is wanted to rescue the subject from the reproach of being a dismal science and a philosophy of selfishness: for it will show us that while industry and thrift are necessary to the accumulation of property, sympathy also and generosity are in the highest degree useful, in promoting the best partition of it.

Many human qualities then, are necessary to the well-being of a nation:—skill and industry, without which little production is possible; thrift, because where that is wanting a family may spend in a day the earnings of a month; moderation also in the pursuit of gain, lest present good fortune should tempt to perilous or ruinous speculation; with sympathy and generosity to spread a part of superfluous riches over the poorer strata of society.

It is consolatory to know that during the last seventy years, *i.e.* since the battle of Waterloo left us to the pursuits of peace, our Parliament has displayed these good qualities, in conformity with the wishes of its constituents, little restrained by the dismal theories of Malthus and the Philosophical Radicals: legislation has favoured savings-banks and friendly societies; has remodelled the poor-laws, correcting the abuses but continuing the relief of distress; has extended these laws to Ireland and enlarged them in Scotland: above all, has promoted education on a grand scale without shrinking from a vast expense, general and local.

A reformed political economy will encourage such sympathetic and liberal efforts, and will condemn without hesitation those who say:—leave the people alone to take care of themselves; abolish your poor-laws and let the destitute perish; repeal your factory-acts; and if young orphans are worked to death let public opinion condemn the practice and bear with it.

THIRD PART.

XVII.

THEORY OF POLITICAL ECONOMY: SCIENTIFIC VIEWS: PRODUCTION AND RE-PRODUCTION.

BUT now as to the theory of political economy: the scientific side of it: the "Science of Social Opulence:" or "Organization of the Means of Living."

I begin with Definitions: generally the latest development of a science, and the most difficult. Malthus in 1827 offered a series of definitions, and they were in conformity with the doctrines then accepted: he began with Wealth, Utility, Value, Production.

It is best to begin with *Property*, and that may be defined as everything capable of appropriation which has a price in money or money's worth. Property may be divided into Gifts of Nature (such as Land, Streams, Natural Forests); and Human Productions (such as tools, crops, manufactures, houses). This distinction is founded on the facts that the Gifts of Nature, being limited in quantity, yield rent, while Human Productions yield profit; and farther, that rent and profit follow different laws (profit generally falling as rent rises). The incomes yielded being different the things must be different. The rent I speak of here is that understood in the "Theory of Rent:" it is what in the "Terms and Definitions" I call "Differential Rent."

But Human Productions require division into Capital and Not-Capital, just as in the last century the grain we call wheat was classed as wheat and not-wheat. Not-Capital merits a name less uncouth and more connotative. If I am a small manufacturer and receive weekly from my customers £110 in payment for goods I have supplied, I may choose to put £100 into my cash-box for the payment of wages and the purchase of materials. This £100 is capital. The remaining £10 I may choose to take home for the maintenance of myself and my children. This I call Self-maintenance.

Here I am at issue with other writers: for no one of them, so far as I know, has given a name to this portion of commodities; just as no one of them, so far as I know, has divided property into Gifts of Nature and Human Productions.

Teachers of the science are to be found who regard as capital the £10 I bring home for my household. Worse than this: a recent Oxford Professor has sanctioned the blunder of calling land, capital: classing land, which yields rent, with the goods in a shop and the iron and timber used in manufactures; things which do not yield a rent but do yield a profit.

But as to Capital and Self-maintenance. The £100 in my cash box is capital: it is intended to be used in carrying on business. Or, if you prefer to say so, it is intended to be so used as to reproduce itself with a profit.

The word *re*produce is an important one, and may be often advantageously substituted for the common word produce. M. J. B. Say defines capital as everything which produces. Steam-engines produce commodities, and therefore they are capital. But my easy chair produces something, namely comfort, and therefore that also is capital: a luxurious dinner produces satisfaction, and therefore that also is capital. The result of such a definition is utter confusion.

If however, you take capital to be money or money's worth which *re*produces itself with a profit, the easy chair and the luxurious dinner are excluded; for though they produce satisfaction they do not reproduce themselves with a profit; as does the capital of the farmer, of the manufacturer, and of the dealer.

I insist strongly on the word reproduce as applied to capital.

The easy chair and the luxurious dinner belong to a different class and require a separate name. I call them Self-maintenance; and I apply this name to all the means of living (or things we consume) whether first, necessaries, as plain food, warm clothes, healthful houses; or secondly, superfluities, as poultry, wine, engravings; or thirdly, luxuries, as venison, champagne, or pictures by David Cox or Muller.

Thirty years ago I first suggested this term, Self-maintenance: some of my other terms I have changed, though without changing the divisions they represent.

What I then called Realty I now call Gifts of Nature.

What I then called Stock I now call Human Productions.

But Self-maintenance I shall continue to employ until a better expression is found.

I may add as to the division of things into Capital and Not-Capital, that some skilled artizans claim to have their skill and faculties placed in the class of capital. They might quote in their favour a passage from J. B. Say:

"A family of mere workmen, which has the means of rearing a child to manhood, without cultivating in him any talent, has none the less accumulated a capital for the profit of the son; for by self-denial and thrift it has produced a man capable of earning wages, and these are the income of a capital called man: for a mature man whatever he may be is an accumulated capital."

The artizans may perhaps insist less on their claim, if they observe that M. Say describes a slave and not a free man: a Turk who has an infant slave and rears it, can sell it as part of his capital. But the English artizan is not a chattel like a slave: he cannot sell himself; he cannot legally sell his wife or his children.

Lawyers since Justinian have distinguished between the law of persons and the law of things; in their eyes artizans are persons; slaves are not persons but things. "All persons," they say, "have rights." Objection :—" What as to slaves ?—Slaves are not persons."

To treat artizans as things, sins against the sound maxim of Malthus which I quote elsewhere :— "When we employ terms which are of daily occurrence in the common conversation of educated persons, we should define and apply them *so as to agree* with the sense in which they are understood in this ordinary use of them." Now what would be thought by educated men if anyone said :—"John Smith has no capital, for he is childless; the absence of capital makes him rich: Michael Doherty has a large capital, for he has ten children; and this large capital makes him poor?"

But, say the artizans, our skill and faculties promote the wealth of the nation as much as capital does. Granted. Nay, it may be held that the skill and the faculties rank far higher, because without them capital would soon disappear, whereas they would accumulate it for themselves even in a wilderness.

Skill and faculties are great *Productive Forces*, without which capital could produce nothing: they are not capital, but something much better.

Thus in the "scientific" part of Political Economy (the explanation of the organization of the means of living) I restrict the name Capital to Human Productions, devoted to earning an income by business.

FOURTH PART.

XVIII.

INSTRUCT BY INTERESTING.

A MOTTO on my title-page is, "Instruct by Interesting:" this expresses what I regard as a fundamental notion.

A century ago (1776) Adam Smith published his celebrated Inquiry into the Nature and Causes of the Wealth of Nations: a book of so clear a style, and of contents so varied and readable, as to fully satisfy the requirement, "Instruct by Interesting." His successors, as I have already said, did not inherit his attractive qualities: Ricardo and the elder Mill, McCulloch and Jevons, are caviare to the general. .

Now as to later authors. Imagine a sensible, earnest American Senator, of little education but of penetrating intelligence; another Cobden, bent as he was on real knowledge. Having determined to learn what his predecessors had said and done, he proposes to study Political Economy, and is recommended to get the late treatise upon it in the *Encyclopædia Americana*. He wants to know what Capital is, and he is told by the Encyclopædia:

"Capital is a social substance, which combining with labour through a social agent, becomes a new substance in accord with the desires of society."

Most readers would shut the book and forget to open it again. But a Cobden is made of robuster stuff. He says to himself:—I am a capitalist: I have wool in my store, and this wool is part of my capital: is it a social substance? At any rate, when I entrust it to spinners and weavers and they make it into cloth, it combines with labour through a social agent, and becomes a new substance.

But I have other capital; my buildings for instance: I do not see that these combine with labour through a social agent and become new substances. The Senator might be wrong, but he would be excused if he placed the volume on the shelf of unreadable books.

If it be objected that definitions are generally unattractive, however necessary, I reply that this is the best of reasons for studying to make them as clear and as little repulsive as possible; and for avoiding an affectation of science which puzzles instead of instructing. In this particular case, it is sufficient to use a few intelligible words, taken, as Malthus advises, in the sense in which they are commonly understood by educated persons. Capital then, is money or money's worth used in business; excluding however, land and other Gifts of Nature. This definition excludes also things in family use, such as clothes, furniture, carriages.

XIX.

JEVONS AND WHATELY REPULSIVE. FIRST PRINCIPLES FOR REFERENCE.

LET us now suppose an educated and thoughtful Englishman returned to the House of Commons, and resolved to fit himself for his duties. Like the American Senator he appeals to political economy: he is told that the " Theory of Political Economy" is one of the latest treatises and an excellent one; having been written by the late Professor Jevons, who was highly esteemed by all, and especially by his colleagues at Owens College.

The inquiring member begins with idly turning over the leaves; he is startled on meeting with diagrams of angles and curves like those of analytical geometry and conic sections, the terrors of his youth. Going on, he lights on this abstruse scrap of the higher algebra or trigonometry, he knows not which.

" The equations of impeded exchange may also be stated in the concise form :—

$$\frac{\phi_1(a-x)}{n\psi_1(ny)} = \frac{y}{x} = \frac{m.\phi_2(mx)}{\psi_2(b-y)}.$$

Concise? says the despairing inquirer: and he thinks of his school Horace, charming by comparison :—Brevis esse laboro, *obscurus* fio."

He throws Jevons aside, and resorts to Archbishop Whately, whom he knows by his Logic to be the clearest of thinkers. He is disappointed: he finds Whately proposing to call political economy *catallactics*, while others talk of *Chrematistics*, and of *teleologic value*.

I grant that in using learned terms, political economy follows the lead of other sciences: the Faculty of Medicine talks of preventives as prophylactics, and of curatives as therapeutics; it uses atrophy and phthisis: lawyers discourse of allodial or feudal lands or lands in fee; of emphyteotic or fee-farm rents; of choses in action and of contingent remainders: terms that may drive a client to despair. But these sciences require many technical terms to express a class of things by a word or phrase, and to give precision to their talk. No such need exists in political economy: the familiar names, property, capital, wages, tell us what we want; and a few additional names such as Gifts of Nature, Human Productions, Differential Rent, go little beyond our ordinary vocabulary.

The American Encyclopædia then, Archbishop Whately and Professor Jevons, have repelled readers by their ostentation of learning.

As to definitions and explanations of terms, it is a thankless task to read a series of these, and most men find it impossible to remember them when so read. Yet the explanation of them is necessary and ought to be easily accessible. I have therefore placed my Terms and Definitions on early pages, but "For Reference only."

As to *First Principles*, it is wise I think, when instructing mature men, to defer the consideration of them until we have discussed the applications of the science to actual affairs. For if we are to secure the attention of those who have ceased to be students or never were such, we must treat of matters in which they are already interested *(instruire en interessant)*: we must follow the advice of the *Ars Poetica*, and instead of beginning Diomede's return with the death of Meleager, hasten *in medias res*.

Experience has convinced me of this. It might have been expected that if anywhere, then at the Oxford Political Economy Club, first principles would have been habitually discussed, since among the members there were besides the Secretary, Thorold Rogers, Professors Henry Smith, Goldwin Smith, T. H. Green, Newman. Yet, during the sessions I attended, the predominant questions were such as these :—In what form, if any, could the principles of Tenant Right be applied with benefit to Ireland?"—"Has the compulsory division of Landed Property, at death, been economically beneficial to France?"—"Can we justify the present monopoly of printing the Bible enjoyed by the Universities and the Queen's Printer?"

It is I think, by discussing such questions that we can secure the attention of men : some of whom will afterwards go on to the study of principles. A school-book indeed, may be constructed logically, with terms and definitions, declensions and conjugations, because attention to them can be commanded.

Two sisters comparing notes as to their German, found that the elder could converse fluently, but could not easily read Goethe or Jean Paul, while the younger could read these authors but could not converse: the elder had learnt from a nurse and a resident governess; the younger had been taught with grammar and dictionary. So in political economy: a man long a member of the Oxford Club, would be familiar with the questions of the day, but might have shadowy notions of capital and rent. With him the concrete should have been followed up by the principles.

Therefore, I say, begin with the concrete and go on to the science. Discuss the questions whether free-trade can be forcibly extended; whether Mr. Herbert Spencer's austerity is a return to barbarism; whether land can be nationalized: go on to Terms and Definitions: and afterwards to First Principles; and to Population, Rent, Wages, Profits, Supply and Effective Demand, Trade, Money.

XX.

CONCLUSION.

IN this Introduction I have tried to sketch the opinions and sentiments of the chapters which follow: opinions and sentiments which to the orthodox, are objects of disgust, or more probably of contempt.

I may apply to such blind followers of authority, some of the words of Hobbes which I elsewhere quote in full. They have not examined the definitions of their masters, and much less have they made definitions for themselves: therefore they are led into absurdities, and are "as much below the condition of ignorant men as men endued with true science are above it. For words are wise men's counters, but they are the money of fools."

Chapter II.

INEQUALITIES OF FORTUNE.

I.

THE GROSS INEQUALITIES: FACTS.

TO young persons first opening their ears to social questions, it seems monstrous that the inequalities of fortune should be such as they see around them. A late noble duke was popularly believed to have the spending of £1,000 a day; and for anything known to the contrary his son and successor may have as much. I know it is said that the popular voice grossly exaggerates such figures, and that it would be safer to lower the £1,000 to £300 or £400. The argument remains the same after the reduction. At the same time with the duke's £300, the farm labourer has to be resigned to 2s. a day, or allowing for the low rent of his cottage and occasional piece-work and harvesting, 2s. 6d. a day. The duke's income then was as great as the joint incomes of 2,000 or 3,000 labourers.

The spinning-jenny was patented in 1769 by Richard Arkwright: he was a barber, and a few years ago his brass door-plate coming into the possession of Professor Thorold Rogers, was with a touch of practical satire presented by him to the University of Oxford. Arkwright was knighted, and died in 1792, leaving a large fortune earned by ability and industry. His son continued the business of cotton-spinning, and died so lately as 1843, at the advanced age of 88, leaving as we are told eight millions sterling. What did he do for the world that he should have so large a share of its superfluities? Nothing that I ever heard of. His means grew by industry and frugality.

Strutt, who is said to have become Sir Richard Arkwright's partner through the judicious use of a bit of chalk, also founded a family, that of Lord Belper, whose title was fairly earned by public services. The family must not be confounded with that of Strutt, Lord Rayleigh, the Senior Wrangler and distinguished man of science; whose grandfather, Colonel Strutt, declined the title for himself, though he earned it for his wife and family by raising a regiment in Kent in opposition to the invasion threatened by Napoleon.

But merits or no merits, it remains lamentable that one man should have £1,000 a day and another only 2s. 6d. It is the more so, because £5,000 a year would give a noble family as much happiness as twenty or sixty times the amount, if only the reduction were general. Talking to a young German baron who was visiting this country, I pitied a certain nobleman for having only £5,000 a year: the young man stared:—"£5,000 a year! that is about 50,000 florins: we Germans should think ourselves well provided having so large an income." No doubt, the noble English duke with £1,000 a day might well spare nine-tenths of it if other great revenues were proportionately cut down.

II.

MITIGATION OF THE EVIL BY A NATIONAL INSURANCE-FUND. OTHER CAUSES OF ENVY.

BUT the evil of inequality is inveterate; and we must content ourselves for the present, with remembering that these vast fortunes are a national insurance-fund against calamity. It is possible, though highly improbable, that the French may some day get possession of Ireland, and hold it for half a generation, as the Carthaginians held a part of Italy. The prodigious expense of modern warfare, in which a single shell costs as much as a great gun cost formerly, together with the frightful disturbance of our commerce, might bring Great Britain to a state of distress such as that of France at the close of the wars of religion, and again after

Louis XIV's reckless ambition followed by ruinous defeats. A large part of the people would be unable to pay additional taxes, which therefore would fall with redoubled severity on the rich. Even Pitt had to impose an income-tax of 2s. in the £, qualified by various remissions: these might be multiplied, and the tax might rise to 5s. or 10s. in the £.: in that case the people at large might rejoice at having this reservoir of the rich.

The case would be like that of an unlimited joint-stock company which fails, in which a number of very rich partners are the salvation of creditors. The first call may be met by nearly all the share-holders; the second by only three-fourths; the third by one-half; till at last even the richest are nearly ruined.

This is no imaginary case. Before limited liability was adopted, the Leeds Bank failed: this was in September, 1864: three years later it was said, that calls had been made upon the shareholders to the amount of £160 per share: that all but seventeen of these unfortunates were ruined, and that even these seventeen had further calls to pay. The final result was I believe even more fatal. The rich shareholders are a reservoir for the nation. The national reservoir is even more secure than the other: for the shareholders of the Leeds Bank might go abroad and evade payment of the calls: but rich men would not thus escape the income-tax, which is levied on lands, houses, railways and other things which could not be carried away: and as to incomes from trades and professions, these can only be carried on by men continuing to live at home. This does not cure the evil of overgrown fortunes, but it is a mitigation.

A man of the educated middle class has no reason to envy the lot of those born to great wealth, provided that he himself has a competency without worry. Yet suppose that fortunes were so far equalized as to remove all ground for envy: there would still remain enough differences between men to disturb the equanimity of querulous persons. The three great sources of worldly distinction are said to be birth, rank, and wealth. The obscure but educated middle-class man, will reconcile himself to the absence of these, if he is the fortunate possessor of practical philosophy; *i.e.* of the predominance of reason over passion. But he will allow himself to enjoy the witty sarcasms he meets with.

> What if your ancient but ignoble blood
> Has crept through scoundrels ever since the flood!

And again:

> What can ennoble sots, or slaves, or cowards?
> Alas! not all the blood of all the Howards.

He will smile when he hears of a man who has said that he prefers his own "Honourable" by birth to his neighbour's "Right Honourable" gained by public services rendered: and at the fatuous senility of a late peer, who valued the Garter because it could *not* be earned by merit. He will not deny that he should like to have been a Pope, or a British Premier, or a Lord Chancellor: but he feels that if he should seriously regret not having early aspired to mount the ladder of ambition and not having reached the top, he would be as weak as the infant who cries for the moon.

Horace, the son of a freedman, sets us a good example. His happiness lay in his Sabine farm the gift of his patron, where, far from the bustle and ostentation of Rome, he could enjoy a frugal feast with his country neighbours, and discuss divine philosophy:—O noctes cœnæque Deûm! He cheerfully conceded his patron's superiority of birth, both in the line familiar to us at school:—Mæcenas atavis edite regibus, "scion of royal ancestors," says Dr. Kennedy, and in the other expression equally familiar to scholars:—Tyrrhena regum progenies. He certainly did not envy his patron in later life, when the old bachelor married a young wife, who behaved much like Lady Teazle, and perhaps gave her husband more solid ground for jealousy than Sir Peter had to complain of. After all, mere birth, with a long unquestionable pedigree, goes for little at the present day: few people are jealous of the butcher in the black country, and the turnpike-keeper, and the London sexton, for their legal right to quarter the royal arms, as descendants of co-heiresses with regal blood in their veins. The

Romans generally may have assigned as little importance to the kingly descent of Mæcenas, as we assign to that of the Irish and Welsh peasants with equal claims. But there remains the fact that if fortunes were equalized other grounds for envy would remain.

III.

MR. GREGG'S FALLACIOUS DEFENCE; MATTERS HAVE BEEN WORSE.

A LATE writer amused himself with the paradox, which apparently he believed, that it was a matter of indifference whether an income of £300,000 a year was enjoyed by one man or was divided among fifty men: the reason he gave was, that the spending of the income gave the same employment to capital and labour in both cases. Indifference! yes, as to capitalists and labourers, but not as to the possessors of the incomes. The duke may have half a dozen halls and parks for residence and sporting: he may travel abroad like a prince: he may buy pictures at £10,000 each. The owner of only £6,000 a year has everything necessary to wellbeing, and with perhaps a better chance of happiness than the duke: and if £300,000 a year were divided, instead of one such fortunate man there would be fifty. For the nation there would be this great gain, that the halls and parks generally unoccupied would then be inhabited. The presence of a great landlord has a beneficial influence: the commissioners on Education some years ago, found that in parishes with a resident landlord the schools were well maintained, while in parishes deserted by the landlord they were starved. The squire and his family could not allow the decay of schools constantly before their eyes. What is true of schools is true of other parish institutions.

The benefits then which would follow from splitting up an income of £300,000 a year into smaller portions, would be, first that fifty families instead of one would have the advantages of affluence, and secondly that there might be fifty centres of civilization instead of one.

But if doubt be possible as to these great fortunes, there can be no doubt as to the poor means of living of the labourers: that cannot be called a reasonable or kindly distribution of wealth, under which one man has £1,000 or even £20 a day and another has 2s. 6d.

It is true that matters have been worse. Compare 1885 with 1842. The lamented Lord Iddesleigh says:—" There was at this period (about 1842) a great deal of suffering among the lower orders, and especially among those engaged in manufactures; there was a scarcity of employment, and *provisions were at a high price.* As a consequence, there was much political discontent. Chartism was exciting serious uneasiness; the new Poor Law, against which the Chartist movement was mainly directed, was pressing hardly upon the people, who had not yet become fully accustomed to it; and who were suffering from it all the more severely on account of the badness of the recent harvests, the slackness of employment, and the growth of the population, which had not yet learned to relieve itself by emigration."

As at that time so of late years, harvests have been bad, employment in towns has been slack; but on the other hand *provisions are not at a high price.* Potatoes ~~also~~ have during two years been cheap: foreign and colonial meat whether imported in tins or as frozen carcasses is at a really low price; and the same may be said of cheese and bacon, and of butterine which we are told on good authority is no "nauseous compound," but the unmixed fat of beef carefully clarified.

Above all, bread the principal food of families on low wages, has fallen to the standard of the last century.

Average Prices of Wheat per quarter during the periods,

44/2	35/4	35/2	32/1	33/3
1706-15,	1716-25,	1726-35,	1736-45,	1746-55,
47/8	54/3	81/2	97/6	78/8
1774-85,	1786-95,	1796-1805,	1806-15,	1816-25.

For many years before the repeal of the corn-laws in 1846, it was 55/. For many years after the repeal it was 50/.

It now varies from 30/. to 40/. as it did from 1706-55.

But farm wages in the mean time have gone up from 6s. or 7s. a week to 12s. or 14s.: and if anyone imagines that the gain is neutralized by the loss of rights of common, let him turn to Hutton's *Court of Requests*, where he will find that in towns, where there was no question of right of commons, the wages of labourers have doubled since the last century.

It might be shown also, that at the present day, the condition of our labourers is far better than that of the labourers of other European countries. But the fact remains, and is humiliating to our civilization, that one nobleman has £400 or £1,000 a day, a fortunate curate has 10s. a day, and a labourer 2s. 6d.: *i.e.* that the nobleman has as much as 800 to 2,000 curates or 3,000 to 8,000 labourers.

A youthful learner will naturally ask why the rate of wages should not be raised: the reply is that attempts were formerly made to fix the rate by law, but generally I fear, to keep wages down and not to raise them; the attempts failed, just as in the case of trying to determine the selling price of commodities. Even in so simple a matter as the stipends of curates, little good was done by interference: for though, early in this century, when the supply of young men for the Church was beyond the effectual demand for them, the law civil or ecclesiastical declared that no curate should be paid less than £60 a year, yet the newly ordained deacons did not get that remuneration, but served in some cases without any payment.

As to farm labourers, during the parliamentary election of 1885 a silly clergyman published a pamphlet advising the men, now they possessed votes, to insist on receiving wages of £1 a week for 8 hours' daily labour, and this besides a cottage and garden: now £1 a week for 8 hours is equal to 25s. for 10 hours and 30s. for 12 hours. The demand then would be, allowing for cottage and garden, about 30s. a week for the present hours. Wages are now 12s. to 14s., and the advance would be at least 15s. a week. Did the wrongheaded, reckless adviser ever ask what would be the result if the labourers succeeded in such a demand? The additional 15s. a week would amount to nearly £40 a year: a farmer employing ten men would have to pay them £400 a year more than he now pays: that would be ruin to those farmers who are not already ruined by the reduced prices of corn and cattle. A very large proportion of the farms would be thrown up, and the labourers upon them would be discharged and reduced to poverty.

Part of the loss no doubt, would fall on the land-

SECT. III.   INEQUALITIES OF FORTUNE.   77

lords. The learner may say, "all of it: for as I hear, the cultivated lands of England and Wales amount to at least 25 million acres, and the rent some years ago was on an average £2 an acre, giving a total of 50 millions £. Imagine the rents lowered to 5 or 6 millions £: this would give a surplus of at least 40 millions £. Say that we have so many as a million rural labourers, the surplus 40 million £ would give each of them the additional £40 a year, or 15s. a week, required."

These figures may be accepted as not far from the truth, and yet the conclusion is unfounded. The imagined reduction of rent would be equal to 32s. an acre on the average: but how would that average be made up? A large part of the land could not have its rent lowered by 32s., because it does not pay so much as 32s. The actual rents vary from £5 per acre to £4, £3, £2, £1, 30s., 15s., 5s., 2s. 6d.: and in the vast tracts paying less than 32s., the extra £40 a year would have to come partly and in many cases principally out of the farmers' pockets: the holdings would be thrown up and the demand for labour would cease. Better leave the rate of wages to fix itself as it does now, and not to ask for more than the farmers can pay.

IV.

IS THERE NO HOPE THEN? MACHINERY: CHINESE IMMIGRANTS.

IS there no hope then? the learner will say: are the opulent to revel for ever in their wealth, while the poor crouch under their penury? I see no probability of any heroic remedy, but mitigation I trust, is at hand. We find generally that the skilled artizan of a village gets fairly paid, even though his neighbour the labourer is in poverty: Arthur Young, more than a century ago, found this to be the case in Ireland; where, while the farm-labourer or peasant was in a condition far worse than that of the English labourer, the blacksmith and carpenter enjoyed as good wages as those of Suffolk: quite recently our consul reported the same peculiarity in so backward a Turkish province as Anatolia. Now there is ground for hoping that the low prices of farm-produce, will stimulate the country population to the same strenuous exertion that is caused in towns by the severe and continued competition of traders: one of the results will probably be the more general use of machinery on farms; and if this should lead to the necessity of mechanical skill on the part of the farmers' men, at the same time with a greatly reduced cost of cultivation, then the rate of country wages may rise to that of the towns. Many dread the change because they fear that improved farming involves clipped hedges, the felling of ornamental trees, the adoption of large fields with straight hedgerows, a formality painful to the eye: while I share this fear, I cannot deny that though a beggar's rags look picturesque I like better to see clothing which is warm, neat, and ugly; and for the same reason I should prefer utility to beauty in our rural landscapes. Thus, machinery, frequently the bugbear of town artizans, may be the salvation of rural labourers in the next generation.

Wages then, cannot be raised by Act of Parliament, nor to any extent by a reduction of rents: they may probably be raised by the use of machinery, which would increase the produce of the soil, and give employment with high wages to skilled labourers.

Governments however, though they cannot raise wages may sometimes remove impediments. Thus, in California, the immigration of Chinese, who are satisfied with low earnings, tends to reduce the wages of the whites, who are said to be illiberal and negligent of political economy, because they would shut out the Chinese in order to keep up their own wages.

Illiberal! because they keep out their enemies. And they are enemies: enemies of the workmen whom they supersede : enemies of civilization and of morality : for, as we are told, so filthy and hateful are their habits that the lowest wretch taken from the most obscene slum of London, would turn sick if he tried to pass a night in a Chinese sleeping room. I am not speaking of the decent Chinese found by Mr. Fortune, forty years ago, in the interior of their empire, of whom it has been said recently, that there is much to admire : "that their conspicuous filial piety, their moderation and peaceableness, their habitual courtesy and politeness, and their outward morality are national traits which deserve the respect and admiration of all." But I am speaking of the migratory race who visit America and Australia for few years and then return to die at home. Now even if these foreigners were as well conducted as whites living apart from their wives and children ; as our soldiers for instance ; and even if they did not introduce the pernicious habit of smoking opium, I should still say that the whites of California and Queensland would be fully justified in forbidding their admission if they lowered the rate of wages. I look upon a high standard of wages as a benefit to all classes : especially to the class which receives them because it gives them a fair share in the distribution of wealth : but also to the richer classes because it relieves them from the charge of selfishness, and gives safety and stability to the foundations of society. A country like Ireland, Italy, or Egypt, favoured by nature with fertility of soil and climate, but in which the lowest classes are ill fed, ill clothed, and ill housed, is a disgrace to humanity, and is in constant danger of disorders, insurrection, and revolution. I fear I must add China, containing perhaps a fourth of the population of the world; a country, says a recent Chinese writer, of which the two great scourges are war and pauperism; a country too, honeycombed with secret societies, hostile to the government of the present (the Manchou) dynasty of foreign usurpers.

Although Government cannot raise the rate of wages, yet it can abstain from interfering with a rise. Formerly even in free England it did not abstain: centuries ago it fixed a maximum rate; until a short time ago it forbade trades-unions. The crude political economy of a generation back (not that of the sagacious Adam Smith) declared with an air of infallibility, that such associations were foolish, and incapable of raising the standard, because there was a certain wages-fund to be distributed among a fixed number of recipients, and therefore any addition to the wages of class A must be taken from those of other classes; a principle never verified by an appeal to facts. Thirty years ago, in my *Science of Social Opulence*, I contested this dogma and appealed to my experience as a manufacturer, to prove that trades-unions were not only justifiable but necessary. Since that time the world has come round to this opinion, and the dogma of political economists has dropped out of sight.

No combination of workmen can raise wages above a certain standard: I have already shown that if farm-labourers' wages were doubled, quantities of land would be thrown out of cultivation, and multitudes of men would lose their work. In British manufactures the standard is determined by foreign competition, and unfortunately the habits of life in Germany and France are more penurious than ours, and therefore wages are lower. All that combination can do is to keep the actual rate up to the highest point that is possible.

Mr. Arch some years ago taught the farm-labourers to combine just as artizans do: they learnt their lesson so well that they succeeded in getting a rise of wages; and though these have fallen again, yet with the low prices of provisions the men are far better off than they were formerly; and as I have shown, have the command of twice the quantity of wheat given weekly to their progenitors of 120 years ago. We may hope that the general adoption of farming machinery and improved cultivation may again double their earnings.

But it is not by peasant proprietorship or spade husbandry that these desirable results can be obtained. Steam-ploughing and harrowing require large fields and much capital: peasant proprietors can scarcely command a good team of horses: everything about them is little and pinched, wanting in those large means which are necessary to the full division of labours. This does not exclude cottage gardens and allotments such as may be cultivated by men and their families living mainly on wages.

The generous mind of John Stuart Mill was pained by the thought that the arrangements of industry should permanently make the servant a dependent of his employer. Yet if he had looked round, he would have seen that dependence is the rule in all classes: that the minister of religion is often dependent upon his flock; the young barrister upon the solicitor; the physician upon the surgeon, and the surgeon upon his patients; the retailer upon his customers; the manufacturer upon the merchant, and the merchant upon the foreigner or the colonist. He might have remembered that he himself and his father before him had been dependent upon the Directors of the East India Company, and might at any time have been dismissed from the important post they successively occupied. The artizan protected by his union is perhaps one of the most independent of men as I can testify after long experience. The farm-labourer now is nearer than he was to the same position.

V.

MEANS OF RISING: COUNTY LABOURERS: NEW VOTERS: A LIMITED DEMOCRACY.

MUCH of the happiness of a class must depend upon the opportunity given to the well conducted and frugal members, of improving their condition. Town-bred men have imagined that farm-labourers have no such opportunity, unless by deserting their occupation, and either emigrating or migrating to a town. Investigation has proved that this notion is unfounded: that numbers of labourers become small farmers, and that multitudes of them have allotments.

A controversy on this subject in 1885-6 grew out of the general election, at which for the first time the farm-labourers had votes. Unprincipled candidates, and in a greater degree their vulgar canvassers, made rash promises to the new voters; even holding out to them the prospect of a share of the land without payment, and perhaps a cow into the bargain. The voters wished to support the candidates whose canvassers had bribed them with false hopes: in the new Parliament the Liberal party at once came into power; they did not proceed to parcel out the land or distribute gratuitous cows: such an election trick cannot be played twice: a very few months or years are sufficient to correct such a delusion.

Labourers will learn the wholesome lesson that if they are to better their condition, they must do it by industry and saving. I wish they started from a higher standard of living, and had better prospects of sharing in the overflowing wealth of the country: but they must be satisfied for the present with seeing allotments and small farms within their reach: and that both allotments and small farms are generally within their reach has been clearly proved.

We must also again remember that low as is the standard of living among our labourers, it is far higher than that of their predecessors of a hundred years ago: far higher too, than that of Irish labourers; for as we are told, an "emissary despatched by the *Freeman's Journal*" (a Parnellite paper) to report upon the English land question, finds himself obliged to bless that which he came to curse. . . . . After vividly picturing the wreck of agriculture in the centre of a great tillage country, and commiserating the ruin of English landlord and farmer, he finds in the position of the labourer the one bright feature. 'There was perhaps, nothing which I learned in the course of my tour which gave me greater pleasure than the consideration which is shown to the agricultural labourer.'"

Add to this that the death-rate is in rural parishes very low, and that suicides are most rare.

The "Reform-Bill" of 1885 is not a measure to be regretted. One might have wished that the two millions of new voters had been brought in gradually: that as in 1832 the £10 householders should have been the first to be enfranchised; proceeding in the next generation to householders generally. But the stride has been made and no revolution is threatened.

Now, seeing that no harm has been done, we may rejoice in the good that has followed, and this is manifest. We had in the rural districts formerly millions of people who if living in towns would have had votes and representatives in the House of Commons, but who in fact had neither votes nor representatives: now they have both: they are conscious of being the political equals of the town populations. In the long run this sentiment of gratified self-respect is a matter of importance.

A more immediate advantage is the social one. The rural labourers have complained of being treated harshly: but such grievances as they have had will attract much more attention, and are far more likely to be remedied now all the householders have votes: a candidate for their support at the poll, must listen to them, and try to satisfy their claims.

Of the different forms of government, a monarchy, it has been found, is often disposed to support the claims of the poor, both from kindness and from a wish to use them as a counterbalance to the presuming rich: an oligarchy (the government of a few rich) is the harshest of all: a wide aristocracy is better, though each member of it cannot possibly realize the fact that his happiness is of no more importance to the world than the happiness of a shoeblack. A democracy is of course, the government most bent on securing the happiness of the many: unfortunately a mere democracy is unfit for the important functions of both legislation and administration, and especially for the management of foreign affairs. We were formerly governed by a limited monarchy: then, after 1688, by a limited aristocracy: now we have a limited democracy; and if the limitations can endure, we and our posterity will probably have the best government of all.

At any rate I regard the Reform-Bill of 1885 as tending to correct, though indeed very partially, the Inequalities of Fortune.

VI.

WHAT CHANGES DESIRABLE? AMERICA. SOCIALISM. SETTLEMENTS OF LAND.

ALL the householders of the three kingdoms are now legally entitled to a vote, and thus possess the means of influencing Parliament and contributing to legislation. What changes ought they to demand?

Certainly not the addition of Socialism, which was tried in France after 1848, and was found wanting. Socialism has two forms; the innocent-foolish and the iniquitous-foolish: the innocent, which desires that the production and distribution of the means of living should be performed by society, *i.e.* by Government: there should be no more private farmers or manufacturers or dealers or bankers, but only servants of the Government, which should employ and pay all these people, and receiving the profits should apply them to—benefiting the people. The slightest investigation of history and of present conditions, must convince us that such a scheme is impracticable and absurd.

Recent painful and alarming disclosures have shown us that government manufactories are unfit for the discharge of their duties: our great guns and our small arms have proved worthless, and that in quantities. Most of the small arms were formerly made by private contractors, and the Government "view" was extremely strict. Now, the Government makes the arms and the "view" is careless and insufficient.

The second form is equally absurd and at the same time is wicked: it proposes to seize by force or fraud the properties of the world, and divide them among the public. Such a scheme of wholesale robbery, besides being in the highest degree criminal, would be an effectual bar to all progress, if it did not put an end to civilization. If man is to be kept from going back to barbarism, it must be by maintaining private rights, and above all the security of property. The stronger term, sacredness of property, is no innovation of the present day, which is threatened with spoliation: it is a term of the last century, when the poorer men were robbed by their superiors; and especially in France, where under pretences of the rights of seigneurs, and under the oppressive *taille*, a tax from which nobles and clergy were exempt, and which was increased as a man prospered and showed his good fortune, no poor man's property was secure. The poor men's friends cried aloud for the sacredness of property. At that time the danger came from above, and was ended by revolution: now the danger comes from below, and threatens to begin with revolution.

Popular socialism rests on the dictum that all our wealth (human productions) is the result of labour, *i.e.* of labour alone. This is a dogma of some modern political economists.

You are talking to an intelligent, unemployed shoemaker, and he founds a claim to assistance on this principle. You reply:—since labour can of itself produce commodities, go and with your labour make me a pair of shoes, and these I will buy. Nay, he replies, but I have no tools. You give him tools:—now make my shoes.—But I have no leather. —My friend, you say, tools are capital, and leather is capital : it seems that without capital you cannot make shoes; how then can you say that labour alone produces commodities?

The shoemaker may rejoin :—you, sir, have tools and leather, and you cannot produce a pair of shoes. —Did I ever pretend that I could? I do not say that all productions spring from capital alone; I say that capital as well as labour is necessary to production; that the capitalist has a claim to his profit just as strong as the claim of the workman to his wages; and that if the capitalist by thrift amasses a fortune, he benefits the workmen by supplying tools and materials abundantly at a low profit.

It is fatuity to say that labour alone produces all our commodities, and that therefore all our possessions ought to be distributed among the workmen.

An anonymous author has said of modern Socialism " There is absolutely nothing new in the substance of the social gospel now preached among the nations. Every one of the tenets of the most advanced of nineteenth-century revolutionists is to be found in one form or other amongst English Fifth-monarchy men, Munster Anabaptists, hordes of wild sectaries right up the stream of the Middle Ages. The repeated *Jacqueries* of feudal France, the memory of CADE at home, of DOLCINO DI NOVARA in the Italy of DANTE, of the fanatical 'heretics' of Africa and of Asia Minor, of the Persian Mazdakites, and of the slave-rebels of republican Rome, establish the continuity and the strength of the anti-social tradition. Every one of these movements was to the full as *advanced* as that which is now paraded to the world as the great discovery of modern thought. Every one of them cost endless blood and suffering to repress. Every one of them ended in failure."

It was imagined at one time that true democracy was a cure for the inequalities of fortune. We can now appeal to the true democracy of the United States, with universal suffrage, and more than a century old. There, democracy has brought no equality of means of living: in New York and Philadelphia there are splendid palaces and miserable tenements: families living in the extreme of luxury, and in the slums families hungry and shivering. The recent death of Mr. Vanderbilt has proclaimed to the world how utterly powerless in this respect is universal suffrage: how it permits the accumulation in one family of a fortune large enough if divided to give a competency to thousands.

We are told that Mr. Vanderbilt's father left 16 millions £ (not dollars) and that the son lately deceased left double that amount. Making allowances for exaggeration, but taking into account the power of American accumulation through the high rate of profit and interest, we may believe that the son had an *annual income* of a million sterling. I have mentioned the case of an English nobleman who was said to have £1,000 a day: this American capitalist had, apparently, £3,000 a day. I calculated that this English nobleman enjoyed an income as large as that of 2,000 curates or 8,000 labourers: Mr. Vanderbilt enjoyed an income as large as that of 6,000 English curates or 20,000 English labourers. It is not democracy and universal suffrage that we can trust to correct the inequalities of fortune.

Some persons look for a remedy to changes in the tenure of land. They say:—abolish the right of landholders to settle their property, and then land will be sold freely. It is not obvious that anything would be thus gained by poor men who have no funds with which to buy. And how far would these innovators go? Would they abolish the present power of settling all property, personalty as well as realty?

In France before 1789 the law did not admit of settlements: the Revolution and the Code Napoléon made no change in this respect: at the present time a wife's property is administered in one of three modes, as agreed before marriage; but the French themselves say that no one of them is so beneficial as our practice of settlement by creation of a trust. All of them are tainted with the power of the husband to lay hold of the principal directly or by harassing the wife into giving her consent.

Some persons imagine that settlements are needless

SECT. VI.   INEQUALITIES OF FORTUNE.   93

in Great Britain now that married women can hold property independently of their husbands; forgetting that there remains to the husband the power of teasing and bullying his wife into giving up her property. Trustees cannot be teased or bullied into a dereliction of duty, because they are liable to be called on to repay any part of the trust fund which is lost. The practice of settlements on marriage and by will has become very general; and even the lower middle class would unwillingly surrender it, knowing how important it is that in case the husband fails or dies, the wife should have a resource.

Probably it is seldom that this kind of settlement is attacked. Men feel, without formally expressing it, that the sense of security is the greatest blessing of civilization: security of person and property. They add when a daughter marries, security of the means of living. Therefore, the dowry is placed in the hands of trustees, so that the income from it though smaller may be safe. But surely no reasonable person would refuse to property in land that security which is given to money: no one would say to a father:—if you give your daughter £4,000, half in money and half in a plot of land, you may settle the money but not the land.

When men object to settlements of land, I believe they are thinking of something quite different: they hear of estates being entailed, and they imagine an entail to be what it was in Scotland till recently, such a possession without any specific settlement that in case of insolvency creditors could not claim the land as part of the assets. No doubt there are entails of a moderate kind in England and plenty of them. The use of them is a survival.

In practice the survival has almost ceased, since the recent Act obtained by Lord Cairns. The authorities say that this "Settled Land Act" has effected a "complete revolution:" that it makes every acre of settled land in England (with the exception of the chief mansion-house and demesne lands) saleable at the unfettered discretion of the person who is tenant for life." Of course, the trustee must re-invest the proceeds of the sale; but the land ceases to be tied up, and therefore, "the *economic* objections to settlements of land are now almost entirely at an end."

Yet so high an authority as Mr. Justice Fitzjames Stephen has declared his opinion that land and other realty ought to be subject absolutely to the same laws as money and other personalty; and that the fusion should be effected by adopting for realty the present laws that regulate personalty. If this were done, no excuse would remain for railing at land-settlements, unless men can be found to declare that all settlements should be disallowed.

VII.

FRENCH EQUAL DIVISION AT DEATH.

THE French practice of distribution of property at death, seems to some persons a step in the right direction, as preventing too great an accumulation in the hands of one heir: the property is by law divided into a number of portions greater by one than the number of the children: the father has the disposal by will of the odd share; so that if there are only two children the father's favourite may have two-thirds of the whole, and if there are six children the favourite may have two-sevenths.

The object proposed by the law I believe, was the promotion of political and social equality; "liberty, equality, fraternity!" being the motto of true citizens. This equality has been so far attained, that France has now few mansions and parks, with their grand trees and beautiful herds of deer, such as are still some of the glories of Great Britain. On the other hand, the object we propose, the securing to all classes of ample means of living, has not been attained. It is certain that in Paris wages are lower than in England, while the means of living are dearer: it is certain that the country population is worse fed, clothed, housed, and educated, than are our farmers and labourers.

This result does not encourage us to adopt the French mode, of distributing a deceased man's property among his children according to a fixed rule. It is maintained also that the practice is injurious by much lessening the parental authority. We see the bad results of such relaxation in the case of English artizans: among these, a boy of sixteen may earn wages enough to maintain him; if he is of a wandering or rebellious nature, he may leave his father's house and shift for himself, and therefore even while he lives at home, the parental authority is weak: among the educated classes a boy of sixteen, if he is not at school, at any rate earns nothing or not more than pocket money; he is therefore obliged to remain at home and subject to his father's commands; besides which the father may threaten to disinherit him. If English law prevailed in France, the peasant proprietor also might threaten an ill conducted or rebellious son; but the son can now reply:—disinherit me? you cannot: my share of your property is my own at your death, however much you may increase it. The power of disinheriting is in England sometimes used capriciously and unjustly, but the absence of the power in France is an injury to every family possessing anything to bequeath. I think it quite possible even, that means may be found hereafter of modifying among us capricious and inhuman wills; perhaps by means of an appeal to a jury: this would be an extension to the acts of a morbid mind, of the control now exercised over the acts of an insane one. At any rate, I repeat, the French practice has not given the labouring classes their due share of the means of living.

Of the many remedies I have mentioned, not one seems available. Of that Socialism which calls on the Government to assume peaceably and justly the functions of capitalists and employers of labour, all we can say is that this system would greatly reduce the annual productions of the country, and while pulling down the rich would do little or nothing to elevate the poor : of that Socialism which would make war on landlords and capitalists and ruin or destroy them, we must say that the proposal is the evil dream of envy and hatred, and that if carried out would bring anarchy and the dissolution of society, which rests on justice and the security of property as its base.

Democracy and universal suffrage offer no better results : since we see in the United States most men living on wages, which house-rent considered, are not sufficient for a liberal competency ; slums with a squalid population, and one great capitalist (besides a multitude of less bloated ones) with an income as great as that of 6,000 English curates, or 20,000 English labourers.

The abolition of settlements and entails gives little hope of improvement in the distribution of property. Mr. Justice Stephen proposes to simplify matters by bringing land and all other realty under the laws regulating personalty. Settlements of land would be on the same footing with settlements of money or of railway-shares; and to abolish the latter would be a heavy blow to the sense of security now enjoyed by parents as to their children.

I may add as to land that if this were made as marketable a commodity as shares, the result, in the opinion of some competent persons, would be an increased number of great estates: for there would be far more estates to be sold, and an overgrown capitalist might take a fancy to become the greatest of landowners; an English Vanderbilt might choose to lay out fifteen or twenty millions sterling for this purpose. An example, within my own knowledge, may show how recklessly he might buy:—a family estate with a magnificent park and a fine mansion was announced for sale; a wealthy manufacturer instructed his agent to buy it; before the auction-day the agent called with the rent-roll of the property and asked for particular instructions; the manufacturer refused to look at the rent-roll, and said, My instructions to you are, *Buy the estate.* A Vanderbilt might on such terms buy and hold fifty great properties, and be satisfied with a revenue from them of 2 per cent. The abolition of land-settlements then, is no cure for the disease of inequalities of fortune.

We see also that the French law of distribution

SECT. VIII.   INEQUALITIES OF FORTUNE.   99

at death, is no cure ; but that it leaves the destitute classes poor by diminishing production, while it also has the baneful effect of weakening parental authority.

VIII.

WHAT SUBSTITUTE PROPOSED? NONE AT PRESENT. DANGER AS IN IRELAND. WEAKENED SENSE OF SECURITY.

IT may naturally be said :—if you condemn all the popular remedies, you must surely have something of your own to put in their place. A common form for discrediting an opponent but an unsound one. In the case of bleeding formerly for pleurisy, a youth who condemned it (as I know) because the patients so treated in a certain hospital died ; it would have been no disproof of his argument to extort from him a confession that he had no other treatment to recommend.

New remedy with any hope of immediate cure I have none to offer : of a rather distant future I will speak hereafter. For the present I may suggest that emigration brings relief. England and Scotland want no fostering in this respect. In my boyhood, emigration like popular education was looked at askance, as not advantageous on a large scale. The prejudice against it has now died out, and the numbers of emigrants from Great Britain, counted by hundreds of thousands, are as high as can well find new countries to receive them.

That is nearly true of Ireland, though her population in some parts still wants thinning. The actual reduction of Irish population is amazing.

The numbers were in 1801 about 5 millions.

They had risen in 1841 to over 8 millions.

They are now under 5 millions.

A reduction of 3 millions out of 8 in 40 years is a marvel. On the other hand the famine of 1846 to 1852, and the fevers that followed are chargeable with much of the diminution: yet the emigrants may be reckoned by millions.

Some parts of the country nevertheless are still overpopulated. How! it will be said: the numbers forty years ago were over 8 millions, and now they are under 5 millions: if forty years ago 8 millions contrived to live on the land, however badly, there must surely be now room for 5 millions. I presume the answer to be that there has been a great reduction in the quantity of land open to peasant cultivation: that this reduction took place during and after the famine of 1846 to 1852, the landlords having taken advantage of the exodus to consolidate their properties by throwing many little holdings into one. The new larger farms are out of the reach of poor men; and only some of these can get employment upon them as labourers, because great farms require far less labour per acre than the little peasant holdings with spade husbandry. Besides; the wet climate of Ireland and its fertile pastures (the admiration of the practical Arthur Young in the last century) favour the rearing of cattle and horses while they discourage the production of grain. It naturally follows that the proportion of permanent pasture as compared with arable land is very large: it is ⅔ of pasture to ⅓ of arable. In England it is ½ of each. In Scotland it is only ¼ of pasture to ¾ of arable. Thus we have Scotland ¼, England ½, Ireland ⅔.

A cry has been raised that the landowners should not be allowed to have so much pasture, but should be required by law to turn a large part of it into arable land. Such interference with the rights of property would be condemned by political economists generally. I do not pretend that this would make me condemn it; for the doctrine of laissez-faire has been grossly abused; and each case to which it is applied ought to be decided on its own merits. This is not the place to consider elaborately the interferences with the rights of landowning which have taken place in Ireland during the last twenty years: but I agree with the *Spectator*, a thoroughly Radical paper, honest certainly if a little fanatical, that the Land-Acts from first to last, while they have harassed the owners have done little or no good to the tenants; and that they have caused incalculable mischief to the three kingdoms by diminishing the sense of security, and thus hindering fatally the increased application of capital to working the land and giving employment to labourers.

In Ireland then, emigration wants the assistance of Government: not that this has been entirely withheld; for the "state-aided" emigrants were in 1883, 17,198; and in 1884, 6348; and these were taken from the western counties, the parts in which the most severe distress prevailed. But if the duty had been earnestly taken in hand by the Government twenty years ago, and if in each year 10,000 young persons had been sent out in addition to the spontaneous emigration, the Irish would have been reduced by more than a quarter of a million, taking into account the children of these young persons who would have been born abroad, and the relations left for a time behind but whom the emigrants would have sent for. I adopt a moderate estimate in mentioning a quarter of a million; yet even this number would probably have been sufficient to banish the extremity of distress except in unusually bad seasons. For these the poor-law authorities ought to provide; or we should have some accumulated fund like that of India for years of famine.

Mr. Tuke, backed by the Duke of Bedford and his friends, has shown by experiment that the destitute people are glad to go and join the millions of their countrymen in America. The priests set themselves against the emigration. I will not say with certain vulgar-minded people, that this is because it lessens their fees on marriages and their feasts at christenings; for few fees can be paid by the destitute, and the disappearance of these paupers reduces the urgent claims upon charity. The good priests oppose emigration, because they shudder at the sight of good Catholics going to places where they are devoid of the offices of their Church, and where multitudes of their children become Protestants at the peril of salvation. The worldly priests lament over the decay of the Church: and no wonder; for the Roman Catholics who in 1801 were probably a third of the people of the United Kingdom, are now only a sixth, making a reduction of one half; not in the absolute numbers but in the proportion of the one church to the other. We as Protestants should not think it right to banish Roman Catholics or to forbid the celebration of mass under pain of death as Cromwell did; but if in relieving distress we reduced the numbers of Roman Catholics, we could not be expected to lament over the altered proportions.

The money cost of assisted emigration would be really far from serious. Part of it might be defrayed by the Irish themselves: the remainder, say £3 or £4 a head, would amount to an annual charge of £30,000 to £40,000: the cost for twenty years would be equal to a payment of a halfpenny in the £ of income-tax, once for all; or 1-40th of a penny per annum.

IX.

PERSONAL IMPROVEMENT WANTED: EDUCATION.

ALL these measures are but palliatives: useful but imperfect. In this as in all social questions, we find ourselves ending with the maxim that all real reforms require an improvement of the people themselves. O'Connell quoted from Byron until the sentiment got hackneyed:—" Know ye not who would be free himself must strike the blow?" As it is with liberty, so it is with well-being: resolution, industry, self-denial, are generally successful, and if these were universal the few cases of congenital weakness, of accident, or inevitable misfortune, would be easily dealt with.

But how improve the people? At best the process is a slow one. Science and mechanical art have made astonishing progress during the hundred years since Watt and Arkwright: the practice of government, I think, has also advanced, though of course the resolute opponents of democracy may say that we have gone backwards and not forwards. This is not a fitting opportunity for the discussion of party politics: I will content myself with saying that I am a Conservative and a pronounced one, but that I look upon the English advance in democracy as a social good, because it tends to reduce the shameful disproportion in the means of living of the highest and the lowest people: so tending because it adds to the weight in the political scale of the poorer classes, and enables them to insist on all possible improvement of their lot.

I repeat the question, how we can improve the people. The action of good executive government is sure but slow, if it is confined to national defence, the maintenance of order and of administration of justice; and sometimes slow even if we add to its functions that of the relief of crying distress.

We want something that will act directly and powerfully on each individual. Laissez-faire denies this, but laissez-faire has had its day. Sunday-schools and clerical influence generally have helped to keep us from relapsing into barbarism, but these agencies have proved too weak to bring about rapid improvement. Apparently, an extension of school-instruction, (or education) is the one course open to us. Without being fanatical on the subject, like recent converts to the cause, I am as I have long been an earnest believer in the importance of working-class schools; and this not only for the instruction given, but also for the discipline practised; for the regularity of attendance enforced; for the decency of behaviour insisted on during school hours. Indirectly too, a very useful task is performed, that of clearing the streets of neglected children of school age, formerly allowed to roam at their pleasure and fall into bad company and vice, but now seized by the Board visitors and compelled to attend school. The Act of 1870, which has virtually brought all British children under these influences, must certainly in the next generation produce admirable effects in the improvement of the people's habits. It is one of the multitudinous calamities of Ireland, that her people share imperfectly in public education, because the priests have set themselves against obliging the children to go to school, while the English working classes have submitted cheerfully to the compulsion, and to its serious inconvenience of robbing the parents of their children's small gains.

Give us a labouring class as well taught as the traders themselves were in the last century, with books at command by means of free-libraries, and taking an intelligent interest in the political knowledge furnished by the popular newspapers, and by the orators of political meetings, and then will follow increased self-respect, foresight, thrift, and a determination to get good wages, or remain unmarried and emigrate. Improve the people and a step will have been taken towards equalization of well-being: a short step but one good in itself as well as in its consequences.

X.

WANTED MODERATION ON PART OF CAPITALISTS.

ANOTHER of our aims should be to moderate the desires of affluent men to become millionaires. We are like the Dutch in the last century, who went on accumulating money until interest fell lower than even the present rate among ourselves. They had to lend it to their own Government at 2 per cent.: and on one occasion, when a loan was paid off the receivers took their principal with tears in their eyes, not knowing how they could re-invest their principal. This we learn from Sir William Temple and Adam Smith. The Dutch patricians were traders, and continued to be such however rich they became.

Many of our traders no doubt, take a wiser course: they buy estates and retire from business. But too many of them fail to do this, and what is worse, extend their business, and even enter into new trades. This deprives younger and poorer men of the chances they would otherwise have: it increases competition and lowers the rate of profit. It often happens that the rich capitalist burns his fingers, subjects himself to years of worry, and loses a large slice of his capital. But though he is rightly punished, that is no compensation to the young and struggling competitor whom he has impoverished and perhaps crushed.

Moderation in the pursuit of wealth would relieve us of a good deal of anxiety and poverty. It would benefit even the labouring classes, because it would leave a wider field open to such of them as save money and wish to embark it in a venture on their own account.

Fifty-five years ago, to make money was the only means of earning distinction in our great towns; as these had no Members of Parliament, not even a seat in the House was within the hopes of aspiring men; but now the greatest towns have their six or eight members, who at present are not selected for their wealth; and these legislators take precedence in society of the millionaire. Municipal honours too, have their attraction, and help to divert attention from mere money-getting.

I wish we had distinctions of another kind, such as to cultivate qualities of a higher class than those which captivate the many and the caucus. In an Essay published in 1871, *The New Academy*, I recommended the creation of an order of merit, such as has been established in other countries, but in this case protected from the influence of political and personal favour. Such an order open to all by reading, reflection, and authorship, and not *in the slightest degree by wealth*, would lead men from the unbridled pursuit of money to something at any rate much better; and by giving precedence to scientific

SECT. X.   INEQUALITIES OF FORTUNE.   109

and literary merit, would rebuke the coarse vice of purse-pride.

It has been objected that the scheme savours of the Chinese mode of governing by Literati, elected through examinations. It is added that the Chinese practice is unsuccessful. The latest information I have met with does not confirm this notion of failure.

The Chinese are divided into four classes: at the head is that of the Literati; then in order of merit come the farmers, the manufacturers, and lowest of all the dealers. To become one of the Literati is an object of such general desire, that for every one who succeeds in each examination, 100 compete: the influence therefore, of the examinations is widely diffused. The desire of success is the more intense, because the honour is extended to a man's parents and family, who become like the man himself, nobles. The organization is the reverse of ours: the honour ascends to a man's relatives; it does not descend to his children and posterity What acknowledged public opinion there is in China is to be found among the Literati, who have a right such as that of the Peers in Great Britian of conferring with the Emperor or his ministers.

We could not fear that the creation of an order of literary merit would disturb the play of our Government: we might hope that it would bring traders to see that there are in the world things more important than swollen money-bags.

XI.

HARRINGTON'S OCEANA AND LIMITATION OF A MAN'S PROPERTY.

THE noble minded Harrington, who whilst thoroughly imbued with liberalism, attended Charles I. on the scaffold, proposed in his *Oceana* a plan for reducing overgrown fortunes: he would have forbidden by law that anyone should own more than a certain fixed estate: such a scheme was more feasible then than it would be now, because the greater part of men's property consisted in land and houses, personalty being comparatively little, when there were no canals or railways, neither gas-companies nor water-companies, and scarcely any public funds or foreign investments.

Yet even now, the difficulty of carrying out such a limitation would not be so great as appears at first sight, because private interest would watch over the execution of the law: for if a certain Dives restrained by law to £5,000 a year, had inherited £10,000 a year, the unlawful £5,000 a year would legally belong to some one else, and this person would demand the execution of the law.

I was struck, years ago, with the efficiency of private interest. A certain barrister with a seat in the House, had made himself obnoxious to his party, and had retired. Long afterwards, it was announced that he had been made a judge; but in a few days we were told that his proposed appointment had been cancelled on account of the earlier scandal. I asked a legal friend how it was that such a small offence was so long remembered, and he replied that another candidate for the judgeship had raked it up.

The same principle appears in France as regards the distribution of an estate on death: if a father tries to evade the Code and give more than the stipulated proportion to one child, the other children invoke the aid of authority, and defeat their father's intention. If a law is to be carried out, it is well to have private interest working in its favour. Thus, even Harrington's maximum might become feasible, if it were proved desirable.

XII.

SUMMARY.

1. THE substance of my Essay then, is this:— my sympathies are with the disinherited of the earth; I regard it as a scandal to humanity that one man, perhaps of less consequence in himself than an honest street-porter, should enjoy an income

of £1,000 a day; an income as great as that of 2,000 curates or 8,000 labourers.

I have no desire for uniformity of fortune, because this is inconsistent with the freedom of each man to earn, share, and bequeath; while this freedom, *curis acuens mortalia corda* (to adopt Hume's favourite quotation) is necessary to the improvement of the useful arts and the greatest possible production of commodities. What we want is moderation.

2. Even the overgrown fortunes are not without their use: they are a resource in case of national adversity, such as that which Pitt had to deal with in the mortal struggle with Napoleon; and which he met by doubling the assessed taxes and by imposing an income-tax of 2s. in the £, with liberal exemptions for the poorer tax-payers.

The middle classes, so far as they enjoy a competency without worry, are foolish if they give way to envy of the very rich: for if fortunes were equalized there would still remain great differences of birth and rank to excite their evil passions. They may if they please, enjoy the sarcasms of Pope and others: but if they are wise they will resign themselves to their mediocrity; remembering that happiness is to be obtained only by throwing off the troubles of life instead of nursing them.

One extravagant fallacy however, needs to be refuted: it is this; that it matters not to the world whether the £1,000 a day belong to one man or to fifty. The reason assigned for this monstrous paradox is, that if the one man spend the £1,000 a day, the fifty men jointly do no more, and that the same employment is given to industry in both cases. This argument overlooks the simple fact that the having money to spend is a satisfaction, and that this is increased fifty fold if it is enjoyed by fifty men instead of one.

3. Shameful as are our present inequalities, they have been worse: in 1842, *e.g.*, there was bitter discontent in the rural districts; wages were much lower than they are now, and provisions were dear. At present they are cheap; bread being at about the prices of the last century before the great war, and wages nearly double. Again; if we compare our farm labourers with those of other European nations we find that our countrymen have decidedly the advantage in wages, house-rent, and poor-law relief.

If we are asked why Government should not insist on the payment of higher wages, the reply is that we learn from past history the failure of such interference. If farmers were compelled to pay at a higher rate than at present, the inferior lands would be thrown out of cultivation, and the labourers on them would lose their employment.

Is there no hope of improvement then? Yes! It is probable that the increased use of machinery, by adding to the productiveness of the land, and by turning the mere labourer into a skilled mechanic, will raise the wages to more nearly those of town artizans.

Government may sometimes and in some countries remove impediments. Formerly, in England, as elsewhere, combinations to raise the rate of wages were illegal, but many years ago our legislature removed these restrictions; not much to the gratification of "orthodox" political Economists, who have gone on even till the death of Mr. Jevons, uttering their baseless fancy, that combinations and trades-unions are useless or mischievous. In other countries, the immigrant Chinese are an obstacle to high wages: I maintain that Governments ought to forbid their landing, except so far as they are wanted for working under a tropical sun.

On the other hand, the ordinary nostrums have been often and justly exposed to ridicule: such are spade-husbandry, and very small farms which make the general use of machinery almost impossible. Mr. Mill's pity for the labourers' dependent condition seems misplaced, since most men who earn their living are equally dependent.

5. The labourers are not without opportunities of rising in the world, by industry and thrift. To an Irishman the English labourers seem objects of envy. The Act of 1885, in giving each of them a vote at elections, secures to them all the consideration they can reasonably claim. It completes our present form of government; that of a Limited Democracy, the best of all forms if the limitations can be maintained.

6. What changes ought to be demanded? Not

the adoption of Socialism, but the stricter confirmation of the security of private property, as an encouragement to the outlay of capital and consequent demand for labour. It is not from *un*limited democracy such as that of the United States that we can expect equalization of fortunes, since we find in New York and Philadelphia overgrown capitalists by the side of starving people.

The abolition of private settlements of land would do nothing for the labourer. Since Lord Cairns's recent act, settlements are no bar to the sale of land.

7. The French law of succession at death is unworthy of adoption, though perhaps means may be found of modifying unreasonable wills.

8. "What is your scheme of improvements then?" I have none, nor am I bound to find one because I object to the present condition of the world. Assisted emigration might mitigate our evils and particularly in Ireland. The Irish Land Laws of the present generation have done harm instead of good, and especially by disturbing the sense of security.

9. I suggest only palliatives. But there is one change which goes down to the very roots of society: improve the people themselves. How? Just and firm administration does this, but only gradually: we want a quicker mode of action: I believe that advancing democracy is an effectual mode, so long as due limitations are maintained.

A speedier mode is that of extended and improved

school instruction, which clears the streets of vagrant children, and which enforces habits of regularity and submission to authority. The modern treatment of vicious and criminal children and youths by industrial reformatories and schools is doing much.

10. I have dwelt upon the inequality of fortune as comparing millionaires with farm labourers: but the evil is not peculiar to rural districts; it exists of course in towns. The artizans may get their 5s. or 7s. a day when at work instead of the labourers' 2s.6d.: but what is 5s. or 7s. compared with £500?

Even the middle classes of towns are many of them very poor. Such penury is caused or aggravated by the discreditable striving for further gains by rich men, who crush beginners and men of small means. This greed is very much owing to the fact that the possession of great wealth is the principal means of distinction. I contend that we might counteract this vicious condition, by formally recognizing literary and philosophical deservings through an Order of Merit, to be given strictly for authorship, as suggested in my *New Academy* published a few years ago. By this means purse-proud men would learn that there are things better deserving of admiration than heaps of gold.

11. I conclude by recalling the scheme of Harrington's *Oceana*, which would limit the amount of property anyone should hold: a scheme not easy to carry out now personalty is so vast, but which might possibly be found feasible under some cir-

cumstances, with the help of the claimants of the surplus.

XIII.

CONCLUSION.

WE must conclude therefore, that shocking as are the inequalities of fortune, no one has discovered a cure, immediate and effective: that nihilism, socialism, "the revolution," would impoverish the rich, and would bring frightful distress on labourers and artizans, by leading the capitalists to narrow their operations and therefore to reduce the amount applied to wages.

But it would be rash to infer that time has no remedy in store. Slavery formerly seemed deeply rooted in human institutions: the Athenians, though as compared with the brutal Spartans and Romans they were gentle with their slaves, yet never dreamt of setting them all free; and to have done this indeed would have been madness if it be true that there were three slaves to every citizen: even the New Testament, with its kindly and sympathetic moral code, let the question alone; and if it had not done so would have raised a storm of alarm and indignation which would have greatly hindered the progress of Christianity. Yet slavery has almost disappeared from the civilized world. Why then, should not fortunes hereafter be equally divided? How, I cannot say: nor could Plato or Aristotle, St. Paul or St. John, say that slavery would come to an end or by what means.

For the present we must be contented with palliatives. Every man must be convinced in the first place that his well-being is dependent upon his conduct. Then, he ought to have the satisfaction of knowing that in the case of inevitable misfortune, the local or the general Government will readily come to his assistance: for I repudiate with abhorrence the malignant doctrine of Herbert Spencer, that all charity is a mistake, and that it is a wise and beneficent policy to leave destitute men and women and children to die the lingering death of hunger, cold, and disease, in order forsooth, that the human race may be improved by the extirpation of the weak and unhappy.

The great palliative is good government; a power at once just, beneficent, and wise: just in securing to every man the fruits of his labour and skill and thrift; beneficent in relieving the destitute; wise in adapting its measures to the actual circumstances of the nation: just in preventing or punishing crime, and in repelling foreign attacks on person or property; beneficent in aiding the weak and unfortunate, and that without grudging the cost; wise in avoiding any means likely to undermine or weaken individual self-reliance, and wise also in consulting the prepossessions and even the prejudices of the people.

Education, in the English sense of school-instruction, is an important palliative, by fostering habits of regularity and obedience, as well as by supplying the means of amusement better than those of the club and the tavern: it may become in the end more than a palliative, by so much improving the labouring classes as to enable them to demand with success an increased share of the means of living.

It is within our reach also, to do something towards reducing that competition in money-getting which oppresses the traders of small means. By establishing an order of merit, not open to Court favour or political success, we might show the purse-proud and the demagogues, that literature and philosophy are of higher value than millions of money and the votes of multitudes.

Chapter III.

MR. ~~HERBERT~~ SPENCER'S BARBARISM.

I.

DEFINITIONS: AUTHORITIES; ADAM SMITH.

READING the title of this Chapter, anyone might naturally imagine that it was suggested by ill will towards Mr. Spencer's mental philosophy. Nothing can be further from the truth: I have no such ill will.

I say this with the more confidence, because my knowledge of his philosophy is of a general and shadowy kind. I was one of his readers indeed, some thirty or forty years ago: but he claims the privilege, to which he is entitled, of adopting new and even contrary opinions as time goes on, as his knowledge widens, as reflection enlightens him.

He even complains that a recent critic has disparaged him as a communist or socialist, whereas his recent work on Social Statics proves him to have renounced that character, and shows that he has become an individualist of the purest water : that now, instead of looking to society (represented by the Government) to regenerate mankind, he looks to men to regenerate themselves without any aid or intereference from above.

But this habit of his, of metamorphosis, from egg to larva, from larva to nymph, from nymph to ferocious dragon-fly, compels us to be on our guard in asserting that we know his present opinions. What these are indeed, as to organized charity I can have no doubt, because I have carefully read his recent declarations.

But what his opinions are as to mental philososhy I only know by general report, and not in such a way as to cause me any irritation or annoyance. I see that he has lately been sharply attacked by Mr. Frederic Harrison for saying that he now believes in the existence of a supreme power in nature : for holding a faith in something like the existence of God. In denouncing therefore, what I regard as his Social Barbarism, I cannot be suspected of using this as a stalking-horse, from behind which to discharge my shafts against his doctrines on mind.

Whatever these doctrines might prove to be, I could bear them with entire tolerance. This does not arise from indifference on my part; as indeed I cannot conceive of indifference upon subjects the most important and the most interesting that can engage our attention. I am tolerant, so far as I know myself, through a deeply rooted conviction of the fallibility of the human mind: of the impossibility of attaining to certainty upon such doctrines, or upon any doctrines which cannot be arrived at by induction from facts, or verified by experience.

The existence of ultimate indivisible atoms was religiously accepted from the Greeks by physicists of the last generation; the doctrine was consistent with many phenomena, and was a convenient mode of classifying or coördinating them: but anyone who doubted it was entitled to claim perfect toleration, on the ground that the doctrine was not arrived at by induction from facts nor verified by producing the atoms; and that therefore the fallible human mind might be mistaken in its hypothesis. The atomic theory is now doubted, and let those who still hold it, as well as those who impugn it, be treated with tolerance.

Mr. Spencer may claim the same tolerance for his intellectual doctrines. But the case is quite different in what I have denounced as his Barbarism. The propriety, the duty, the social necessity of sympathizing with our distressed neighbours, and of expressing that sympathy by acts of kindness, carefully directed and systematically practised, is a matter open to proof by induction from facts and by the verification of experience. I do not feel tolerant towards an author who advises the withdrawal of all such sympathy in action; founding his advice not on experience and observation, but on a barren generality of a metaphysical kind. Such a philosopher is a revolutionist of the worst kind, and I have no tolerance for unnecessary and destructive revolution.

It is because he is an enemy to Charity that I denounce Mr. Spencer. I do not use the word Charity in the wide sense intended in such expressions as " live in charity with all men ;" " Charity covereth a multitude of sins ; " " Faith, Hope, and Charity, these three, but the greatest of these is Charity."

Nor do I use it in the narrow sense of almsgiving: as in the expressions, " he carried coppers to distribute in charity;" "Roman Catholics regard charity (alms-giving, even indiscriminate) as a sacred duty;" "before the Reformation, beggars crowded round the convent gates at the hour of charity" (almsgiving).

I mean by the word, *all* assistance rendered to the needy : "the inhabitants of asylums live upon charity;" "charity is especially useful, when it rescues neglected children." Such charity is not mere almsgiving; it requires thought and labour : nor is it in itself the quality of love which is superior to Faith and Hope, even though it springs from that supereminent quality and is supported by it.

By Barbarism I do not understand inhumanity, cruelty, barbarity : I use the word in the sense of absence of civilization. I am far from accusing Mr. Spencer of wilful inhumanity, cruelty, barbarity : I only accuse him of striving to rob us of our civilization; of striving to carry us back to a savage or barbarous state. No doubt, inhumanity or cruelty, prevails more in a barbarous condition than in a civilized condition: therefore, if Mr. Spencer could have his way, he would land us, first in barbarism and then in barbarity. But a philosopher may be expected to see the probable results of his own teaching: he is responsible for those results if they are produced: therefore, I might, if I had been so minded, have written "Mr. Herbert Spencer's barbarity."

To remove a stumbling-block at the threshold of this discussion, I notice that two of the greatest and most independent of modern economical writers, are favourable to the exercise of charity, and of public charity. The two writers I mean are Adam Smith and Jeremy Bentham: Adam Smith, the apostle of freedom of commerce; and Jeremy Bentham, the founder of the Radical School.

Adam Smith (Book i, cap. 10) strongly objected to one part of the English poor-law but not at all to the charity it practised. What he disapproved of was the law of settlement. After disparaging or condemning the hindrances to migration caused by the action of town corporations, he says:—" The obstruction which corporation laws give to the free circulation of labour, is common, I believe, to every part of Europe. That which is given to it by the poor-laws is, so far as I know, peculiar to England" (not Great Britain). "It consists in the difficulty which a poor man finds in obtaining a settlement, or even in being allowed to exercise his industry in any parish but that to which he belongs.

"It is not the labour of artificers and manufacturers only of which the free circulation is obstructed by corporation laws. The difficulty of obtaining settlements obstructs even that of common labour."

I must observe that the law of settlement came in where corporation laws ceased. Birmingham, not being formerly a municipal town, had no corporation laws: no law requiring every artizan to belong to a trade-company. But if a stranger came to live in the town, he was called upon by the overseers of the poor to show that he had a settlement there, or failing that, to show that if he were allowed to remain, he was not likely to become chargeable to the parish. This happened to William Hutton, the antiquary and local historian: he began business as a little bookbinder, and he had considerable difficulty in persuading the overseers to allow him to remain. This was about the middle of the last century.

Adam Smith condemns the law of settlement: he does not condemn the administration of relief. Yet McCulloch dishonestly suggested that he did so; for we find in the Index to his edition of the Wealth of Nations, "Poor laws, account of the rise and nature of '*this disorder*:'" we turn to the page given and find that the disorder is that of the law of settlement, and does not in the slightest degree condemn poor-laws generally. "The difficulty *of obtaining settlements* obstructs even that" (the free circulation) "of common labour. It may be worth while to give some account of the rise, progress, and present state *of this disorder.*"

It is remarkable that even Malthus, the next great economical writer after Adam Smith, took a view the opposite of Smith's on both points. Malthus, in the fervour of his zeal as a discoverer of truth, disparaged poor-law relief, as tending to increase population; whereas Smith regarded such relief as necessary: Malthus approved the law of settlement, as tending to discourage early marriages and increase of population, whereas Smith censured the law of settlement as hindering the free circulation of labour. Malthus indeed, in his later days, almost forgave the relief administered, in consideration of the eminent benefits conferred by that law of settlement which Adam Smith disparaged.

II.

JEREMY BENTHAM.

NOW let us come to Bentham.—"*Of Indigence.*"
"In the highest state of social prosperity, the great mass of the citizens will most probably possess few other resources than their daily labour, and consequently will be always near to indigence—

always liable to fall into its gulf, from accident, from the revolutions of commerce, from natural calamities, and especially from disease: infancy will always be unable, from its own powers, to provide the means of subsistence; the decays of old age will often destroy these powers. The two extremities of life resemble each other in their helplessness and weakness. If natural instinct, humanity and shame, in concurrence with the laws, generally secure to infants and old persons the care and protection of their family, yet these succours are precarious, and those who give them may stand in need of similar succours themselves. A numerous family, supported in abundance by the labour of a man and his wife, may at any moment lose the half of its resources by the death of one of them, and lose the whole by the death of both.

"Decay is still more badly provided for than childhood. The love which descends, has more power than that which ascends: gratitude is less powerful than instinct: hope attaches itself to the feeble beings who are commencing life, but has nothing more to say to those who are closing it. But even when the aged, receive every possible comfort, the idea of exchanging the part of a benefactor for that of the recipient of alms, pours somewhat of bitterness into favours received, especially when from decay, the morbid sensibility of the mind has rendered painful, changes which would otherwise be indifferent.

"To put an end to these evils" . . "gathering round poverty" . . . "there are only two methods independent of the laws—*Economy*, and *Voluntary Contributions.*"

"*If* these two resources were constantly sufficient, it would be proper to guard against the interference of the laws for the assistance of the poor. . . . The motive to labour and economy is the pressure of present, and the fear of future want: the law which takes away this pressure and this fear, must be an encouragement to idleness and dissipation. This is the reproach which is reasonably" (plausibly) "brought against the greater number of Establishments created for the poor."

"*But* these two means are *in*sufficient, as will appear upon a slight examination.

"With respect to economy, if the greatest efforts of industry are insufficient for the daily support of a numerous class, still less will they be sufficient to allow of saving for the future. Others may be able, by their daily labour, to supply their daily returning wants; but these have no superfluity to lay by in store, that it may be used when required, at a distant time. There only remains a third class, who can provide for everything, by economizing during the period of labour, for the supply of the period in which they can no longer work. It is only with respect to this last class, that poverty can be esteemed a kind of crime. 'Economy,' it is said, 'is a duty. If they have neglected it, so much the worse for them. Misery and death perhaps await them, but they can accuse only themselves: besides, their catastrophe will not be an evil wholly wasted: it will serve as a lesson to prodigals. It is a law established by nature—a law which is not like those of men, subject to uncertainty and injustice. Punishment only falls upon the guilty, and is proportioned exactly to their fault.' This severe language would be justifiable, if the object of the law were vengeance: but this vengeance itself is condemned by the principle of utility, as an impure motive, founded upon antipathy."

"Again, what will be the fruit of these evils, this neglect, this indigence, which you regard in your anger as the just punishment of prodigality? Are you sure that the victims thus sacrificed will prevent by their example, the faults which have led to their suffering?"

"Such an opinion shows little knowledge of the human heart. The distress, the death of certain prodigals . . . even their death itself, would have little influence as instruction upon the laborious class of society. . . . Would those to whom this lesson was most necessary, know how to give to such an event the proper interpretation?" In the absence of publicity as to the causes of the misery and death; "Might they not attribute this catastrophe to unforeseen accidents? . . Instead of saying, 'Behold a man who has been the author of his own losses, . . might it not be said . . .

'There is an unfortunate person, who has taken a thousand useless cares, and whose experience proves the vanity of human prudence?'"

Bentham goes on to private charity. "Let us proceed to the other resource—*Voluntary Contributions.* This has many imperfections:—Its uncertainty: The inequality of the burden (falling upon the humane but sparing the sordid rich): The inconveniences of the distribution." . . . .

"From these considerations it appears, that it may be laid down as a general principle of legislation, that a regular contribution should be established for the relief of indigence."

I have here quoted from Bentham at great length, principally because it serves the purpose of my argument; and the more willingly, because my citations disprove the common opinion that he wanted the power of writing when he pleased clearly and with vigour: with a perspicuity and strength far beyond the powers of ordinary men. It was his whim to often use a strange jargon: as when, living for a time in the country, he described to Sir Samuel Romilly his walks before breakfast and after dinner, as his "antejentacular and postprandial excursions:" or introduced similar pedantic expressions into his serious works, so as to justify the sneer at his style as "Benthamese."

If he had written for the booksellers or for the public, such a jargon would have been avoided. But he wrote for himself and the narrowest of circles during the greater part of a very long life (1747 to 1832 = 85 years). He asserted entire independence, both in style and in matter: this adds greatly to the weight of his authority: the authority of a most original thinker; of the founder of the now predominant school of Radical-democracy; of one much disposed to take as his motto in legislation, "Whatever is, is wrong:" of one who sneered at the British constitution, "the Palladium of liberty;" who disparaged the use of juries; who thought lightly of Delolme and Blackstone, of Burke and the Whigs. It is encouraging to find such an image-breaker stoutly maintaining the old principle of the Poor-Laws.

We have in the sagacious and rather cynical Adam Smith, as well as in the original and iconoclastic Bentham, a foundation on which we may rest securely.

III.

MR. SPENCER'S OPINIONS.

WE will now see what are MR. HERBERT SPENCER'S opinions and the reasons he assigns for them.

"In common with its other assumptions of secondary offices, the assumption by a government of the office of Reliever-general to the poor, is necessarily forbidden by the principle that a government cannot rightly do anything more than protect. In demanding from a citizen contributions for the mitigation of distress—contributions not needed for the due administration of men's rights—the state is, as we have seen, reversing its function, and diminishing that liberty to exercise the faculties which it was instituted to maintain."

The next passage was written long before the Californian, Henry George, had turned the heads of many kind and sympathetic Englishmen.

"The wrong done to the people at large by robbing them of their birthright—their heritage in the earth—is, indeed, thought by some a sufficient excuse for a poor-law, which is regarded by such as an instrumentality for distributing compensation. There is much *plausibility* in this construction of the matter. But as a defence of national organizations for the support of paupers, it *will not bear* criticism."

"The usual reason assigned for supporting a poor-law is, that it is an indispensable means of mitigating popular suffering. Given by a churchman such a reason is natural enongh: but coming as it often does, from a dissenter, it is strangely inconsistent. Most of the objections raised by the dissenter to an established religion, will tell with equal force against established charity. He asserts that it is unjust to tax him for the support of a creed he does not believe."

The dissenters will look suspiciously at this appeal to them; for they were led into a quagmire once before by Mr. Spencer. About forty years ago he was a contributor of weight to the new *Nonconformist*. When the Government first offered to pay part of the expenses of day schools of whatever denomination, he urged his friends not to accept a share of the grant, and he induced them to refuse it. The results were such as the dissenters have long since bitterly regretted: their schools were starved by the want of funds, and the quality of the instruction given was damaged by the absence of Government inspection. After 1870, they generally surrendered their schools to the Boards, a course not adopted by the Church and two other bodies. So late as 1883, of the Government grant not very far from half was allotted to the Church.

The exact figures were: of the whole grant the Church took 46 per cent., the Roman Catholics 5 per cent., and the Wesleyans 4 per cent., while the *un*denominational took 8 per cent., and the Boards 30 per cent., leaving 7 per cent. to all others.

The Church may say:—you have given us the education of a majority of the Protestants and we have ceased to fear you: we are grateful to Mr. Spencer.

He says again:

"In truth there could hardly be found a more

efficient device for estranging men from each other, and decreasing their fellow-feeling than this system of state-almsgiving. Being kind by proxy! Could anything be more blighting to the finer instincts? Here is an institution through which, for a few shillings periodically paid, the citizen may compound for all kindness owing from him to his poorer brothers."

"And thus we have the gentle, softening, elevating *intercourse*" (not charity) "that should be habitually taking place between rich and poor, superseded by a cold, hard, lifeless mechanism, bound together by dry parchment acts and regulations—managed by commissioners, boards, clerks, and collectors, who perform their respective functions as tasks—and kept agoing by money forcibly taken from all classes indiscriminately."

We scarcely expected to find Mr. Spencer justifying the ways of God to men: yet in the following passage so it is, or seems to be: with the unhappy result of leading his followers into barbarism.

"The poverty of *the incapable*, the distresses that come upon the imprudent, the starvation of the idle, and those shoulderings aside of *the weak by the strong*, which leave so many 'in shallows and in miseries,' are the decrees of a large, far-seeing benevolence. It seems hard that an unskilfulness which with all his efforts he cannot overcome, should entail hunger upon the artisan. It seems hard that a labourer incapacitated by sickness from competing with his stronger fellows, should have to bear the resulting privations. It seems hard that *widows and orphans* should be left *to struggle for life or death.* Nevertheless, when regarded, not separately, but in connection with the interests of universal humanity, these harsh fatalities are seen to be full of the highest beneficence—the same beneficence which brings to early graves the children of diseased parents, and singles out the low-spirited, the intemperate, and the debilitated, as the victims of an epidemic."

" There are many very amiable people . . . . who have not the nerve to look this matter fairly in the face. . . . All defenders of a poor-law must be classed among such. . . . these sigh-wise and groan-foolish people, bequeath to posterity a continually increasing curse."

Prophecy is unsafe: we cannot anticipate the verdict of after-ages in the cause of Herbert Spencer *v.* Adam Smith and Jeremy Bentham. We may conjecture however, that advancing democracy will scatter to the winds Spencer's hasty inferences from the barren principle of laissez-faire; just as advancing democracy has already scattered to the winds the ill-founded assertion of orthodox political economy, that workmen's combinations, trade-unions and strikes, are not merely absolutely wrong but useless.

If we cannot learn from our successors, we may learn from foreigners, who partly take the place of them by their independence of us, and who have been called a quasi-posterity. I quote two passages, not as showing what Frenchmen think of the cause and the just verdict, but as showing what they understand Mr. H. Spencer to mean on the whole, despite his honeyed words: "the gentle, softening, elevating intercourse" (not charity but intercourse) that should be habitually taking place between rich and poor."

Mr. Spencer says a Frenchman, "condemns charity" (*i.e.* all charity) "because of the action which charitable donations produce on the reserves *(l'encaisse)* of banks; and he condemns that foolish philanthropy which helps the least deserving to propagate their race, by rescuing them from that mortality to which their ill deserts naturally devote them."

Again, Spencer maintains that :—

"The quality of a society falls in its physical relations, by the artificial preservation of its weakest members: it falls in its moral relations by the artificial preservation of the persons least capable of taking care of themselves."

It is interesting to find similar sentiments expressed in France during the last century, several years before the Revolution of '89. Melchior Grimm (not to be confounded with the brothers Grimm of later days) was possessed of so much capacity, that it was said of him by Diderot, himself a man of genius :— d'Alembert is my inferior, and I am just as much the inferior of Grimm.

Here are Grimm's opinions. The spirit of the Gospel is fundamentally inconsistent with good government: and if modern nations have degenerated from the greatness of the ancients, the fault is due to the establishment of Christianity and its charity. "What I know," he said, "is, that if the executive of a state were entrusted to me, all the asylums would be demolished, even at the risk of leaving to die in the streets those who had failed to provide a retreat for their old age."

IV.

FACTS.

MR. Spencer's opinions are quite intelligible. First, he is opposed to the relief of poverty, whether by the general goverment, or by local government. His reason is that *for a bad purpose* you tax the ratepayers and prevent their saving and depositing money in banks.

The purpose which he pronounces bad is the saving of life: and he condemns it because if men, women or children, are so poor that they are suffering the pains of hunger and cold and nakedness, pains that will only cease when death releases them, this fact shows that they are helpless, feckless creatures who are an encumbrance to the Earth. If you place yourself between them and death, you keep alive an inferior race, and interfere with the natural and beneficent law :—the survival of the fittest.

These are fine words, but we cannot realize their meaning till we apply them to facts.

I was lately staying at Clifton, and lodging on Durdham Down in a house which at the back overlooks a mass of mean cottages. My nights were poisoned by the constant wailing of a young child down below. It was ascertained that the infant was dying of incurable disease. But suppose that it had been hunger and not disease :—let the child suffer and die, says Mr. Spencer: if the father or even the widowed mother, is so poor that food is wanting, that proves the family unworthy of life; and social expediency requires that father, mother, family, should all be cut off. If the wailing is too painful to you, change your lodgings.

A follower of Mr. Spencer may be less harsh and may say :—you are bound to relieve the child : it is only the giving relief by a governmental agency that I condemn.

Take another case. During a hard winter, out of door labourers are thrown out of work for weeks or months, and they suffer great distress : it is customary in the large towns to form temporary associations to relieve them. On Mr. Spencer's principle, such organized associations, and all organized associations, are injurious, as tending to prevent the deaths of the very poorest people, who because they are the poorest ought not to live.

However efficiently such associations are conducted, they fail to aid many of the really suffering. During one of these severe winters, a butcher saw a man steal an ox-head from a hook: the butcher followed, traced the man to his house and fetched a policeman. When the butcher and the policeman opened the door, they found the thief and his family tearing the raw meat from the head and greedily swallowing it. The butcher was a humane man: he did not claim what remained of the ox-head: he did not give the wretched man in charge; and if he had done so, no magistrate would have convicted him: the butcher took care that the family should receive assistance till work was to be had.

Mr. Spencer's follower, nay Mr. Spencer himself, would no doubt, have done as the butcher did. None the less, Mr. Spencer would have condemned his own act, would have protested against the organization for preventing such scenes, and would have carefully secluded himself during the dearth to spare his sympathy and to escape the temptation to beneficence.

But why should we trouble ourselves with facts, when we have a principle well established? I reply by another question:—can any moral, or any economical question be so safely established as to be independent of appeal to facts? Mathematical principles generally are so, because they rest on demonstration; though when a learner advances to the Calculus he may doubt whether the demonstration is to be trusted; and Auguste Comte said that the truth of the Calculus is proved partly by demonstration, and partly by our experience that it leads to accurate results, that is by facts. It is not like Euclid's celebrated 47th proposition, which though a little complex, appeals to unquestionable demonstration at every step. Even as to this proposition, it is worthy of remembrance, that Whewell, before he became Master of Trinity College, used to verify it to his class (or "side") by drawing a right angled triangle on card-board, describing squares on the sides, completing Euclid's figure, and then cutting it up and placing the fragments of the two smaller squares so as to exactly fill up the largest square. This was done, not for induction, but for verification.

It would be a relief to a perplexed student of the Calculus, if one could present to his eye the indefinitely small quantities or tendencies assumed: such verification is impossible: the student must be content to wait until, after years of familiarity with mixed mathematics, he gets the verification he wants or becomes indifferent to it.

An accomplished mathematician is apt to treat Whewell's proceeding as frivolous: he may be equally contemptuous towards anyone who tests by experiment the doctrine of probabilities. I have myself spent hours in tossing up a coin and recording the proportion of obverse and reverse: I have spent a morning with a friend in testing by tossing up a coin, what odds, whether 2 to 1, 5 to 2, or 3 to 1, should be given at whist by the winner of the first game; with the result of confirming the mathematical dictum that the true odds are 3 to 1. I hope that in doing this I was not as weak as I might seem to be in the eyes of the thorough-bred mathematician.

But such verification is far more wanted in moral, social, and economical questions. In these, truth is commonly best reached by induction from history and present observation: but if it is alleged to have been reached by deductive reasoning, it ought never to be received until it has been submitted to experience. If a Sciolist, strong only in his self-reliance, maintains that the best way to feed a people is in all cases to leave the supply of corn or meat to follow the demand for them, and if he is a man in power, he may bring frightful calamities on the people under him. The fatal Orissa famine is an exmaple. The newspapers cried out that if Government intervened it would interfere with private traders, who if left to themselves would dispatch the necessary food: "leave things to the natural operation of supply and demand." Things were so left: the necessary food was not dispatched: the unhappy people died off by hundreds of thousands.

This was because the Sciolists, audacious with their deductive principle, neglected to verify it by facts. If they had taken the trouble to verify the principle, they would have learnt that the law of supply and demand is a general principle and not a universal one: they might have learnt from Adam Smith that demand without means of payment is the desire of a beggar for a coach and six: they would have discovered that not every demand but only an *effective* demand causes supply; and that the desire or demand for food on the part of the Orissa ryots was not an effective demand because there were no means of paying for the food.

Mr. Herbert Spencer might learn a lesson. He believed that he had got at a truth. Bentham and others had shown that the first duty of a government is to protect the people from foreign violence and home depredation. The first duty? says Mr. Spencer: it is the only duty. He believes that he proves this: not by history and recent experience, but by reasoning from the nature of things. Those who differ from him may fairly say that they do not object to his reasoning from the nature of things, but that they call upon him to verify his result by facts, by history, by recent experience.

I will offer a few facts, taken from the experience of France. We owe the account of them to M. Maxime Du Camp of the Académie française; a gentleman by birth and education, and one who has his time at command, so that he can write for pleasure and not for bread. An impetuous man: a great traveller, especially in the East: an intimate of many of the most popular French writers, including the epileptic Gustave Flaubert (the author of *Salammbô* and Madame Bovary) and including Prosper Mérimée, the most obscene of talkers.

M. Du Camp has lately given us short and very interesting biographies of many of these, not forgetting the *Bohemians* among them. But it is his account of an organized charitable institution that I propose to use in order to throw light on our subject. This institution, the Little Sisters of the Poor, well known in England, is founded on the basis of a Roman Catholic sisterhood, and we are quite safe from having its merits exaggerated by M. Du Camp, a Parisian *littérateur*.

M. Du Camp had an excellent literary training; for though he had been unsuccessful in his attempts at light literature, he had obtained a seat in the Academy. When he was about *fifty* (in 1873) he published an account of the sewerage of Paris, to the amusement not without disgust, of Gustave Flaubert, who regarded light literature as the only business of life, and rallied his friend in good, set terms. Take care! You are going down an incline: you have already adopted steel pens, like a weak soul. And he fixed on him the name of Égoutier (Scavenger). We have a little autobiography which reminds one of Gibbon's celebrated narrative of his feelings when he had finished his Decline and Fall; and reminds one also of an extract from a pastoral which reads like a Persian or European production, but which was really written by a Chinese statesman-poet of the time of our Norman Conquest.

"The slanting rays of sunset surprised me sitting on a fallen tree, silently watching the restless swallow flitting about her nest, or the cunning hawk pouncing on his prey. The rising moon found me still and contemplative. The murmur of waters, the rustling of leaves fast fluttering in the wind, the charm of an unclouded sky, soothed me into a gentle reverie; all nature spoke to my soul; I forget myself as I listen, till advancing night slowly leads me to the threshold of my home."

In M. Du Camp's notes we learn how the light French writer's reverie occurred. Until middle age he had enjoyed an unusually good eyesight: he was proud of it; for it had withstood the burning sands of Syria; the dazzling snow of the glaciers, and the breezes or calms of the sea; no one could better mark down a covey of partridges, or read more indefatigably. But at *forty-three*, his eyes pained him, and on consulting an oculist he found it necessary to order spectacles. One day while these were being adjusted, he went to sit for half an hour on the Pont-Neuf. There were a hundred sights all familiar to him: a cargo of timber floating down the Seine; a swimming-bath preparing for use; the chimney of the Mint pouring forth its smoke; on the quay were cabs, omnibuses, policemen, a prison-van and carts.

"Why did this well-known scene so strongly move me? Why through the tumult did I see a manifestation of superior foresight? I cannot say: but Paris suddenly appeared to me as an immense body whose every function was the result of special organs, watched over and attaining singular precision."

"I fell into a day-dream, all the more intense for the movement and uproar. There I sat without motion, absorbed in my thoughts; and when twilight recalled me to myself, I forgot the optician who had been awaiting me two hours. But I resolved to study one by one the wheels of the social machine of Paris."

This happened in 1865, and since that year M. Du Camp has been fulfilling his resolution. He prepared for his task by a series of investigations made at the cost of severe and continued labour and sacrifice. "I was led to try every employment: I lived at the Post Office; I was all but a clerk in the Bank of France; I knocked down oxen; I accompanied the detectives and the superintendents of loose people and of lodging-houses; I sat down in the cells of prisoners; I went to the guillotine and the dissecting table; I visited paupers and slept on a hospital bed; I assisted the agents of the octroi in watching smugglers; I travelled with the drivers of fast trains; I shut myself up in a madhouse to study the inmates. I may say that I recoiled from no possible investigation, from no fatigue whatever, from no cause of disgust."

The result was his work in six volumes, on "Paris, its organs, functions, and life, in the second half of the XIXth century." After his studies and labours he came at last to a description of the Little Sisters of the Poor.

We can trust such a man better than another who merely resolves to write a book, and such a book as shall be read; who therefore, selects the striking and interesting, and leaves in shadow, or omits altogether, the uninteresting and repulsive: we can trust him far better than one who enters into a contract with a publisher to furnish a certain quantity of copy every week, until a projected book is complete: the practice of Georges Sand, who probably owed to it those rather frequent pages and chapters, uninteresting and even wearisome. For myself, after reading a large part of what M. Du Camp has written, I rely on him confidently.

V.

LITTLE SISTERS OF THE POOR.

I PROCEED to the history of the Little Sisters. In reading it we learn a good deal of the French indigent classes, of the insufficiency of unorganized relief, and of the results of leaving extreme misery to shift as it may.

"Who can forget the parable of the grain of mustard-seed, almost invisible, but the parent of a plant in which the birds take shelter? Such is the work of the Little Sisters of the Poor, humble at first and almost despicable, but which has grown into the dimensions of a public benefit. It started in a district used to a struggle with the elements and often visited by misfortune: in the little town of St. Servan, the twin sister of St. Malo." There, the cruel sea often swallows the seaman, leaving his family to hunger and his old father to beggary. "In the time of my youth, at every corner of a street there was a medicant, telling his beads and begging for alms."

"It is a commonplace, that want stirs compassion: but for the most part such compassion is satisfied by dropping its indiscriminate alms. Thoughtful compassion is rare, such compassion as is seriously bent on doing good." . . . . .

Generally, it is the poor who help the poor. But goodwill is not enough: there needs a directing intelligence, bent on doing good, with such moral resources as give permanence to the work. This want was supplied on the day when the Little Sisters came into existence, founded by two young workwomen, and an old domestic servant, backed by a humble priest.

The old servant, Jeanne Jugan, had her biography

written and laid before the Académie française, which recompensed her devotedness. She was born in 1792, and her early years witnessed the long wars, the cruel conscription, the blockade, the dearths and high prices. She went out as a servant, grew to be a tall, bony, abrupt woman, remained unmarried, and finally entered the house of an old maid who was kind to the poor. There she served her apprenticeship to beneficence.

When the kindly mistress died (1838) Jeanne was 46 years old: instead of getting another place, she set up as a sempstress, and earned a poor livelihood; cooped up in a garret, sometimes working at home, and at other times hiring herself out for the day. She had a little hoard of £25.

She saw that there was no asylum at St. Servan, where she was living; no refuge for the old and poor: the unhappy creatures died unrelieved on their pallets, or dragged their limbs through the streets, or knelt at the church doors and begged.

The winter of 1839 was a hard one; the sea had swallowed some of the boats; the weather was cold and food was scarce. An old woman infirm and blind, lived on the alms collected by her sister. This sister died, and the alms ceased. Abandoned by all, helpless in her blindness, the poor creature was dying of want, muttering her prayers.

Jeanne Jugan hearing of this from a young friend, visited the sufferer, carried her to her own garret and contrived a bed for her. She nursed, fed, and washed her: the cost was a heavy one to her small means, but she worked the harder.

Soon afterwards, she heard that another poor woman, who had lived by begging, had become so infirm that she was unable to stir out: she had the strongest claim to assistance; for having been in service with a master who failed, she had continued to wait upon him till he died, and this without any wages. Jeanne brought her also into her garret, which was now so filled with the three beds that Jeanne had to sew sitting outside on the landing.

Strong in faith, and driven into a change, she ventured to hire a house: but she was soon as crowded as before; for she could not resist the cries of the paupers around her: within a month she had twenty old women to provide for, all of them helpless, ragged, infirm, or bedridden. Resolute as she was, it was beyond her means to provide for all these, even if she could give up to work her nights, already too short: her savings were exhausted, and she had sold everything she could spare: yet she could not turn out of doors the poor creatures she had adopted; nor could she leave them to die of hunger.

Then it was that Jeanne Jugan, advised by her priest, took the step which led to prodigious consequences. All her inmates had previously lived on alms: she made a list of the persons who had supplied these and resolved to call on them. Dressed in black serge and a mob-cap, she went basket on arm and besought alms for her poor. She did not ask in vain: she brought home crusts, cheese-parings, old clothes and shoes: she made the best of these with the assistance of the least helpless of her charge.

Her efforts were talked of. "Good or bad, example is contagious. Kind-hearted people of St. Servan and St. Malo subscribed and bought her a large house, in which her poor would have room to breathe and move: but they warned her if she went beyond the bounds of prudence, it would be at her own risk. She promised to be prudent, but nevertheless her numbers increased from year to year, until at Christmas 1844 they amounted to *sixty-five*.

"The infirm have an asylum: Jeanne not only receives them; she searches them out, carries in those unable to walk: the house seems to grow in order to shelter vagabond and miserable old age: 'Knock and it shall be opened to you.'"

The priest (himself a great promoter of the good work); the mayor, the municipal council, agreed that such unfailing self-denial deserved distinction and reward: they sent a memorial with confirmatory documents to the Académie française: the committee for the prizes of virtue recommended a gift of £120 from the Montyon fund and that sum was given.

It is on this legal memorial, accepted by the Academy, that the history now given is founded, and we may therefore accept it without hesitation.

The Little Sisters of the Poor sprang from the heart of Jeanne Jugan, but required more ability and cultivation than she possessed.

Two young ladies, of devout aspirations, and bent on a life in a religious community, quietly assumed the direction of the enlarged institution but Jeanne Jugan continued to be the factotum. The two Sisters (not sisters by blood) introduced a sort of monastic rule: they divided the day into hours of work and hours of prayer, leaving no hours for amusement. They acted under the advice and authority of a young priest, Le Pailleur.

"The older I get" said Georges Sand in 1836, "the more I worship kindness, because I see that it is the advantage of which God has given us the least." One might quote against Georges Sand the saying of Dr. Johnson, that on entering the world he was surprised to find so much kindness and so little honesty. My experience is with Johnson. But at any rate, Le Pailleur is said to have possessed the quality of kindness in the highest degree.

He and the two ladies had no ambition of founding the widely spread institution which now flourishes: they only proposed to do the good that was within their reach: to mitigate the suffering they saw, to solace the wretched, to rescue old age from the wandering life of mendicity. They made no provision for the future; they lived from hand to mouth as did Jeanne Jugan; and their successors do the same. They sought no foundations or permanent revenues; they asked only for daily bread: in fact they have sheltered thousands upon thousands of poor old people, who but for them would have died on a dunghill of hunger or of drink in taverns.

The asylum was full: the sisters slept where they could; in the cock-loft, or on the landing place; yet many indigent were left unaided. There was land outside the house, but there was no money in the drawer. The sisters themselves began to dig out the foundations and to fetch in stones. The labourers around pitied them and took their places; a contractor lent his carts; money came in: a new house was built and received 40 inmates.

The abbé Le Pailleur used his influence and authority wisely: he saw the danger of aiming at too much: the Sisters were receiving the indigent of all kinds; foundlings, orphans, sick children; the abbé limited the admission to old people falling into dotage. "I imagine that as a pupil and as a seminarist along the walls of St. Malo, in the road towards Cancale, in the hollow lanes of the environs of Rennes, he had often met dotards, ragged, begging, or drunk, with hanging lip and lacklustre eye, pestered with vermin, and in an abject condition the more shocking because respect to age is innate in our hearts. The old beggar" (pace Sir Walter Scott and Edie Ochiltree) "is a drunken vagabond, a prey to every vice which he scarcely tries to cast off."

M. Du Camp adds his own experience. "I know little of Brittany at the present day; but I remember that on a walking tour there in 1847, begging was a sort of institution, aggressive and almost threatening, from which it was really difficult to escape. More than once Gustave Flaubert and myself were stopped by bands of wretched creatures whose demands it was difficult to satisfy. In the Morbihan, at Baud, as we returned from the château of Quinipilly, we had to appeal to the gendarmes to release us."

"The abbé Le Pailleur must have witnessed many such scenes: as a man he must have pitied the misery; as a priest he must have been horrified at such vice: his intelligence and kindness taught him that to save the soul the body must often be cared for."

The work prospered: more sisters came in and relieved the overworked nurses: the collectors of alms multiplied. It was then remembered that other places besides St. Servan had their miseries. Le Pailleur had seen these at Rennes where he had studied. In this former capital of Brittany, there were swarms of beggars. The Little Sisters opened a house there, and succeeded so well that a larger house was provided for them.

They were gratified by a proof of the estimation in which they were held: "the soldiers, the loafers, the drunkards, removed the furniture to the new home, and far from seeking payment dropped their mite into the treasury."

The next town they adopted was Dinan, of which the former seigneurs were the ancestors of the heroic Du Guesclin: in 1846 the mayor of the town proposed to establish a gratuitous asylum for old men: the Little Sisters exactly suited him, for they asked nothing but opportunity. At first they got an old gaol, so damp and unwholesome that it stood empty: they took possession and made the best of it; they had one difficulty; that they had not money enough to alter the locks which were so put on as to keep the prisoners in and not to shut trespassers out. At the end of a year a fitter abode was found for them.

In the course of time they came to Paris, where up to 1883 they opened five houses, with 1200 inmates and about 100 Sisters. There as elsewhere, they have no regular income, but live on the alms they collect: it is said that any surplus money they receive beyond the needs of the day, is not kept for future needs, but is sent to the head institution. These Parisian houses were opened between 1851 and 1864: what must have been the anxieties and sufferings during the siege and the commune of 1870-1! Since that time they have found their way across the Channel: we have for years past seen them in England: going about their work quietly; never mentioned in the newspapers; holding no meetings in public: *quêting* with a modest reserve which secures courtesy and alms for the poor: aided by Protestants as well as Roman Catholics.

But in France they have had their enemies: those fanatical enemies of all religion, who lately banished the priests from the bedsides of the dying in the public asylums, and decreed that all orders, including that of the Little Sisters, should cease: that lay nurses should take their places. "*Laicisation*" is their watchword. "With Frederic the Great they say '*écrasez l'infâme*.' Word equally harbarous!— Ah! I know too well these lay nurses; I have seen them at their work; I know what sausages and absinthe they carry in their pockets."

The Little Sisters on the other hand, are the mothers of their charges: mothers tender, fondling, smiling, as is fit with second childhood. "I have seen young Sisters, with the freshness of youth, walking with a band of sons, the youngest of whom was 75: I have seen them casually, engaged in their daily occupations, and not arranged to be looked at. What struck me the most was their gaiety: a smile always on their lips as if a part of their discipline." *The tear forgot as soon as shed; the sunshine of the breast.*

As we have already seen, the Little Sisters make no pretence of confining their charities to the "deserving poor," no more than do our workhouses. In the houses of the Little Sisters there come to an end lives which surpass in strangeness that of the most imaginative of romances. But the biographies are not revealed. No doubt they resemble those of the drunkards and outcasts of other countries: such as those which were lately given to the world of London in general terms. The following were inmates of a London common lodging-house, charging 4d. a night for a bed.

1. One who had been a paymaster in the Royal Navy.

2. Two who had been friends at Cambridge, now equally degraded.

3. A medical man, son of a physician, and who sold fuzees in the Strand.

4. A clergyman who had taken high honours, now a drunkard.

5. A Master in a celebrated college, and F.R.S.

6. An ex-officer, turned begging-letter impostor.

7. Sons of officers, contractors, wealthy traders: one of these sons a low potman at a tavern.

8. The wife of a west-end physician.

All these sinners and criminals can if they please throw themselves into the workhouse and escape starvation: all of them as they grow old would be received by the Little Sisters. There are persons to be found who hold, that our workhouses and the Little Sisters, by helping such people, encourage vice: they believe that if men and women were left to reap the natural consequences of their misdeeds, vice would cease, or nearly cease. Among such pseudo-philosophers is Mr. Herbert Spencer.

He indeed, would go much further: he would not only discourage vice and improvidence by leaving the bad and the spendthrifts to the natural consequences of their misconduct: he would extend his icy philosophy to the innocent unfortunate. In the following case, as it seems to him, society did just what it ought; though if it happened in England, the newspapers from London to Berwick and Land's End would denounce the cruel neglect of the neighbours and the authorities.

"Going by chance into an old shed, I found a wretched creature, shapeless and motionless: I made out that it was a former servant of my mother" (a Russian lady) "once a pretty, laughing girl, now paralysed and a prey to some strange disease. This skeleton lying forgotten among the rubbish had no tie to bind her to the world: no one cared for her, except that a kind soul sometimes filled her water-jug. She wanted nothing more: she showed that she lived, if life it could be called, by her eye, and by a voice like the whisper of the marsh-sedges."

She managed to relate her misfortunes. Going one evening to listen to the nightingales, she had a bad fall: the unknown disorder seized her, and robbed her of one function after another till every possible enjoyment was gone. Her betrothed was greatly distressed, but what could he do? He married another, and she trusted he was happy.

For many years her only occupation has been to listen to the church bell and the humming of the bees. Sometimes a swallow comes and flits about the shed, and that is a great event for her. She does not complain: her neglect is that of other unfortunates: she is grateful to those who give her water.

This is a fancy picture. But it is painted by the genius of Tourguénef, who, writing in Russian, may be trusted to have given a true representation of the daily habits of his countrymen.

To Mr. Spencer, the sight of the shed and its suffering bundle of rags, filth and vermin, would be heartrending; and he would fly from it as he would fly from the operating table of a hospital. But none the less would he say that both the neglect and the surgery are wholesome: the one to get rid of a diseased limb, the other to get rid of a diseased member of society.

Well may we dread a Government of Philosophers! of men, says Hobbes, who in the absence of true definitions, are "as much below the condition of ignorant men, as men endued with true science are above it."

VI.

THE LITTLE SISTERS OF THE POOR: LESSONS.

WE may learn many lessons from the careful and trustworthy narrative by M. Maxime Du Camp.

France has no general and organized system like our Poor-Law. We see the results. First, Beggary, open and legal. In England, as we all know, there is still a good deal of beggary but it is illegal. In fact beggars as such are frequently brought before the Police Courts: I cannot say that they are often punished; if they are infirm or emaciated they are probably sent to the workhouse; robuster ones are warned, and generally undertake to tramp on to another place, and they keep their promise. If there were no workhouse and no tramp-ward, they could not be punished or threatened. "What am I to do? I am out of work and I have not a penny to buy a crust of bread." You cannot punish that man: if you do punish him for begging, he must steal or die. We can punish a man in England because he has the resource of the workhouse.

The stationary beggar then, is unknown. Compare France where the starving man must beg or steal. I say France; but this is not true of Paris; there, the institutions for relief are numerous and even lavish; the sums spent on paupers are twice as great as those spent in London; that is, Paris has half the population and spends about as much as London.

Paris avowedly does this mainly from prudence and fear of insurrection: if charity were the mainspring, the same aid to the poor would be rendered throughout the country. "The *Public Assistance* in Paris is a social institution: it does a work of charity no doubt; but it does it mostly for *public safety;* in receiving the sick, in locking up madmen, in adopting infants, foundlings or not; in giving alms to paupers driven to beggary. What are the millions expended, compared with the dangers threatened by the 300,000 persons relieved every year?"

"The day when the Public Assistance disappears, the footpaths will be invaded by the infirm, epidemics will rage, infanticide will grow frightfully, and the bakers' shops will daily be in danger from rioters. Paris in protecting the miserable protects herself."

The lavish alms are given for expediency, and with the worst results. But no such profusion appears in other places. We have seen the facts: M. Du Camp twice visited St. Servan, once in his childhood and again in his youth; on both occasions he saw at every corner a beggar telling his beads and imploring charity. Probably, the father or son, who would have supported the mendicant, has been wrecked and drowned. Other wretched beings suffered and died unrelieved, or as long as it was possible dragged their limbs through the streets and knelt at the church doors: one of these, bedridden and blind, was maintained by her sister who begged for her and nursed her.

What would Mr. Spencer do with a man who places himself at the corner of a street? Say that all passers by are induced to refuse alms: the man swoons away; is he to be left lying there till he dies? Impossible! he must be picked up and fed. He returns next day and every day. You cannot flog him: you may imprison him, but in that case you must maintain him, and your gaol becomes a workhouse.

Sturdy beggars are still worse. In Brittany M. Du Camp in 1847 met bands of these, asking or rather demanding alms, with threatening looks and hostile attitudes, discontented and grumbling, whatever they got, blocking the road to enforce their extortions and requiring the authority of the police to drive them off.

England had full experience of such people long ago. In the years preceding the reigns of Edward VI. and Queen Mary, the change of manners which caused the dismissal of crowds of retainers who had hung about noble mansions, together with the enclosure of farms found necessary for increased sheepbreeding and diminution of tillage, together with the cessation of almsgiving at the gates of convents recently suppressed, threw upon the world multitudes of needy men, who banded together to exact by threats what would be refused to each of them singly. It was soon after this that a statute of Queen Elizabeth established, not asylums but *work*-houses, in which these vagabonds should be gathered and made to labour. Thenceforward sturdy beggars could be punished, because they had a refuge to which they could betake themselves.

I have said that at St. Servan, begging often arose from the loss at sea of the bread-winner of a family. But inland towns were not free from it: at Rennes, for instance, mendicants swarmed. They are more common in wealthy places than in poor ones, for there is more to be got; more common in old towns than in new ones, because indiscriminate almsgiving, doles and fixed charities carelessly administered, attract a race of idlers and waiters upon providence. Rennes was formerly the capital of Brittany, the seat of a Parliament, the abode of many noble persons. There you would see abundance of those wretched old men shocking to the eye.

The old French vagrant is often a drunken scoundrel, a prey to every vice, and a willing prey; pestered by vermin, with hanging lip and glassy eye; a liar and cheat and often a criminal. Compare a knot of such outcasts with an equal number of old men in the ward of a well-conducted English workhouse: in decent uniform, clean, well fed, civil, apparently contented: not so indulged as to make outsiders desirous of surrendering their liberty by coming in, but rescued from the bondage of vice and misery. St. Servan, Rennes, every town and village of France, might be saved from the plague of vagrants on the same terms.

Mr. Spencer will not deny that as regards mendicity we are more fortunate than the French. But he will say that the price we pay is too high: that price is the interference with nature's law, the survival of the fittest. By keeping alive a number of men, women, and children, who under the fiat of "the highest beneficence," are condemned to die with the long torture of cold, hunger, wounds undressed, chronic disease unrelieved; by supplying food, clothing, shelter, surgical assistance, and medical attendance; we disregard the moral laws of the universe, and from a weak desire to mitigate present suffering, do infinite damage to future generations, in causing the continuance of those portions of our race who are unfit to live. All defenders of a poor-law must be classed among those "sigh-wise and groan-foolish people, who bequeath to posterity a continually increasing curse."

Mr. Spencer tells us what people they are whom he would condemn to slow death: the poor through incapacity, imprudence, idleness, weakness, unskilfulness, sickness; the poor through losing husband or father; (Soc. Statics, 1868, 364) all these are to be regarded as unfit to survive and therefore fit sacrifices to the god of expediency, the expediency of improving the race. The breeder of short-horns or Devons, out of his calves annually produced, selects those with bad points and condemns them: but he does not leave them to die of cold and starvation; he kills them off. Mr. Spencer would practise more humanity, if he would administer prussic acid or strong chloroform to the idle, the unskilful, the widow and the orphan. Am I wrong in my title, The Barbarism (or Barbarity) of Mr. Herbert Spencer?

The narrative of the Little Sisters gives us some examples of those to whom prussic acid should be administered. We have the two poor sisters, living in a garret, on alms; both ought to have been poisoned off, though to be sure at their age there was no danger of transmitting their beggary to a family: both however, must be left to die, or more humanely poisoned off. One of them escaped the danger by dying a natural death: the other was left, without even the resource of begging; for she was blind and infirm: prussic acid ought to have supplied her last meal.

Another example suggests a different view of the case. Mr. Spencer assumes that paupers have become such by bodily or mental incapacity; for it is assumed that if people fell sick to death, or are deprived by

SECT. VI.   INEQUALITIES OF FORTUNE.   165

accident of husband and father, that is a proof of such incapacity and unskilfulness as calls for cutting off from the human race by death.

Try this opinion by the sketch of Isabel Quéru's career. She had been a domestic servant: her master was suddenly ruined: she would not leave him, but remained and waited on the family till they died. She served them and took no wages: she was therefore unable to save anything for her old age. When this came upon her she had no resource but begging.

The cause of this old woman's pauperism was not idleness, or unskilfulness, or improvidence, but generosity. Mr. Spencer may say that her generosity was improvident, and so far blameable that it helped to keep alive a family unthrifty or unfortunate, and fit for death. Administer prussic acid to the family and to Isabel herself: away with them! they are unworthy to live!

It may be said that in the absence of a poor-law, exceptional cases may be left to private charity. Now at St. Servan there was no poor-law and these exceptional cases were delegated to private charity, and this left the poor creatures suffering the pangs of cold and hunger. They were rescued from death at the last moment, but how many others had died? " Generally compassion is diffuse, and satisfies itself with slipping a coin into the hand of the beggar." Indiscriminate charity! which encourages mendicancy. "It is not sufficient to give, it is necessary to know how to give, a difficult art."

Private charity, and organizations lay or religious, do much; but the poor-law is still wanted. We see how much it was wanted at St. Servan, to relieve these poor and deserving women. Besides; if lay or religious organizations did supply the place of a poor-law, they would be open to the same objection that is made to a poor-law: they would keep alive the idle and the unfortunate, and transmit their children to the next generation.

I have heard kindly men speak of the English system as the cause of the pauperism around us: I have heard this especially from elderly men, survivors of the early days of the Westminster Review, a periodical founded by the followers of Bentham, who disagreed with their master on this important matter. Let such devotees of *laissez faire, laissez passer*, ponder the lesson that is taught us by France, with no poor-law but with pauperism and mendicity rampant.

I should also like to know Mr. Spencer's opinion as to a general system of insurance. Would he think it advisable that all labouring men in town and country, should pay a small weekly sum to provide an annuity for their declining years? No doubt he would think it advisable. Let us go a step farther and suppose that the Government enforced these weekly payments, and applied them to supplying annuities for the old and relief for the young; a scheme that Prince Bismark has more than dreamt of for Germany. Mr. Spencer might object that in doing this the Government would be going out of its province which is to protect citizens from home and foreign violence.

He might also say that a fund so raised by compulsion would be equivalent to one raised by a poor-rate, and would be employed like that in propagating the inferior portions of our race. I agree with him as to the equivalence of the two funds: I regard the present poor-law as a vast insurance company, with an annual income of six or seven millions applied to relief: an income to which every householder contributes and on which every person has a claim. I hear it said that the poor impudently assert *their right* to relief: it seems that they have a right to it, since they and their relatives and friends all contribute to the fund in the form of poor-rates. In the great towns the rates are generally compounded: the landlord pays them and gets them back from the tenant as part of the rent: in the country the labourer is often excused from paying, and the gap thus left, is filled up by an increased contribution from the farmer and the landlord. But if the poor-law were an avowed compulsory insurance company, the same compounding and the same exemptions would, no doubt, take place.

Many of Mr. Herbert Spencer's admirers disagree with him as to this singular application of the doctrine of the survival of the fittest. Living in the world and acquainted with men and women as they are, they know that they cannot poison off or allow to die, those hundreds of thousands of persons whom the Union workhouses receive within their walls, or whom the Guardians by small allowances enable to tide over days of distress and sickness.

Some of these dissidents will excuse their master on the ground that his intentions are excellent: that he desires to do his part in regenerating, purifying, strengthening the race of man. A few years ago, a Swedish pastor adulterated the sacramental wine with poison, and administered the deadly mixture to a few of his parishioners. The poor creatures died. The pastor was suspected, accused, tried, and convicted. For his defence it was urged that his intentions were excellent: that the poisoned persons were old, decrepit, miserable, and that death was a relief to them: that they could not die more happily than in receiving the Communion. On the other hand it was conceded that the pastor acted from kindness: that his *motive* was a desire to diminish suffering. But motive and *intention* are different things: the pastor's intention was to put certain persons to death illegally and without any pretence of a warrant, and he carried this intention into effect. If this had happened in England, it might have been thought harsh to hang the pastor, but he certainly would not have escaped many years of penal servitude, or confinement as a madman.

Mr. Herbert Spencer may be actuated by the most amiable of motives in desiring to regenerate the human race: but his intention when he tries to induce us to withhold bread from the famishing, clothes from the naked, shelter from the houseless, and medicine from the diseased, is odious, detestable, and barbarous.

To accept a good motive as an apology for cruel deeds, may lead to frightful consequences, such as would naturally follow the impunity of crime. A mother puts her children to death, foreseeing for them in this world nothing but poverty, sickness, sin, and crime: she dismisses them as she thinks, to a better world, during their days of innocence, before they have incurred a worse fate. Brought before a jury, she is probably declared mad and is condemned to a lunatic asylum, that is really to a prison. She may be sane, but her good motive will not exempt her from the severity of the law.

Attempts have lately been made in France to rehabilitate Robespierre, just as a similar foolish attempt has been made in England to rehabilitate Henry VIII. Robespierre's life, it is said, before 1793, was virtuous, and that to an uncommon degree: he desired to be irreproachable: he carried his virtue into politics; he was convinced that it was for the true interest of France to get rid at once of royalists, of aristocrats, of priests, and of their abettors:

patriotic expediency required the sacrifice of tens of thousands of victims, innocent in the eye of the law but obstacles to the common good: the guillotine was set to do its work.

In the opinion of Louis Blanc and a few other fanatics, Robespierre's virtuous patriotism excuses or gilds his atrocities: the world contemptuously or angrily dismisses the plea, and continues to look upon Robespierre as a monster of iniquity.

Beware of doing evil that good may come! Far from us be the fatal error of founding our morals on a narrow imaginary expediency!

VII.

FURTHER CONSIDERATIONS.

THE case as I have given it seems fairly complete: so conclusive indeed, that I cannot help asking myself whether I have not been fighting with a shadow: I cannot help suspecting sometimes that I have misunderstood Mr. Spencer, and that he does not really mean to advise the abolition of all poor-laws and all organized almsgiving.

I turn for correction to his admirers and followers. I find that they understand his utterances as I do. I can point to one of them, a man, rich, self-denying, industrious, earnest, who formerly took an active and zealous part with his friends in works of charity, but who now says, *ipse dixit:* the master has declared that so-called works of charity are pernicious and debasing; and that they are to be classed with the indiscriminate charity of giving to beggars, a wicked folly that all Protestant philanthropists condemn. This man now, will no more take part in a committee for aiding orphans and widows, than he would take part in a mission for converting the Hindoos or restoring Solomon's Temple.

Mr. Spencer's meaning is unquestionable: it is the decree of an overruling power that the incapable should die, in order that the human race may be rid of them: that the widows and children should also die that they too may not hand down incapacity to future generations. As a Frenchman has interpreted the doctrine :—

" The quality of a society falls in its physical relations, by the *artificial preservation* of its weakest members : it falls in its moral relations by the artificial preservation of the persons least capable of taking care of themselves."

No wonder Mr. Spencer himself says that there are many very amiable people who have not the nerve to look this matter fairly in the face. I would suggest as nearer the truth that people generally have not the barbarity to look unmoved at men, women, and children, dying of cold and hunger, to satisfy the dictates of a pedantic philosophy.

I cannot help recurring to a simple case such as is happening every-day, but which a freak of memory reveals to me. I was in my countinghouse while my people were at dinner: opening my door, I saw a mechanic whom I had long known, and who had evidently become blind; I state his case in his own grotesque language:—"Some months ago, I was working till Monday dinner, and then I went to my garden, and the blight took me, and I went into the hospital, and I suffered martyrs, and when I come out I was quite dark."

A kind-hearted gentleman had offered him a trifling weekly allowance, if he could get others to join, and make the pension enough to maintain the poor fellow. The matter was so arranged, and the blind man had the small occupation of constantly calling on his benefactors. Thus he lived, and after a few years he died without having suffered the humiliation of going into the workhouse, and without having known the extremity of want.

According to Mr. Spencer the blind man's benefactors were enemies of society; for they artificially kept alive one whom the beneficence of an unseen power doomed to perish. This beneficence required that the victim should be left to beg or steal: in fact to steal, since the beneficence of nature forbids the giving of alms, and the hungry man's only resource would have been to help himself from a cook's or confectioner's shop, or to smash windows and so get board and lodging in a gaol.

"But the workhouse!" you will say. Mr. Spencer would abolish the workhouse. The gaol alone would remain, the wretch's only resource. If he had too much self-respect to enter there, he must throw himself down in an outhouse and suffer cold and hunger till a lingering death relieved him.

It has been said that no cruelty is so unsparing as that of false philosophy.

But what is the difference between giving casually to a beggar and on the other hand such charity to a blind man as I have just described? The distinction is clear. In giving to a beggar whom you do not know, you are probably helping to maintain an idle vagabond, who will not work and is not ashamed to beg: for after all that has been said and done, there are still professional mendicants, some of whom disdain to be called beggars, but dub themselves *askers*. It was said to be a boast of Archbishop Whately that he had never given a penny to a beggar: some persons thought that the Archbishop liked to save his money under the cloak of practical philosophy, but they abandoned this unworthy notion of him when they learnt that during his lifetime he had given away in thoughtful charity not less than £20,000. He was no abettor of Mr. Spencer's cold fanaticism. He saw too the distinction between indiscriminate and regulated charity.

I should like to know what Mr. Spencer has to say to the support by Government and by voluntary helpers, of Reformatory and Industrial Schools: the former established for the maintenance and reformation of young criminals; the latter for the maintenance and reformation of vicious children on the verge of crime. Nominally, the parents are called upon to pay part of the cost of these outcasts: in practice, the greater part of the cost is defrayed by the state, and some part by local taxes. These waifs and strays are for the most part the children of the vicious and criminal classes, and may be supposed to inherit the taint in the blood of the parents: left to themselves the children would many of them die off through neglect and vice: our reformatory and industrial schools keep them alive and make them into healthy, industrious men and women. It is found that three-fourths or four-fifths are really reclaimed.

Mr. Spencer may say that it *is* a great misfortune for us to have such institutions for preserving artificially a bad race, which left alone would to a great extent die out through vice and want: but that on the other hand the institutions are really a part of our police system; that it is found better and cheaper to reform these youngsters than to allow them to grow up into hardened adult criminals; that this is proved by the gratifying reduction of juvenile crime of late years. But this strange consequence follows: honest men's pauper children should be left to die; rogues' pauper children should be cared for. In other cases honesty is said to be the best policy, but here roguery and villany are the best policy. Besides: by these schools we continue the breed of the vicious and criminal, while we do our best to kill off the breed of the unfortunate but honest.

Such are the inextricable perplexities which attend a doctrine that disregards the teaching of common sense: meaning here by common sense, not the ordinary sense of mankind, but the sense common to competent judges generally: that sense which has prevailed in mental philosophy since the teaching of Reid and Kant: that sense which tells us that we are to day the same persons we were yesterday; that there really is a world external to us; that as fire has burnt certain substances in past times and still burns them, so it will burn them in future: that sense in short (or reason as distinguished from reasoning, or Practical Reason as distinguished from Pure Reason) which supplies the fundamental certainties on which all our knowledge rests.

When Lucian's sceptical slave denied his own existence, his master with a cudgel compelled him to retract: he drew out of him a sort of anticipation of Descartes' famous *cogito, ergo sum*; only that the slave varied the phrase "I think, therefore I am," into "I suffer, therefore I am:" besides that Descartes, as it seems, really meant:—thought is being, and as I possess thought I possess being. We do not now use whipping, chains, and straw, to drive out the evil spirit of the slave's thoughtless so-called philosophy, but we appeal to common sense, to the sense or reason of competent judges generally. To this tribunal I appeal against Mr. Spencer's madness.

I appeal to the earliest historical times, to every known moral system, to men of all shades, black, brown, yellow, and white; to rulers and subjects, to legislators and philosophers. I appeal especially to that ancient and extraordinary race, once the chosen people of God, now the butt and victim of ignorant Christians; that race of whom a French philosophical traveller has lately written:—

"Faith is deed's uniform in principle and results. The God it worships takes diverse forms: the actions it inspires are the same great deeds under every latitude and in every temple. I have travelled much and among various nations: I have watched the lives of many, and have heard the prayers of a multitude of sects: in my life's career what race have I found the most beneficent, the most helpful to others?—The Jewish race, whose faith has resisted all hatreds and all persecutions."

I appeal even to the Romans, the hardest-hearted of great nations; who according to St. Augustine burst into applause, at the well-known sentence of Terence:—Homo sum; humani nihil à me alienum puto.

I find all agreeing in this: that men are bound to deny themselves that they may minister to the widow and the orphan, the maimed and the blind. But

SECT. VII.   INEQUALITIES OF FORTUNE.

Mr. Spencer recks not of the superstitious Jew or the more superstitious Roman: he cares nothing for the testimony of Buddha or Confucius: he wraps himself up in his newly-discovered philosophy, which he has not arrived at by induction, nor verified by observation. But he will not overthrow the consensus of competent judges of all ages and all nations, by the miserably thin objection that perhaps in acts of kindness you are perpetuating the breed of weakness and improvidence. I say advisedly:— perhaps.

In a notice of the late charming Princess Alice, the Queen's daughter, I find that she died at the early age of 35, but that "her virtues, her charities, and her constant solicitude for the poor, the sick, and the miserable, will long be remembered at Darmstadt. The memory of an English Princess whose life lends a lustre of its own to the reign of Queen Victoria, will not soon fade out of England."

Mr. Spencer will agree with the greater part of this eulogium: he will concede that the Princess was an excellent daughter, wife and mother, and a woman of unusual cultivation and enlightenment: but, he will add, she was misled by a false philosophy, or a want of philosophy. If she had been properly instructed, she would have not shown any solicitude for the poor, the sick, and the miserable: on the contrary she would have tried to teach the Germans that all those who are weak and improvident enough to be poor, sick, and miserable, ought to be left to the fate intended for them by a beneficent overruling power, which dooms them to death by neglect and starvation.

Under this new political philosophy, it will become necessary to reconsider every form of philanthropy, (or misanthropy shall we say? speaking etymologically): the question being not which form is good and which is bad, because all forms are bad as preventing the destruction of the weak and miserable; the question being, which forms are especially bad.

Of the many works hitherto esteemed good, but which we may find it necessary to condemn, on this new principle of "the fittest to die"(or the "death of the fittest") is one that has hitherto stood high in the opinion of mankind. I mean the transfer to another country of the offspring of drunkards and criminals. It has been believed that children removed from the filthy and degrading associations of their parents, might if taken quite young, be transformed into honest and useful citizens.

Several voluntary agencies have attempted this work. Most of the volunteers have been women: partly no doubt, because their time is more at their disposal, but chiefly because a spirit of devotedness to the good of others is far less common among men. But if more uncommon it is not unknown, as we see in the examples of Xavier and other missionaries, as well as of many of the clergy in great towns.

One layman, Mr. John Middlemore, has rivalled

Miss Rye in her efforts; by getting together scores and hundreds of young outcasts; housing, feeding, clothing, and instructing them for a time, and then himself taking them over to Canada; where they are not cast adrift to sink or swim, but are delivered to the charge of a Receiving Home in London, Ontario. They are then distributed among people willing to take charge of them, and who are well remunerated by their services, in a country where hired servants are rare. Mr. Middlemore himself annually visits Canada and gets the assistance of a paid agent and of clergy and farmers. About 1000 outcasts have been thus sent out in a dozen years, and are in a fair way to become decent members of society.

Admirable as this work appears to an unenlightened world, to Mr. Spencer it must seem abominable. Not on the ground that it is open to abuse, and that possibly in some cases the young emigrants may be ill treated and even wilfully led into vice: the objection is much deeper and goes to the very root of the matter. For these children, thus restored to society, are of that odious and degraded race, the opprobrium and scourge of mankind; and it is to be feared that they carry out to Canada the seeds of corruption, weakness, misfortune, which have ruined their parents. Why use all these efforts to keep them alive? The sooner that vice and misery put an end to them, the better for the world.

Let us see what these people are, and whether they are not eminently fitted to die out. "There are few, if any, who see and hear more of the sufferings of the women of Birmingham than we at the Emigration Homes. We allude principally to those forms of suffering which result from the desertion of husbands, from drunkenness, and from sheer starvation. The saddest element in the case is that the sufferings in question appear to degrade rather than purify the women who are subject to them. The poor creatures generally seem to acquiesce quite passively in their doom, and even sometimes to think that it is one common to all poor women. They are without hope, and they can make no picture in their minds of a life brighter or purer than their own."

Such are the women whose children Mr. Middlemore rescues from rags and famine: women so weak that they have not resolution to throw themselves into the workhouse: no, not even when their children are crying for bread. Surely, the world should rid itself of so bad a breed!

I can imagine Mr. Spencer addressing Mr. Middlemore. "You think yourself doing a good work. I give you full credit for being actuated by the best of motives: you believe that you have saved a thousand children from hunger, cold, beggary, vice, and crime: I concede that you have done this or something like it. But in accomplishing it you have unintentionally done a great wrong to the human race: you have kept alive a corrupt breed, the offspring of weak mothers and debauched fathers; a breed which left to itself would for the most part be killed off by vice, imprisonments, and the gallows. In rescuing the few you have depraved the blood of the many: though you have given a new moral tone and happiness to a thousand, you have injured future millions: you have not added to the sum of human well-being, but have reduced it.

"You are acting like these foolish creatures, weaker even than you are, who give halfpence or sixpences to beggars: for these ragged outcasts are made happy for the moment with the glass of gin supplied, while society is damaged by the encouragement to mendicity.

"If cretins or lepers still abounded in England as in the middle ages, you would not carefully collect them and send them to a colony, where they would propagate their corruptions; on the contrary, you would do all that was possible to let their diseases die with them: but the parents of these children are moral lepers, drunken, debauched, weak or unfortunate; let no one stir a finger to rear their children: let these submit to the decrees of beneficent nature and groan out the few years they have to live."

Mr. Middlemore would be greatly astonished by such a discourse: the common sense of mankind would reject it with scorn and indignation.

VIII.

EXPEDIENCY.

IN a volume on Taxation, published many years ago, I maintained that the duty of government in levying taxes, requires it to take into account, first justice, secondly mercy, and lastly expediency. What is true of taxation seems equally true of all the measures of government.

That expediency is important in taxation, all agree. The Manchester School say that our annual levy of 75 millions £ of taxes is excessive, and that we ought to go back, if not to the 50 millions £ of forty years ago, at any rate to the 55 or 60 millions £ of the first year of the Crimean war. But the only probable mode of accomplishing this is to make taxation as irritating as possible; and as direct taxation is far more irritating than indirect taxation, therefore use the direct form only. If a poor man buys half a pound of tea for 9d., he may possibly say that 3d. of this goes to the Treasury: if the custom-duty on tea were repealed, and a tax on wages were imposed instead, the same poor man would be ready for socialism or rebellion when the collector called on him for his contribution of 5s. Therefore, say the Manchester School, have a wage-tax, in order that the annoyance caused to the whole population may drive the government into dismantling the navy, cutting down the army, reducing the civil list. Make your taxation as disagreeable as possible.

Expediency by all means, say reasonable people; and on grounds of expediency, follow the advice of Adam Smith, by collecting your taxes in the way most convenient and least annoying to the people. The amount of national revenue necessary is not before us, but it must be remarked that if you cut down the national expenditure by 10 millions £ a year that would save a labourer's family a penny a day, and might expose them to the danger of invasion, ravage, and ruin. Far better collect this penny a day as a duty on tea, tobacco, beer and spirits, than harass every poor household by an annual demand-note for 30s. in hard cash.

But however the Manchester School and reasonable people may differ on the amount of taxes and the mode of collecting them, they agree entirely in appealing to expediency: the one party in favour of direct taxation the other in favour of indirect. Now this political and social expediency has been misapplied by Mr. Spencer.

Expediency indeed, of one kind, is the foundation of his reasoning. He does not say that it is *unjust* to succour the distressed at one's own expense: he cannot pretend that to do so is inconsistent with *mercy*. He alleges that it is inexpedient, because it hinders the action of beneficent nature, which left to itself would kill off the vicious, the weak and the unfortunate, to the great advantage of future generations; while we by our weak charity, and impelled by a drivelling sensibility, keep alive and comparatively happy, the blind, the deaf, the cripples, the widows and children, to propagate an inferior race. It is expedient that these should be left to die for the benefit of the world.

Even if this odious doctrine were well founded, there would remain the question whether other political and social expediency would allow it to be carried into practice. And I may ask whether we ought not to take into account the fact, that this disregard of the sufferings of the distressed would corrupt the race by hardening their hearts. According to the Darwinian principles fully accepted by Mr. Spencer, each generation hands down its acquired qualities to the next generation: we harden our hearts, our offspring would inherit this inhumanity, our grandchildren would be still more perfect in it, till at last sympathy outside a man's own family would cease to be; that is sympathy with distress, since sympathy with the happy and successful might grow proportionately. Mr. Spencer may say that I misrepresent him, that he does not denounce sympathy, but only almsgiving. What! when I am fully fed and warmly clothed, am I to go into a cottage where the husband is weakened by privation, the wife half

SECT. VIII.   INEQUALITIES OF FORTUNE.   185

dying of starvation, the children wan and emaciated, the house devoid of fire and food ; and am I then to express my deep sympathy with the sufferers, but to tell them that my philosophical principles forbid me to give them food or fire or clothing, and that their duty is to lie still and die as weak creatures who only encumber the earth ? Can anyone seriously maintain this extraordinary application of laissez faire?

But let us see whether the carrying out of the principle would not lead to dangerous consequences. John Wesley complained that the reformation of morals among his converts carried in it the seeds of corruption : the new Methodists gave up drinking and drabbing : they became industrious and frugal : they earned more and spent less : they ceased to be in debt to the baker and the publican : they accumulated some provision against sickness and age : in the eyes of political and social economy, they became exemplary citizens. But, said Wesley, there is a law higher than that of political economy ; the law of Christ : I find that this good citizenship is bad religion ; my converts as they grow rich become worldly minded, and wander from the purity of their early faith. I see only one cure : let them every Christmas follow my example, by giving away all their savings. John Wesley was unmarried *had no family*.

Civilization also generally carries with it the seeds of corruption and decay. It gives protection from foreign enemies and from home depredators: it defends us in the enjoyment of the fruits of labour and frugality: it thus stimulates us to a largely increased production and accumulation: many become affluent or easy, some grow very rich. But the many remain comparatively poor; not on the verge of starvation like savages and half civilized races, but still comparatively poor. Therefore you have Wat Tyler and Jack Cade, the French Jacquerie, the peasant massacres of their seigneurs during the French Revolution, the Whiteboys and the Fenians of Ireland: it is vain to remonstrate for hungry bellies have no ears.

The jealousy of the poor as regards the rich takes different forms. In England it is directed more against the landowners, though this jealousy is much tempered by the fortunate creation of numbers of small freehold houses built by working men during the last generation. All the owners of these are landowners, and like the peasant proprietors of France dread revolution and nationalization of land.

But there is also jealousy as regards capitalists, and this especially in France. Yet the labourers ought to see that these are their best friends: for if a capitalist goes down to a poor village and builds a factory, unpleasant as this change may be to the squires, and the clergy and the maiden ladies, the labourers are greatly benefited by the demand for their services, and by a rise in the rate of wages. Suppose a millionaire, moved with compassion towards the destitution of Western Ireland, were to invest his property in the successful establishment of a vast fishery, giving wide employment on liberal wages: that capitalist would deserve a statue of gold.

But after all, the jealousy would remain. The village factory-hands, the western fishermen, would go on saying that their employers earned their great incomes by the sweat and blood of the labourers.

It cannot be doubtful that this jealousy is troublesome and even dangerous: the smouldering discontent and envy felt by the many, is easily blown into a flame; then come riot, insurrection, and perhaps civil war.

Can nothing be done to mitigate the danger? Much can be done; much has been done; much is being done. And it is these very things of which Mr. Spencer complains, which he denounces without hesitation, and which he would sweep away in hope of improving the blood of the human race: a fallacious hope of amending its physique at the expense of ruining its morale.

Of all our institutions that directly tend to mitigate jealousy towards the rich, the greatest is the Poor-Law, the special object of Mr. Spencer's condemnation: "there could hardly be found a more efficient device for estranging men from each other." Now let us compare this opinion with that of Louise Michel, the special representative of Parisian Radicalism and Communism, that is of the quintessence of poor men's jealousy. When she was in England in 1883, the system was exhibited to her in its practical form. It did not seem to her that it was an efficient device for estranging men from each other: she found in it an elaborate, orderly, successful mode of mitigating distress, without much encouragement of idleness and extravagance: a mode of sheltering the widow and educating the orphan, of nursing the sick and aiding the needy; and all this without any vexatious inquisition into the honesty or vice of the recipients. She went back to Paris full of admiration of the institution. I should like to hear her opinion of the proposal to abolish it.

I will give another example of the way in which rough French people appreciate institutions of beneficence. One of these in Paris is the "Hospitaliers de Saint-Jean-de-Dieu." This is an offshoot of a Spanish society, founded by Jean Ciudad, a saint, madman or enthusiast, who was born so long ago as 1495, who was by turns, shepherd, soldier, and thief, and who narrowly escaped the gallows. This reprobate in his forty-fourth year after hearing a celebrated preacher, was seized with a paroxysm of penitence, confessed his sins aloud, rolled in the dust, tore his beard and his clothes, and ran through the streets of Granada, imploring the mercy of God, followed by a crowd of children crying "Madman!"

Locked up in an asylum, and cruelly scourged, in the fashion of that day and of much later days, in order to drive out the demon which possessed him, he gradually recovered his reason, and devoted himself to good works; supporting himself on a pilgrimage he had vowed, by gathering the dead branches of the forests he passed through and selling them as fagots in exchange for food and shelter.

Returning to Granada, he undertook a work singularly like that I have described as performed three centuries later, by Jeanne Jugan, the foundress of the Little Sisters of the Poor; under still greater difficulties than those of Jeanne, since she had a little money to begin with and he had none. He hired a house, begged for alms, got together 46 cripples and dying men, and maintained them. So much reason was there too in his recovered senses, that he far outstripped the other hospitals in organization. While these huddled their patients together, many in a bed, he gave every patient a bed to himself: while these crowded together sane and insane, surgical cases, typhus, and smallpox, he classified his inmates and assigned rooms or wards for special purposes; so that it is said of him that he was the inventor of our present methodical hospital.

He died early, worn out by his incessant labours. But his work survived him and his system spread into other countries; among the rest into France, where it is still at work. M. Maxime Du Camp visited one of these hospitals, or rather asylums (*hospice* rather than hôpital).

"In this house are received not only the sick but also those blind from their birth, whose infirmities exclude them elsewhere. These poor creatures are horrible to look at, with their milky, goggle eyes. They require special treatment and are separated from the other patients. I saw them reading with their fingers their dotted books, inclining their heads like birds to catch the voice of others, seeing by touch, and supplying the deficient faculty by the sharpness of the other senses.

"I attended their music lesson: five of them, sitting in their perpetual night before five pianos, were playing each a different tune, in the midst of which their teacher, himself blind, never lost himself, but felt his way from one to the other. Hearing a voice he stopped the pianos, appeared surprised on touching my sleeve, but stroking the gown of my guide, said, 'Good morning, reverend father Gaëtan.' The children began to play again, and not badly. The blind have a passion for music: harmony is their light."

I have said that rough Frenchmen highly appreciate this beneficent institution. Once however, they struck it a mortal blow; one indeed, not directed especially against it, but dealt against all institutions managed by religious orders.

A decree of the National Assembly of the 15th February, 1790, pronounced the abolition of religious vows. This opened the convent gates and set free the slaves of a monastic life, and this was right but it drove out the persons who wished to remain, and this was wrong, for it was an infringement of liberty; and it was even a despotic thing to prevent persons from living in the way they desired.

What was worse, no consideration was shown towards the inmates of charitable institutions supported by religious orders: the blow fell cruelly upon the paupers, the infirm, the orphans, the blind and the sick. Five thousand of these were turned out of the houses I have been describing: turned out to perish, most of them, of hunger, cold and neglect.

Mr. Spencer, I am sure, is no friend of revolutionary violence, but he would say that there is a soul of good in things evil, and that this tyrannical dissolution of religious orders did a good work unintentionally in purging the world of five thousand wretches unfit to live and propagate a bad breed.

Such however, is not the opinion of the roughest Parisians at present. I have said that in 1790 the revolutionary National Assembly pronounced the abolition of religious vows, and forcibly expelled the monks and nuns, overlooking in their haste the fact that this would be ruin and death to thousands of the sick and helpless. Again, during the last few years, the same anti-clerical spirit has prevailed: once more the religious orders have been dissolved and forcibly turned out of their convents. So far has this hostility towards religion been carried, that about Midsummer 1883 the Parisian authorities ordered the expulsion of all chaplains from the hospitals.

"There are no longer any chaplains, that is clear." Yet, says the eminent Charles de Mazade, himself no clerical, "if anywhere a priest is in his place it is in the home of the pauper, of the sick and the dying, for whom the state no longer provides the last consolations."

Yet even these thoughtless and illiberal agnostics have spared the institution I have described. The question of how it should be treated, was discussed by the Paris Municipal Council, the most intolerant of corporations: so high was the appreciation there of the good work it did, that to abandon this was not even suggested; the only matter deliberated upon, was whether it should be entrusted to laymen: but it was acknowledged that laymen could not be found to execute work so repulsive. "No layman, would for silver or gold undertake such a task . . to secure such services there must be coin which is not of this world." The institution had hitherto received from the municipal funds the small allowance of £60 a year, and this was continued.

The people in the streets are equally cognisant of the admirable services rendered. They are taught, as to priests generally to denounce and insult them: but an exception is made for these worthy fathers; no one insults them in their walks; and when they take their young charges abroad for fresh air, men even raise their hats to them.

A remarkable proof of their popularity was given in 1871, during the short reign of the Commune, when the richer supporters were driven out of Paris. The good fathers saw famine staring them in the face. But without solicitation, the municipal authority came to their assistance, and supplied the necessary food. "Thanks to them the inmates did not die of hunger."

Can anyone doubt that the maintenance of such institutions blunts the edge of the envy and jealousy naturally felt by the poor towards the rich? and that if we closed our hospitals and dispensaries, our workhouses and infirmaries, and made an end of out-door relief, of district-visiting-societies, and of all the charities which cluster round churches and chapels, the easy and the rich would be popularly regarded as selfish, hard-hearted, and deserving of hatred and insult? Many just people refuse to help in these good works: they are the worst enemies of the rights of property. If Mr. Spencer had his way, he would multiply their numbers, at the risk of revolution and anarchy.

Therefore, setting justice and mercy aside, expediency requires the exercise of charity.

IX.

CONCLUSION.

ON the whole, the propriety and necessity of assisting the needy, may be regarded as a part of political economy the truth of which is unquestionable: the best mode of performing the task may be discussed, though for myself I have no doubt that a judicious and liberal poor-law supplemented by private effort, is far more efficient than any voluntary organization: I have come to this conclusion from a comparison of the social condition of England, Scotland and Ireland as well as other countries, in past and present days. But at any rate, whether by public or private organization the duty of charity is one of the highest obligation.

Yet we find a proposal to refuse all help to the needy, the disabled, the diseased, even to widows and young children dying of cold and hunger: this would be a return to barbarism, to a state in which all are too poor to assist their neighbours in want: nay to a state worse than barbarism, because the comforts, the superfluities, the luxuries of the rich would add a sting to the miseries of the distressed, and would develop a hardness of heart disgraceful and ruinous to society.

I have summoned to my assistance the great and original thinkers, Adam Smith and Jeremy Bentham; both of whom supported without hesitation the claims of the needy, and maintained the necessity of a legal provision for them: I appeal also to the opinions and to the example of the wise and good of all civilized ages and nations.

After recalling these authorities, the question recurs:—is Mr. Spencer in earnest when he puts forth this eccentric and monstrous opinion, or is he playing with the credulity of his readers? Undoubtedly he is in earnest; and we shall believe this the more readily when we look at his late contribution in *The Man and the State* to the doctrine of laissez-faire; and find him condemning all the triumphs of philanthropy in Acts of Parliament forbidding truck, limiting women's and children's hours of labour, granting compensation to injured workmen, organizing and assisting national education. Yes! he would leave even education to take its chance!

And all for what? To leave uncorrupted what he regards as the grand solvent of all difficulties:— the Survival of the Fittest.

The phrase is of Mr. Spencer's invention. It would seem that he is so enamoured of it that there is no room left in his heart for sympathy with the afflicted, for pity towards the erring and weak, nay even towards the unfortunate. He involves in the same doom, the criminal and the vicious, the impotent and the deserted by their kindred: "they have come of a bad race, let them suffer and die, so that the next generation may be free from their contagion." Such is his flippant and pernicious philosophy.

Now here is an example of the folly of trusting a logical inference without verifying it by an appeal to facts. We are told that after Newton had completed his Principia, he deferred the publication several years, because one astronomical phenomenon, as it was reported, was inconsistent with his theoretical conclusions: that after a certain time renewed observations corrected an error in the preceding ones, and removed the previous contradiction: that then the masterpiece was given to the world. If Mr. Spencer had possessed a tithe of the modesty and the philosophical caution of the great philosopher, he would have refrained from putting forth his marvellous dogma until he had tested it by application to known facts.

I have tried to execute this neglected task: I have sketched the history of the Little Sisters of the Poor, and I have asked what would have followed if that and similar institutions had been nipped in the bud as Mr. Spencer would have advised.

There would have been in the towns multitudes of beggars; one at least at every street corner, and others dying slowly of cold and hunger in outhouses and cellars: in the country idle men wandering in bands about the roads and demanding alms with threats of violence. We know to what proportions mendicity grew in England before workhouses were established, and in Ireland during the first half of the present century. Victor Hugo, in his grand fiction *Notre Dame*, gives us a vivid picture of the *gueux* in Paris about the time of our Henry VII., and Scott in his *Fortunes of Nigel* sketches Alsatia the sanctuary of Whitefriars : M. Maxime Du Camp has told us what he has seen in our own days.

In the absence of a formal system of relief, vice and crime would have continued unchecked. Here and there is found a prudent or even miserly tramp or pauper, with bank notes hidden away, but as a rule indiscriminate alms are wasted in drunken orgies. Crime follows ; for imprisonment though irksome has few terrors for the outcast. We know what horrors may be bred by hunger : for have we not lately seen a wrecked ship's crew eating their companions, and even killing them for that purpose ? Abolish charity, and you might have on land as well as at sea, in times of famine, cannibalism fed by murder.

Again : from Mr. Spencer's barbaric, unsocial philosophy, there is but a short step to legalized homicide, and that on a great scale : for since the weak and unfortunate are to be got rid of, better cut them off at once with prussic acid or chloroform than leave them to suffer the pangs of hunger and cold: we should come round to the opinions of a certain American Dr. Dana.

"In a few decades, the death-rates in hospitals have fallen from 20 to 10 per cent. . . . But are we not saving lives that would be better extinct? (the weaklings in mind for one instance, and the weaklings in body for another, who propagate and multiply)."

Dr. Dana is quite correct in saying that "the idea of eliminating the incurably insane or hopelessly imbecile by a carbonic acid bath is *at first* shocking and repugnant:" Eliminating is a cunning substitute for "murdering."

We might return to ancient practice as described by M. Gaston Boissier. "Is it not remarkable that in the civilized and humane days of the Cæsars and the Antonines, it should have been regarded as a matter of course that a father should expose his infant before his door to die of cold and hunger? . . . . Yet this practice lasted till the reign of Constantine, without any cry of virtuous indignation; Seneca himself not showing any surprise."

If the poor-law were abolished, and still more if private charity were discontinued, there would soon be a renewal of sedition and machine-breaking such as disturbed the sleep of our fathers: there would be political discontent, bread-riots, new Wat Tylers and Jack Cades, an English Jacquerie, socialism rampant, socialism, nihilism, revolution, anarchy, followed by a despotism welcomed as an escape from political licence. Mr. Spencer and his followers are the worst enemies of legal order and of the sacredness of private rights. From such systematic barbarism there might come avowed child-murder and possibly cannibalism.

Chapter IV.

DEPRESSION OF TRADE, 1885.

MY present chapter is founded on an address delivered by Mr. Goschen in Manchester on the 23rd of January, 1885. It may appear presumptuous to do more than give the substance of that pamphlet. I can only say in my defence, that eminent economist as Mr. Goschen is, he cannot perform impossibilities, and that no one can give a reasonable form to a heap of materials, within the time that he would devote to the preparation of a lecture. I have probably used a week where Mr. Goschen used a day, and yet I am much dissatisfied as to the result.

I have another advantage over Mr. Goschen. Since his Address, we have received the Report of the Royal Commission on the depression of Trade; and this gives us an opportunity of correcting or confirming our opinions.

I.

OUR FARMERS AND TRADERS ARE DISTRESSED.

THAT farmers and their landlords are distressed is unquestionable: and the cause is open to the world, since every family buys food, and knows that the prices of it have fallen seriously; bread being cheaper than it has been for a century, and fresh meat much lower than it was lately: while imported tinned meats, cheese, and bacon, have gone down within the reach of the very poor. From a household book of about 50 years ago, I find the prices of the time: I add those of the present day.

About 50 years ago—

	7d.	10d.	6s.	10d.	8d.	7d. to 10d.
	Bread,	Bacon,	Tea,	Lump Sugar,	Brown Sugar,	Cheese.
1886	5d.	6d.	2s. 6d.	3d.	2½d.	5d. to 8d.

The importations of these articles (except bread) and of millions of quarters of Indian and American wheat and flour, have driven our farmers to the verge of despair.

A lamentable proof of this is given by Dr. Ogle in his paper on Suicides, where he shows that the number of these has much increased among farmers. Suicides ought to be few among industrious men, whose nerves are not overwrought by education and sentiment, who live much in the open air and who are well fed, even though it is suspected that they hurt themselves with drink. Many of their recent suicides are attributed to the pressure of anxiety: this opinion is supported by the fact that the failures among them have been painfully numerous; those of 1879 having been double those of previous years, and those of 1879 and 1880 taken together having been nearly double (more by 4-5ths) those of each of *four* other years.

The Report of the Royal Commission confirms this unfavourable opinion. " There can be little doubt that even the fairly good seasons of the last *three* years have scarcely compensated for the diminished *production* of the *eight* years which preceded them; while the steady *fall in prices* has, of course, affected the agriculturist even more seriously than the diminished yield of soil."

But is it equally certain that trade is depressed? This question may be answered by another:—does anyone doubt it? I reply that doubts have been expressed, if indeed we may not say that a flat denial has been given, and this by a politician high in the late liberal ministry. At a meeting of the Social Science Congress in 1885, he denied the distress; and though his remarks met with little favour, he was not undeceived but afterwards reiterated his opinion elsewhere.

I recommend that politician to listen to the talk of traders themselves; to read the complaints made by the writers of financial articles; to notice the reduced earnings of railways and banks, and of joint-stock companies generally.

What will he say to the state of our foreign trade?

		£.	
The value of Exports of our productions was in 1873	255	mills.
,, ,, ,, ,, ,, 1885	213	,,
A falling off of	42	,,
The population had increased by 13%; had the Exports kept pace with the population, they would have grown by	33	,,
The total falling off may therefore be put at, population only considered	75	,,
If, however, we take into consideration, both the rate of increase of population, and of the Exports from 1860-62 to 1872-73, we find that exports in 1885 should have grown to	487	,,
They had actually fallen to	213	,,
The total falling off may therefore be put at	274	,,
In other words, Exports of home produce which, for the 12 years before 1872-73, had shown an average yearly *increase* per head of the population, at the rate of	6 per cent.
Since 1873 have shown a decrease of . .	2¼	,,

I know that a foolish objection has been attributed (falsely I presume) to a man eminent in natural science:—that the less we export, the more is left at home for ourselves. A reply seems almost superfluous. Compare the case with that of a manufacturer, who complains that his sales have fallen off, and is answered that the less he sends out of his factory the more he has left for himself. The manufacturer, when he has recovered his breath, knows that the goods in his warehouse are of no use to him for his own consumption: that they are made for sale, with a view to profit; and that without sales his income ceases, as do the wages of his workmen. It is the same with our foreign trade: we produce manufactures for the purpose of exportation, and failing that our capitalists get no profit and our workmen get no wages.

Then again: when we export our manufactures we do not *give* them to foreigners, but sell them: we get foreign commodities in return; part of these being raw material such as cotton wool and sheep's wool, which being worked up give wages to labourers and profit to capitalists; while a large part consists of necessary food, with superfluities, and luxuries. These cannot increase unless our exports increase, though not in the same proportion, since the proceeds of the sales of some of our exports are invested abroad.

		£			£	
In 1826 our exports were	38	mills.	and our imports	43	mills.
,, 1840	,,	53	,,	,,	60	,,
,, 1854	,,	97	,,	,,	152	,,
,, 1870	,,	200	,,	,,	303	,,
,, 1872	,,	256	,,	,,	355	,,
,, 1884	,,	233	,,	,,	390	,,
,, 1885	,,	213	,,	,,	371	,,
,, 1886	,,	—				

Whilst our exports then, have grown so have our

imports; and it would have been impossible for us to pay for these unless our exports had multiplied.

We are therefore right when we rejoice in seeing our exports increase, and in lamenting that between 1873 and 1884 they had not nearly kept pace with the growth of population, much less with their previous rate of increase.

Some one may think that the figures prove too much, since the excess of imports over exports was

$13°/_\circ$ $\quad$ $13°/_\circ$ $\quad$ $55°/_\circ$ $\quad$ $52°/_\circ$ $\quad$ $67°/_\circ$
in 1826 ... 1840 ... 1854 ... 1870 ... 1884.
An excess of 67% in 1884, compared with one of only 13% in 1826 and 1840 is startling.

It is partly explained however, by the growth of the annual interest we receive on our colonial and foreign investments; investments which are known to equal two or three times the amount of our National Debt; whereas so late as 1847 instead of looking abroad for investments, we had great difficulty in supplying at home the principal necessary for completing the railways begun.

The falling off of our exports therefore, is a sure indication of the depression of trade: we send fewer goods out and we bring fewer productions in; less of the raw materials which give employment to capital and labour, and less of foreign articles for our consumption.

I am aware that the *quantities* of goods we export have not fallen nearly so much as their *value*, because prices have been seriously reduced: but there is no comfort in this, since the fall of prices has itself principally arisen from the depression of trade. Tell a manufacturer that he has nothing to complain of since he is selling as much iron as before: he will reply that he is truly, selling his old quantity at half the old price, and that this change means half wages to the workmen and no profit to himself. Is not this a depression of trade?

We cannot doubt that manufacturers and merchants are distressed; but we find that the suffering is unequally distributed. For many facts and figures on these subjects we are indebted to Mr. Goschen's address.

He tells us as regards the textile manufactures, that the number of spindles at work in the cotton-trade had increased from 44 millions in 1879 to 47 ,, ,, 1883: that the number of persons employed had increased from 483,000 in 1879 to 513,000 ,, 1883.

But the manufacturers complain that there has been much disturbance and injury to themselves, by the growth of joint-stock and coöperative associations. It is not alleged that the workmen have suffered by having companies for their employers instead of individuals; and it is believed that the public is benefited by a reduction of prices; for as it is said, the companies, borrowing a large part of their capital at a low rate of interest, easily get a sufficient remuneration on their own capital.

We who live outside the circle of great northern factory-owners, many of them possessing untold wealth, sympathise more with the smaller capitalists, who by means of the shares in joint-stock companies are able to invest with profit the savings from their wages or their little retail trades; and sympathies apart, economists will rejoice in this correction of the lamentable tendency of modern times, to heap up mountains of gold in a few hands, without a *proportionate* improvement in the condition of the many, though not without a great improvement.

II.

FACTS OF DEPRESSION CONTINUED.

WE have seen that notwithstanding the complaints of bad trade and low profits, cotton manufactures have grown, as proved by an increase both in the number of spindles at work and in that of persons employed. But the figures given took no account of the additions to population generally in the three kingdoms; and if it should turn out that these were proportionally greater than the augmentation of the cotton trade, it would appear that this trade had fallen off. The reverse of this however, is true. The spindles and the hands increased in four years by about 6 per cent., while the populalation increased only by 4 per cent.

But if the state of the cotton trade is better than we should have expected to find it, the woollen trade presents a still fairer picture, as Mr. Goschen tells us. On the 8th November, 1884, the reëlected mayor of Bradford reminded his fellow citizens how a year earlier, he had foretold that the commercial cloud hanging over Bradford was about to disperse: he said that his prediction had been verified; that at no period of its history was Bradford, he believed, doing so much work: and that not only was there employment for all the operatives, but *machinery was standing still for want of more of them.*

I wish that as much could be said of the hardware towns: but unfortunately the reverse of this is true: machinery is not standing still for want of hands but for want of orders; there is nothing like employment enough for the workmen existing; thousands of them are idle or half-employed.

For proof of this, no figures are available such as those of the spindles and persons in the cotton trade. But we have estimates of the condition of the "Black Country" with which the hardware trades are closely connected. According to Mr. Goschen, the profits of the ironmasters had in eight or ten years fallen by more than one half (from 7 to 3 mills. £); the profits of mining by about one half (from 14 to 7 mills. £): so that the capital employed in mining and ironmaking had found its annual income reduced by 11 mills. £.

I cannot accept this assertion as to the reduction of profits: with the figures before my eyes I see its inaccuracy; this being one of the cases which bring statistics into disrepute, because men draw from accurate figures inferences quite erroneous and often absurd.

Annual Profits of Ironworks:

2 to 3 mills.£	5	7	7	4	3	3 mills. £
1870 to 72	1873	1874	1875	1876	1877....	1882 to 1884

Annual Profits of Mining:

5 to 6 mills.£	6½	9	13	13	13	6 mills. £
1870 to 72	1873	1874	1875	1876	1877....	1882 to 1884

It seems that the profits in 1882 to 1884, both in ironmaking and mining, were about the same that they had been fourteen years before: that these had risen greatly between 1873 and 1877 and had then subsided. We all know the explanation: that the Americans, in order to rapidly construct thousands of miles of railways, had to come to us for their materials: that the price of iron rose suddenly to a degree ruinous for those makers who had large contracts on hand; and that the price of coal far more than doubled in a very short time.

We cannot wonder then, at seeing the profits on iron rise from 2 up to 7 mills. £; and the profits on mining from 5 up to 13 mills. £: but this leap was quite independent of the general trade of the country. So also, when the profits of iron fell again from 7 mills. £ in 1874-75, to 3 mills. £ in 1882-84, and the profits of mining from 13 mills. £ to 6 mills. £, we should not say that this proved a depression of trade generally; any more than we should speak of a depression of trade if we saw the profits on firearms which had increased fivefold in 1854-55, recede on the conclusion of peace, to their former level.

We see then that in 1884, the condition of the iron-trade and of mining, was no proof of a depression of trade generally: this is true even if we allow for an increase of population by one-seventh between 1872 and 1884.

I do not doubt however, that trade is depressed. Those who deny it, allege that our savings are as great as they ever were. What do they know about the matter? Nothing. All they can say is, that the deposits in the savings-banks go on as usual: they forget, if they ever knew, that most of the accumulations of the nation do not go into savings-banks: a trader employing £50,000 in his business, and satisfied with earning £5,000 a year may have found himself between 1850 and 1875, earning £10,000 to £15,000 a year; and if he saved the additional £5,000 or £10,000 a year, he would thus find himself in 1875 possessed of £200,000 or £300,000. The quarter of a million he has amassed he may have applied to enlarging his business; and not a penny of this would appear in the accounts of the savings-banks.

These are much used by middle-class people of small means: now a depression of trade such as the present, with cheap food and clothing and a great reduction of house-rent, is favourable to widows and spinsters with fixed incomes, who at such times are able to put by a little for a rainy day. Then again the banks may be used by artizans at present more than in seasons when they can apply their small hoards to starting a trifling business.

I say therefore that no argument can be founded on the state of the savings-banks.

Pauperism is quite another affair. A bad state of trade, by diminishing employment and wages, must inevitably drive many of the poorest people to seek parish relief. But the following are the figures.

Expended in relief of the poor (including the cost of pauper lunatics, law, official charges, &c.).
Under 8 mills. £   7¼   8   8½ mills. £
   1870 and 71   1876   1880-1881   1884

Allowing for increase of population by one-seventh, the expenditure in 1884 is less than it was in 1870-71, *i.e.* several years before the depression began. But the expenditure depends considerably on the cost of food, and especially of wheat: in the present case this is important, because while

in 1870 and 71 the average price of wheat was 51s. 9d.
in 1884 it was only ,, ,, ,, 35s. 8d.
a difference which would account for a good deal
of the low expenditure of 1884 : for the low price
of wheat and therefore of bread acts doubly:
first by enabling many of the poorest families to
maintain themselves without parish help; and
secondly by reducing the cost of food supplied by
the guardians.

As a proof of depression of trade therefore, the
present moderation of the poor-law expenditure cannot be trusted.

The so-called penny dinners to school children,
which are in many cases halfpenny dinners, and
in some cases farthing dinners, give a proof of the
marvellously small cost at which it is possible
to feed a family. I have been behind the scenes
and have known the accounts made up by a professional accountant, the inventor of the farthing
dinners: the result is that when 500 children can be
brought together, they may have a dinner of a bowl
of nutritious soup and a slice of bread and jam,
which cost together one farthing, and this dinner
is enough for the younger children; the soup and
bread being as palatable as those on a gentleman's
table. I can vouch for the accuracy of this
astonishing fact.

The low prices then, of wheat as well as of potatoes, cheese, tinned meats, peas and rice, reduce
both the number of paupers and the cost to the

guardians of supporting each one; and therefore the moderation of the poor-rates does not disprove the depression of trade.

Thus it appears that the alleged depression of trade really exists: that the exports instead of *growing* in amount at the rate of nearly 7 mills. £ a year as they did for a generation after the repeal of the corn laws, have *fallen* in amount since 18|3 by 3 or 4 mills. £ a year: that instead of rising to 370 mills. £ as they should have done, population considered, they have fallen to 213 mills. £. We could not indeed rationally expect that they would go on growing indefinitely, so as to amount hereafter to 750 or 1000 mills. £. Nevertheless we find the cessation of growth unwelcome.

It has been thought a smart answer to this conclusion, that though the *value* of our exports has fallen off, the *quantities* have not much diminished. I have already said that I do not see any force in this reply.

I need not recall what I have said on the comparative numbers of spindles at work, on the woollen trade, on iron and mining, on savings-banks and pauperism: none of these seriously affect the conclusion that trade is much depressed.

III.

INCOME-TAX: ABSOLUTE OR COMPARATIVE? HOUSES.

BUT there is another problem to be solved; and one apparently of much difficulty. Trade you say is bad; farming is even worse: traders and farmers then must have had their incomes reduced: the income-tax therefore must have fallen off. Look at the figures.

Incomes assessed during the last 17 years.

Mills. £. 430 435 445 466 482 514 543 571 Mills. £.
          1868 1869 1870 1871 1872 1873 1874 1875

579 570 578 578 577 585 601 613 629 631 Mills. £.
1876 1877 1878 1879 1880 1881 1882 1883 1884 1885

We are not concerned at present with the figures of 1868 to 1875; it is an undisputed fact that trade was good during these years: it is with the years 1876 to 1884 that we have to do.

At first sight it is marvellous that while there was no growth between 1876 and 1880, there should be a large one between 1880 and 1884, and the largest of all between 1883 and 1884.

Several important considerations however, have to be taken into account: first, that in one very large source of income, the profits of trades and professions (Schedule D), the assessment is made on the average of three years; so that the amount appearing under 1884 is really that of 1881 to 1883; and that this Schedule D is not very far from being as heavy as all the other schedules together. Even in other schedules the return under 1884 is really the income of 1883. The annual assessments therefore, appearing in the returns, are those of years before. If we pursued our investigation we should find how the recorded assessments under other heads lag behind the facts: for example, a person has saved money and has deposited it in a bank: if this appears at all it will be as yielding a very small income: afterwards it may be invested in brick and mortar, but it will not add to the assessments until the building is completed and in use.

Another and more important matter is the increase of population. In order that a nation should be even stationary as to prosperity, its aggregate income should increase as fast as its population. England and Wales doubled in numbers between 1801 and 1851: if its aggregate income had remained the same in 1851 as in 1801, there would have been during the 50 years, intense and regularly growing distress: if the aggregate income had increased by one-half the distress would have been only very great: if the aggregate income had increased just in proportion to population, that would indicate a stationary condition, one which Adam Smith denounces as miserable. Now from the figures I have given it appears that the aggregate incomes assessed, had risen between 1876 and 1884 by 50 millions £, while in proportion to the augmented population it ought to have risen by 2 millions £ more than this: it follows that between 1876 and 1884 the nation as judged by the income-tax was in something worse than a stationary condition.

IV.

INCOME-TAX: THE SCHEDULES A, B, &c.
RETAIL TRADES.

THE assessments then, have scarcely kept pace with the increased population. Even if they had, we should still ask whether they had grown in each schedule: for the marvel we have to account for is the favourable amount of assessments in the face of distressed trade and distressed farming: despite these distresses the total assessments might be kept up by heavy returns of houses, canals, gas works.

But the assessments have not quite kept pace with population: and unfavourable as they have been, they would have been worse but for the great increase in the rents of so-called Houses: I say so-called because the word includes factories and retail shops. I am not speaking here of the house-tax but of the income-tax: the house-tax is levied on dwelling-houses only; the income-tax is levied also on factories and retail shops. The assessments on Houses, including factories and shops,

were in 1876 97 mills. £.
In 1884 they were 127 ,, ,,

an increase of 30 mills. £ in 8 years: this sum being not very far from half as much again as the annual interest on our National Debt, and about as much as our annual outlay on army and navy taken together. Reading the figures for the first time, you rub your eyes and look for your magnifying glass: yet after repeated glances you are convinced that there the figures are: an increased assessment of the rents of buildings amounting to 30 mills. £ in 8 years!

Now in estimating the whole assessments of 1884, the more there appears under Houses, the less there remains for the other schedules. If "Houses" had not increased at all, the entire assessments in 1884 would have been alarmingly reduced.

The particular schedule however, with which we have to do, is D: "for all gains arising from any profession or trade." Under this heading are included "railways, canals, mines, gasworks, waterworks, &c." If we want to know what were the profits of manufacturing, dealing, and banking, together with the professional incomes, we must deduct from the amount published under schedule D, the profits of railways, canals, and gasworks, amounting in 1884 to nearly 10 mills. £ more than in 1876. After this deduction we find that the earnings under this reduced schedule D, were in 1884, 281 mills. £ against 272 in 1876, or allowing for increased population, in 1884, 257 mills. £ against 272 in 1876. That is, traders and professional men paid, population considered, on 15 mills. £ less in 1884 than in 1876. A falling off of 15 mills. £ may seem to be no great matter, being not much over 5 per cent. : but any reduction is distressing, and is especially so after a whole generation of prosperity and rapid increase.

It may also have happened that certain branches of trade have been prosperous, leaving the deficiency of the total to fall on others. We cannot judge of this by common report, because traders habitually disparage their own business with a view to keep out fresh competitors : and the unusually prosperous may be excused if they forbear from proclaiming in the market-place the fact of their success.

Mr. Goschen is of opinion that during the general depression, retail trades have been good : he argues from the facts, that while retail trades have smaller returns and smaller incomes than wholesale ones ; and that in the income-tax returns there are proportionally more small incomes now than formerly ;

these additional small incomes must be those of retail trades. The *Economist* however, disputes the conclusion : not denying that it *may* be true, but maintaining that it may be false : for the additional small incomes may be otherwise accounted for : it may be that the wholesale traders have many of them had their returns reduced from great to small ; from £3,000 a year to £2,000, from £2,000 to £1,500, from £1,000 to £500 : thus the proportion of small incomes would have grown.

Probably, both opinions are partly true. I think it likely that many retail traders have been making uncommon profits. I found this conclusion partly on the extensive, splendid, and costly buildings erected of late years for shops : I do not mean that the outlay on these has been supplied by the recent unusual profits I speak of : it has been supplied principally no doubt by previous accumulations of capital : but a retail dealer would not build or hire a shop at a vastly increased rental, unless his business were decidedly flourishing.

Besides this, I know from a long experience of buying and selling, that a reduction of cost is profitable at first to the seller, who does not at once give the full advantage to his customers. In wholesale business the seller's additional profit is short-lived : the keenness of the buyers and the competition of the sellers quickly reduce profit to its ordinary rate and even below it. The case of retail trade is quite different : among the affluent middle classes, ladies who are generally the housekeepers, are not keen buyers, and the shops get the best prices in their power.

Sugar formerly, it was said, was sold by the retailer almost without any profit; at present, after reading merchants' price lists, we must believe that even the present wonderfully reduced prices give a profit to the retailer.

Coal-dealers in my own neighbourhood must have been earning unusual profits lately. The ordinary price of the best deep house-coal was for many years 16s. delivered within two miles from the town: in 1874 to 1876 the price rose by one half and in some cases far more than that: then it fell again. Very good house-coal, disguised as "cobbles," may now be had at 12s.: but old fashioned people are content to pay 14s. or even 16s. as they paid formerly. Yet the price at the pit-mouth is far lower than it was before 1874-1876, partly because many new pits were opened during the flush of 1874-1876, and partly because the demand ~~for it~~ is reduced by the bad condition of the iron-trade.

The butchers again, have found their trade of late uncommonly lucrative. In my younger days I paid 7d. a lb. for the best joints of beef and mutton: the price increased by steps to 11d. or 1s. The wholesale prices had risen in the same proportion: but of late years while the wholesale prices have steadily gone down, the butchers have refused as long as possible to give their customers the benefit of the fall: the exorbitancy of their charges has been proved in some places by the action of the farmers, who have killed their own fat animals, and distributed the joints retail in the towns, at prices lower than those of the butchers and with a good profit for their trouble. It may turn out hereafter, that butchers may to a great extent be dispensed with, just like other middlemen: they will then find that in their cupidity they have killed the goose which laid the golden eggs.

We have lately had a remarkable confirmation of the opinion that we are charged exorbitantly for our meat: it comes from one who signs himself a "Retired Sussex Farmer." He says that we pay 4d. a lb. too much, and his figures seem to prove that we pay at least 2d. too much. It seems that in the trade a beast is divided, illogically, into *5* quarters; the illogical *5th* quarter consisting of the skin, the head, and the offal. Formerly, this 5th quarter was the butcher's profit; and meat was sold to the public at the price per lb. given to the farmer for the four quarters. The price now given to the farmer is 7d. and therefore the public ought to get their meat at 7d. whereas they pay 11d. that is 4d. too much.

It is not true however, that in my own neighbourhood the retail price is 11d. it is only 9d. to 10d. Besides; the inferior parts fetch considerably less, so that the liberal butchers get for the whole sheep of the best quality only about 8½d. and the other butchers 9½d. We may hope that they may have to lower their prices by 2d. a lb. We may expect this reduction, taking into account the increasing quantity of land laid down to grass, and the vast importation of lean cattle. A "Northern Landlord" supports the "Sussex Farmer," asserting that his farmers get only 3d. a lb. from the butchers, and ought therefore to sell the best joints of the best meat at 7d. a lb. and the inferior parts at 4d. to 5d. In the mean time, as we see, this retail trade is an unusually profitable one.

Milk-dealers have acted like other retailers: formerly their price in Warwickshire was *3d.* a quart; then it rose to 4d. a quart; till 1886 though the price of cattle and of all farm produce had fallen much, the price of milk continued to be 4d. a quart: it is now sold to frugal housekeepers at 3d. The milk-dealers have been coining money on a small scale. They allege however, that the milk, under pressure by the Acts against adulteration, has improved in quality: that what is now sold is milk, not milk and water.

Outside the body of retail traders generally the increase of profit is unknown and can only be guessed. But there are two exceptions, and very important ones: first that of the London Civil Service Stores, and the remarkable changes which took place there between 1880 and 1885. During those five years the sales grew by one fourth in price and far more in quantity. The *gross* profits rose from 380 to £615,000, reduced by additional expenses incurred partly by more liberal accommodation in sending the goods home. The *net* profits grew nevertheless, and about doubled. The *Statist* says:—"the inference arrived at is that the selling price of goods has been to a large extent maintained during the time that values in the wholesale markets have been falling."

The second exception is that of the coöperative societies and their retail sales. The *Economist* says:—"profits, instead of being curtailed during the three years of greatest trade depression, have continued to expand. If there is any fault to find with them, it is not that they are too small, but that they are on far too large a scale. To us, profits of from 27 to 57 per cent. upon the share capital appear to be altogether out of harmony with the spirit of coöperation."

I find further evidence as to retailers generally, in the following paragraph of May, 1886:—" In the new number of the *City Quarterly Magazine*, Mr. Ellis discusses the question how it is that, while wholesale prices are unprecedently low, retail prices have fallen but very slightly; and he correctly suggests that one reason is the want of education, skill, and capital in retail business. The retail business is not organized properly, and therefore, is extravagant and wasteful."

In the absence of proof I much doubt Mr. Ellis's explanation. My experience has convinced me that, as I say elsewhere, when cost-price falls selling-price follows gradually and not at once: that in retail trades the middle class buyers are generally ladies and that these are content to pay prices that are unreasonably high. As to Mr. Ellis's notion that education is wanting, I believe that to be a mistake: if a man can read, write, and sum, he will be as good a man of business as a senior wrangler or a senior classic, and probably much better. Skill is obtained by going through the grades of clerkship. It is hard also to believe that capital is scarce when we look at the splendid shops and their contents.

Whatever weight Mr. Ellis may have, it is lessened by his desire to have prices fixed; not by Government indeed, but by some acknowledged authority. An assize of bread would be possible, but what as to an assize of tea, or calico, or furniture? (things having every variety of quality).

While then, I differ from Mr. Ellis as to the cause, I agree with him in his opinion that consumers have not received the full benefit of the reduction in the cost of commodities. Another proof has recently presented itself in the important article of malt liquor. In October, 1886, the Messrs. Guinness of Dublin proposed to turn their business over to a Joint Stock Company, if one could be formed: the necessary capital was eagerly subscribed at once, though this was no less than 6 millions £, all to be paid down to the seller. The profit per hogshead was in

1872 to 76 :	1877 to 81 :	1882 to 86 :	*1885*
8s. 2d.	10s. 5d.	11s. 10d.	13s. 5d.

We see that between 1872 and 1885, when trade was so depressed that our exports *fell* from 256 to 213 millions £ (omitting increase of population) the profit on each hogshead of liquor sold by Mr. Guinness rose from 8s. 2d. to 13s. 5d.

The grocers, the coal-dealers, the butchers, the milkmen, the brewers, and the Civil Service Stores, confirm the opinion that of late years retail traders have made unusual profits. But the greater their share of the assessments under Schedule D, the less is the share of other men of business; and since it seems that all the assessments together under Schedule D were in 1884 less by 15 millions £ (population considered) than in 1876, it follows that the *wholesale* assessments generally must have fallen greatly. Therefore, the income-tax returns when analysed, cease to be "astounding," as Mr. Goschen calls them.

It is then, consistent with those returns to believe, that the incomes of professional men and of wholesale traders have fallen considerably, and indeed must have fallen, population considered. Among the clergy there has been a reduction in the value of tithes and of glebe-land, besides, no doubt, some backwardness in the payments of town congregations. Lawyers have suffered more. They like to fish in troubled waters, says the popular voice: but it was long ago explained to me that when, after a revulsion of trade, the crop of difficulties and failures has been gathered in, a flat condition of affairs brings few clients for sales and purchases, few costly indulgences in suits and appeals for the gratification of anger. The business and the high fees of barristers are reduced for the same reason.

The gains of the important profession of accountants follow the same rule.

So do those of the faculty: with empty purses men shrink from a heavy doctor's bill, and still more from the fees of physicians.

The reduction of income then, is shared by professional men with wholesale traders, consisting mainly of manufacturers (including brewers and distillers), merchants, and bankers. But these last seem for a time to have escaped: yet in 1885, the joint-stock banks were unable to pay their usual dividends, and the two great companies, the London and Westminster and the Union reduced theirs by $2\frac{1}{2}$ per cent., Lloyds by 5 per cent. The manufacturers and the merchants no doubt suffered far more.

V.

SUMMARY OF INCOME-TAX.

AFTER the multitude of particulars I have had to give as to the Assessments for Income-tax, a careful and rather elaborate summary is required.

How can we reconcile the unquestionable depression of trade, with the favourable income-tax returns? Favourable, these surely are: for the returns of 1884 are nearly 50 millions £ more than those of 1876. It is true that 1876 was a year of revulsion after the prosperous 1873, 1874, 1875: but the assessments of 1876 do not indicate the *incomes* of that year but the *returns* made that year of the incomes of an earlier period; partly of 1875, and in great part (under Schedule D) of 1873, 1874, 1875: therefore, in comparing the returns of 1884 with those of 1876, we are really comparing the incomes of 1881, 1882, and 1883 with those of the prosperous years 1873 to 1875. Nevertheless the assessments of 1884 are greater by 50 millions £. What explanations can be offered?

First, there is the growth of population: between 1876 and 1884, this was nearly 3 millions or one-eleventh part of that of 1876; but the growth of the income-tax assessments during the same years was rather less than one-eleventh. If therefore the period of 1883 to 1885 had been as prosperous a one as that of 1873 to 1875, the increase of 50 millions £ in the assessment would have created no surprise: the astonishing thing is that the later and adverse season should have given anything like the same proportionate assessments as the earlier and prosperous season.

Our astonishment is the greater, because we know that land has not yielded its ordinary income; the landlords and farmers together returning, if we allow for growth of population, 10 millions £ less in 1884 than in 1876.

From what sources then, do the additional assessments come? Principally from the amazing growth of "Houses," a heading which includes factories and retail shops. Adding the enlarged railways, canals, and gasworks, there is an addition of nearly 30 millions £, even after deducting one-eleventh for increase of population.

But this is not enough. The retail trades at home are supposed to account for a good deal, since, as it is found, falling prices are commonly favourable to them, and since we know that the Civil Service Stores have earned unusual profits.

We must also remember that the complaints of flatness of trade come very much from men whose notions of prosperity and adversity were formed during the generation which saw our exports grow from 50 to 250 millions £. The adversity, though real, is not so severe as these men believe.

I must add, from the Report of the Royal Commission:—(1) that the growth of the assessment is largely attributable to the increased efficiency of collection: (2) that in some cases the tax is paid on profits which have not been earned, owing to the unwillingness of traders to make known the losses they have sustained.

Compare this with the insufficient assessments of prosperous times: remember the case of the trader who made no return and was assumed by authorities to be making £5,000 a year; a sum raised next year to £10,000, and a third year to £30,000, at which point the trader cried, enough.

If there were a considerable number of such cases, they would much disturb the comparison between good and bad years.

VI.

CAUSES: WANT OF FIELD FOR EMPLOYMENT.

IT is of course a satisfaction to find the total incomes of the country increase about as fast as the population: a satisfaction to the Chancellor of the Exchequer, the Ministry, the Parliament, and above all to the tax-payers, who see that at this rate the national expenditure may grow by 6 or 8 millions £ every ten years without calling for any additional taxation. Still they all look back with regret to former periods, such as that from 1870 to 1876, when in six years population advanced 6 per cent. and incomes 30 per cent.

Manufacturers and merchants too as well as artizans, complain bitterly that their trades are flat; that profits and wages are low: they ask why this is so; why the exports have *fallen* from 256 millions £ in

1872 to 213 millions £ in 1885; *i.e.* by 43 millions £, or taking increased population into account, by 78 millions £: instead of having multiplied as in former years.

It is no answer that it is to a considerable extent the value and not the quantity of exports which has fallen: on the contrary, this fact is an aggravation, because the reduction of prices proves the reality of the alleged fall in profits and wages: it is a grievance that we should have to give the same quantity of our productions for less money.

What are the causes of this depression of trade? Thoughtless " Fairtraders" will answer glibly that one cause is sufficient, the foreign protective system, which shuts out our manufactures. Now I share the opinion that that system is so injurious to us that we ought to retaliate; and I have tried elsewhere to show how we could retaliate without any considerable risk to ourselves. But this is far from saying that this foreign system is the sole cause of our present depression: for this is recent, while foreign protection is of long date: our depression has taken place since 1876, while the United States adopted protection more than half a century ago, and their present exorbitant tariff was imposed as a consequence of their civil war of 1861-65. Nor have such changes taken place of late in the custom-duties of European powers as to account for our flatness of trade.

Besides; the want of wages and of profit is not

confined to Great Britain: it is the grievance of America, France, Germany, Belgium, of all the civilized world. In the United States, the rate of interest, generally far higher than it is here, lately sank for a time to nearly our level: wages, at any rate in the iron trade, sank in the same way.

We want to find some cause common to all the civilized world. The pure political economists, the followers of Ricardo and *James* Mill (I will not say of M'Culloch whose theoretical political economy is contemptible) tell us that the cause exists in the stupidity of the producers; *i.e.* of manufacturers and merchants. Where there are capital and labour, they say, the proper application of them will yield wages and profits. Men and their families have various wants unsatisfied: let one portion of these men produce food, a second portion clothing, and a third portion furniture, or superfluities and luxuries: these things will exchange for each other, and thus capital and labour will have employment.

The error of these economists is that they do not try their theories by facts. Principles are useful and even necessary, but they require to be verified. Verification would have shown the economists that their principle was false. But this inquiry will involve the first principles of Political Economy. When we investigate these, we shall find that James Mill and others were ignorant of what capital is, and confounded it with what I have called self-maintenance. The explanation of this distinction must be deferred.

All who have to do with producing and dealing, know that what we are suffering from at present, is the want of gainful occupation for labour and capital.

Political economists, or some of them, now concede that besides capital and labour it is necessary to have a Field for Employment, if production is to be carried on profitably. The elder Mill and his friends said that capital itself furnished that field: the younger Mill threw his father's opinion overboard. The want of a field for employment is the cause of our distress.

But how has this want arisen? Not from foreign protection, though this is an aggravation. The cause must be of a wider and more general character, since not only Great Britain, but the civilized world has been suffering from commercial flatness.

VII.

EXAMPLE IN CHINESE POSSIBLE RAILWAYS. WARS.

PERHAPS we shall see the cause of a want of lucrative employments, if we consider what would be a relief.

Let us suppose that the present depressed condition of farming stimulated landlords and tenants to the same anxious restlessness which is general at all times among manufacturers: that it was found possible to grow wheat and rear cattle so as to fairly compete with American and Indian productions, while yielding fair wages, profit, and rent. Suppose farther, that to do this required a liberal outlay of capital; so liberal as to amount to £20 an acre throughout the kingdoms: *i.e.* to amount to nearly a thousand millions £, or more by a third than the National Debt; or more than the present capital of all our home railways. If all this expenditure took place rapidly, there would be a demand for capital such as that of 1845 to 1847; and trustees would again be able to obtain for their beneficiaries 5 per cent. instead of the present 3½ per cent.

Descending from the cloudland of 1000 millions £ to mundane reality, we find that one item of improvement might cost 70 millions £. After the "Health Exhibition" of 1885 in London, a number of handbooks were published, and this passage has reference to them.

In Professor Acland's essay on "Health in the Village," he sketches the condition of an English village in the "pre-sanitation period"—say thirty years ago: charmingly picturesque of course; an exquisite group of low cottages, with crumbling walls, round an antique weather-stained church, tinted with mosses and lichens; bright flowers in the little garden patches—in short, an ideal bit of sunny rusticity. But pestilence lurked everywhere; and at last it was recognized that typhoid fever "ravaged the dwellings of the agricultural labourer as certainly as the alleys and courts of our large towns." The discovery resulted in rebuilding and reform on an enormous scale. *It has been calculated that it will cost seventy millions sterling* to rebuild the hundreds of thousands of farm cottages which need or did need rebuilding; the work being almost entirely carried out by great landlords like the Prince of Wales, the Dukes of Bedford and Northumberland, Earl Spencer, and managers of estates such as the Ecclesiastical Commissioners and her Majesty's Commissioners of Woods and Forests.

Let us imagine again, that China with its 300 or 400 millions of people, were to begin eagerly the construction of railways, disregarding the disturbance of ancestors' bones. If these new railways were (in proportion to population) as numerous and as expensive as those of Great Britain, there would be a demand for capital amounting to seven or eight thousands of millions sterling, or ten times our National Debt. So vast a sum, taken in a few years from the whole world, would produce in every country the same kind of commercial activity which was seen in England in 1845 to 1847, when the overhasty construction of railways absorbed the unfixed capital of the country and cried aloud for more. If such a railway-mania were to invade

China it might give full occupation to the unfixed capital and the unemployed labour of the earth.

We may better appreciate the results of Chinese railway-construction, if we observe what is actually going on elsewhere. The United States, we might have supposed, is abundantly provided with railways: yet at the beginning of 1887 it was announced that new lines were to be made, at a cost of perhaps 70 millions £. "The demand for steel railways on a scale like this must give extraordinary activity to the ironworks of the country. All the old works will be set going, and new works will be started. There will be an eager demand for labour, and an equally eager demand for capital to carry on the works." Orders for steel had already been given to Great Britain.

If such results follow an outlay of 70 millions £ what would an outlay of 700 millions produce?

This suggests a question:—whether the comparative cessation of railway construction is not one of the principal causes of the worldwide commercial depression now prevailing. It was in the year 1845 that the mania for construction began in England: in 1847, the commercial Revulsion-Panic brought a severe check; but the lines begun had to be finished and were most of them ultimately finished, at the cost of distress to multitudes and the ruin of many persons unable to pay up the calls on their shares. Afterwards, new projects were more carefully scanned, but many of them were approved:

other countries, European and American, were tempted to follow our example, and even India after a time got some great lines formed.

Gradually however, the world found that only a certain number of lines could be laid down with a chance of profit. Then came the years before 1875, and a mania for new lines in the United States; and this was carried to such a stupendous extent that half the new lines afterwards paid no dividends, and a large part of these were bankrupt.

The *Economist* gives us the figures for two years.

```
                            1884.
45 Railways went under "receivership," capital 112 mills. £.
37     ,,     ,,    ,,   "foreclosures"    ,,   204   ,,
                                                      ――――  316 mills. £.
                            1885.
51     ,,     ,,    ,,   "receivership"    ,,   118   ,,
29     ,,     ,,    ,,   "foreclosures"    ,,    56   ,,
                                                      ――――  174   ,,
                                                Total  490   ,,
```

So that in two years the capital of the American railways that went into liquidation was half as great as the capital of all the British railways. We shall wonder the less when we look at the rate of construction.

```
Thousand                                          Thousand
  miles.   7     10    11½    7     4     3       miles.
         1880   1881  1882  1883  1884  1885
```

Thus there were constructed in the United States during the five years 1880-1885 more than twice as many miles of railway as there are now existing in the whole of the United Kingdom.

This prodigious folly may have benefited the American nation by increasing its means of communication permanently. The previous "boom" of 1872-75 certainly benefited us by the demand it caused for our iron; our exports of all kinds of goods to the United States being so high in 1872 as 46 millions £, but dwindling in the following years, until in 1878 they fell to 18 millions £. If China would but enter on the same career! Poor as she is when compared with America, she might relieve us for a time of the heavy cloud which hangs over us, by giving us occupation for our unemployed labour and capital.

Besides the diminution in railway making of late years, there has been a great reduction in the contracting of foreign loans. Some twenty years ago there was a mania for such loans, and most of us have seen examples of the results, when the lenders became aware that they had been imposed upon, and the income they expected suddenly disappeared: most of us have seen the sufferers fallen into dejection, despondency, despair, imbecility, or madness; their careers cut short, their happiness gone, their lives a wreck.

Between the years 1860 and 1867, the national and colonial debts of the world are said to have augmented by a thousand millions sterling; a sum greater by a third than our huge national debt; and all this world-wide debt of a thousand millions was incurred in seven years. The greater part of it no doubt, grew out of the gigantic civil war in the United States; but there were also loans to Turkey and Egypt and to such half civilized countries as New Granada, Salvador, Venezuela, Morocco, in some of which cases the money advanced remained to a great extent in the hands of middlemen as commission, and what the Americans call *stealings*, we, more civilly, *perquisites*.

Of this thousand millions a large part went from Great Britain, and it did not go from us in gold and silver; for if it had, we should have felt such a want of sovereigns as would have driven us to the use of one pound notes, as in the case of the Peninsular War under the Duke of Wellington: our share of the thousand millions went from us in manufactures: in any case, the ultimate payment being made with our manufactures.

Then again in the ten years 1861 to 1871 there were two great wars which swept away prodigious amounts of unfixed capital: a large part of the cost of the American civil war was supplied by loans contracted between 1860 and 1867, though there was in addition a great amount raised by taxes, and a destruction in the South of fixed property which had to be replaced. A few years later came the Franco-German War, which in a single year cost the French many hundreds of millions sterling.

A man who would wish for a great war between other nations as a means of restoring our prosperity must have the heart of a savage; but it cannot be denied that it would clear away the surplus unfixed capital and for a time raise the rate of interest, while perhaps giving our workmen employment.

The cause then of our depression of trade is generally speaking, the want of a field for employment of capital and labour: a real cure would be effected if capital were widely applied to improved agriculture; or if the Chinese were to follow the example of the Japanese in adopting European customs and rapidly constructing railways in proportion to their vast Empire: even the curse of war would relieve our present glut of the means of production.

VIII.

ALLEGED ENHANCEMENT OF GOLD: DENIED.

SOME persons are found to write that without question, dearness of gold is at the bottom of the general fall of prices.

Others pronounce that cheapness of commodities and dearness of gold are the same thing: for cheapness of commodities means, that a ton of iron or a quarter of wheat or a bale of wool, will exchange for less gold than usual; and dearness of gold means that an ounce of gold will exchange for more iron, wheat, or wool than usual: now to the holder either of the commodities or of the gold, the two conditions are the same. Yet to the nation they are not the same. If in a country without money, a quarter of wheat usually exchanged for 2 quarters of oats, and if in a particular season a quarter of wheat exchanged for only 1 quarter of oats, this might be either because wheat was excessively plentiful or because oats were excessively scarce. The two men who made the exchange might be indifferent which was the case, but to the community the distinction would be highly important, since in the one case consumers would be abundantly supplied and in the other case imperfectly.

So it is with gold and commodities: if as in the years following 1851, gold is unusually plentiful, and continues so, prices will gradually rise and gold as compared with commodities will gradually fall: but the quantity of commodities to be consumed will be as great as before: if on the contrary, while the quantity of gold is unchanged commodities are scarce or dear through bad harvests or war, prices will rise and consumers will be pinched. Therefore, when prices rise or fall, it has to be considered whether this happened through a change in the quantity of gold or a change in the quantity of commodities. Gold can become dearer only by scarcity in proportion to demand, though we admit that the scarcity is caused by increased cost of production. Yes, say these economists, and scarcity has arisen through the lessened supply from the gold-fields:

the world was receiving 40 millions £ a year, and is now receiving only 20 millions £.

It never seems to have occurred to these economists, that the annual supply of 40 millions £ may have been beyond the effectual demand, and if continued might have caused a growing depreciation of gold. It has to be considered whether the present annual supply of 20 millions £ is not as much as is wanted.

An attempt indeed has been made to show that it is not enough. But the calculations are vitiated by a ludicrous exaggeration of the quantity required to replace losses by the wear of coin. There are men to be found, who in the true spirit of Conjectural Statistics, declare it probable that the wear of the gold coin of the world is equal to 5 or even 10 millions £ a year: how astounded must they be when it is proved to them that instead of 5 or 10 millions £ a year, it is not one million and perhaps not half a million, or a quarter.

I do not speak without authority when I mention the high estimates formed: for example, there is Mr. Robert Montgomery (Manchester Statistical Society, 1882-3, p. 71), who says :—"probably, then, after all deductions, we shall be right in assuming that 2 millions £ a year will provide for the wear and tear of our gold coinage." Two millions a year for the United Kingdom! If we believe that the gold currency of the world is six times that of England with the small quantity of Scotland and

Ireland, it seems to follow that the annual wear throughout the world is 12 millions £, though this is a false inference.

Now for the disproof. It is found by examination of the dates of our current coin, that the life of a sovereign is 30 to 50 years: it is also probable that our gold coin amounts to 110 millions £, viz. 90 of sovereigns and 20 of halves (*i.e.* by tale 90 millions sovereigns and 40 millions halves). Let us call the life of a sovereign 40 years and the amount of our gold coin 120 millions £.

Thus we should apparently require three millions of new sovereigns every year. Then, as the gold coinage of the world is supposed to be six times that of this country, the world would appear to require a recoinage of 18 millions £ of sovereigns or equivalent coins every year. At the first glance this may seem to justify the statement which I have called a ludicrous exaggeration.

What is meant by the life of a sovereign? By the life of a *machine* we mean the term of years during which it can be used, and after which it is broken up as old iron of little value. By the life of a sovereign we also mean the term of years during which it can be used: but after this time, though it is broken up and melted, its value is not little; it is nearly as great as that of a new coin. The sovereign should be withdrawn from circulation when it has lost 1% of its weight, *i.e.* when it has lost gold worth 2½d.: if it is said that it is not really withdrawn so soon, and further that other nations may be less precise than we are, then let us say that such coins lose six pennyworth of gold before they cease to live: it follows that the 18 millions of sovereigns withdrawn every year throughout the world would cause an annual demand for gold worth 18 million sixpences, or nearly half a million sterling, against the 5 or 12 millions conjectured. But I will soon show why even this half million is an exaggeration.

We learn from the *Economist* (29th May, 1886) that during the year 1885, the amount of gold currency withdrawn and recoined in the principal countries of the world, excluding Russia, was £1,310,371.

If the deficiency on each of the withdrawn coins was 3d., the gold consumed in recoining would be £17,000 (or less)

If the deficiency on each of the withdrawn coins was 6d., the gold consumed in recoining would be . 33,000 ,,

If the deficiency on each of the withdrawn coins was 1s., the gold consumed in recoining would be . 66,000 ,,

Adding for other countries, the world's cost might be (even at 1s. per coin) £100,000

Or $\frac{1}{10}$th of a million £ against the many millions conjectured.

But by a certain calculation I arrived at an amount many times as great as this small sum: I reply that I there carefully used the word "apparently," leaving the truth of the appearance for reconsideration.

The fallacy of my former result is easily explained, by the fact that it omitted an important element. We have seen that gold coins do not require to be withdrawn till they are 30 to 50 years old: call the time 40 years: it follows that no recoinage is yet required of coins struck ~~before~~ 1847. But most of the gold currency of the world has been struck since 1847.

Now there was little gold circulation in the world in 1846-47 beyond that of England and of Portugal with small quantities in France &c. But to say nothing of Scotland and Ireland which use 1£ notes with small bank reserves of gold, England has grown in population in 40 years from 16 to 26 millions, whilst its commerce has increased four-fold: therefore its gold currency if now 110 millions £, may then have been only 70 millions £ and it is principally in this limited sum together with the small Portuguese currency that the recoinage is required. The recoinage does not touch the whole 660 millions £ of the world's gold coin, but little more than a ninth part of it. This accounts for the startling difference between the actual figures of the *Economist* and those of my previous calculation.

Everything confirms the opinion that the quantity of gold used in *re*coinage is so small that it may be disregarded.

The proofs, being clear and decisive, do not seem to require any confirmation: yet no evidence can be deemed superfluous in a matter so complex, and in which the estimates of loss vary from a few thousand pounds sterling to as many millions.

Let us revert to Mr. Montgomery's paper. He gives the quantities of gold coined at our mint, and finds that from 1873 to 1882, the annual average of new gold coined was £871,000, or less than a million. He omits to say that in 1882 there was none (as there was none in 1883). Another omission however, is more serious: he forgets to take into account the mint in Australia: yet we imported from that country in 1881 3¼, 1882 2¼, millions £ of gold coin. This vitiates all reasoning on the figures above.

Let us look again at the conclusion:—" Probably we shall be right in assuming that 2 millions £ a year will provide for the *wear and tear* of our gold coinage." Recoinage then, costs us 2 millions £ a year. Let us see how many coins in number must be withdrawn, melted and recoined, every year. Suppose that all the coins withdrawn are sovereigns, and that the loss on each sovereign withdrawn were so high as even 1s.: then 40 millions sovereigns would be recoined annually if the loss on each were 1s. But if the loss on each were less than 1s. we must recoin more than 40 millions sovereigns to incur the loss of 2 millions:

If the loss were only 6d., we must recoin twice as many, *i.e.* . . . : 80 millions sovereigns
If it were only 3d. (as we are told) four times as many or 160   ,,

But we have seen before that the whole recoinage of *the world* is not supposed to exceed 1½ million £ instead of 40, 80, or 160 millions £. Whilst, as the total gold coinage of England does not exceed 110 millions, it is obvious that we must recoin every sovereign once, some twice, a year!

It is true that I have made my calculations on the supposition that all the coins withdrawn are sovereigns, but in the face of such a disproportion as 1½ to 40, 80, or 160, it is useless to carry the inquiry further. It confirms my previous inference, that the loss by wear and tear of coin is so small that it may be disregarded.

Though the demand for gold by recoinage is very small, there are other demands of really large amount. Eastern Asia it is said, takes so much as 3 or 4 millions £ a year.

The greatest demand however, has of course been that by countries which have substituted a gold currency for a silver one. During the last fifteen years Germany has done this and has swallowed up large quantities. In 1870, all her gold specie (coin and bullion) is supposed to have been only 4½ millions £. In 1884 it had risen to 78½ ,,
This gives an increase of 74 millions £ or 5 millions £ a year.

Italy also, has possessed herself of large quantities. In the United States, the gradual resumption of specie payments after the peace of 1865, required much gold. The amount coined was in

Mills. £	11	9	12	16	19	7	6 mills. £ (not dols.)
1878	1879	1880	1881	1882	1883	1884	

The amount of American gold coin and bullion was

58   122 mills. £

in 1879, 1884, an increase of 64 millions £ in 5 years, or nearly 13 millions £ a year.

If such German, Italian, and American demands had arisen now, since the supply from the mines has fallen off, scarcity and dearness would certainly have followed.

A large quantity is used annually in the arts, *i.e.* in jewellery, gold plate, and gilding. But those who estimate the amount are apt to overlook an important fact; that a considerable part of this does not come from the mines, but from gold refiners: these men buy broken ornaments, and everything which contains a trace of gold. I saw an example of this formerly. Before electroplating was invented, metals were water-gilt: *i.e.* grain gold was mixed with quicksilver, and the amalgam was spread over the metal surface; then this was exposed to a hot fire, which drove off the quicksilver and left a thin layer of gold: but the mercury carried with it some little gold, and a part of this was intercepted by the bricks of the flue: after this flue had been used a certain number of years, a gold refiner gave some pounds for the bricks and mortar, and extracted the gold. It is said also that butlers in charge of gold plate, sell for the same purpose the leathers they have long used. A considerable part of the articles marked at assay-offices must be composed of such second-hand gold.

The quantity consumed in the arts is certainly large. A correspondent of the *Economist* in March 1884 believes that in England between 1857 and 1883 it was worth . . 47 millions £.
Or during the 27 years less than 2 millions £ a year. In the autumn of the same 1884, it was estimated that in America the quantity used in the arts during the year was 1¼ millions £. The two countries together therefore, were using about 3 millions £ a year. How much of this was new gold we cannot say.

France must use a good deal, and every country a certain quantity, but the problem, how much new gold they consume taken together is insoluble. Dr. Soetbeer however, has made an attempt to solve it. The figures he gives are nearer to those I have used than I should have expected to find them. I said that the British consumption in manufactures was less than . . . . 2 million £ a year.
He sets it down as . . . 1¾ ,,
He estimates the quantity so used throughout the world as (I believe this is besides old gold used again) . . } 8½ ,,

From this amount there ought probably to be a large deduction: for an estimate carefully made in 1886 by an experienced and able official, who consulted a large number of jewellers besides the assay-offices, reduces the estimated amount used in Great Britain from "under 2 millions £ a year" to perhaps 1 million £ a year.

Let us see whether more can be learnt from another point of view. It is alleged that gold has become dearer through comparative scarcity. Let us concede that a former annual production of 40 millions £ has gradually fallen to one of about 20 millions £. From this it has been hastily inferred that gold has become scarce: but as I have already remarked, the only true inference is that the quantity existing is far less than it would have been if the annual production had continued to be 40 millions: so far it remains doubtful whether all this larger quantity was wanted to replace the annual loss and consumption, or whether the production of 20 millions is sufficient.

These questions would be answered if we found that the quantity now existing had increased as fast as the population: and we should infer, in the absence of other disturbances, that the diminished annual production had been sufficient. Now we have so lately as November 1885, an elaborate and careful estimate by the American Director of the Mint, of the quantity existing first in 1870 and secondly in 1885. The figures are these:—

1870. Gold of the world, coined and uncoined, 700 mills. £.
1885.   „   „   „   „   „   866   „
        Increase 24%, or   .   166   „

Probable increase of the population of the gold-using nations in 15 years (the estimate is my own), 19 to 23%.

If these estimates are correct, it is evident that the stock of gold has more than kept pace with the population.

There are two other facts rather inconsistent with the existence of scarcity: the first that recently, the stocks of gold in the cellars of the three great banks of England, France, and the United States, taken together, were far beyond their usual amounts: the second fact that while the gold, coined and uncoined, of the world was set down in 1885 as . . 866 millions £.
The bullion and coin in treasury
and in banks of 38 various
countries was set down as . 207 ,,

If gold were so scarce as to raise its value and to depreciate prices, we should not expect to find unusually large stocks in these great bank cellars, nor almost a fourth of the stock of the world lying idle.

I am glad to appeal to the editor of the *Economist*, who says in an article of the 29th May, 1886:—

"It cannot be reasonably contended from these figures that what is called the dwindling product of Californian and Australian gold production is here reflected in any force. A new gold coinage in the chief mints of the world of more than 13 millions £

exclusive of £1,310,371 of light coinage reintegrated to its full weight, does not argue any dearth of gold, seeing that the world's supply of gold bullion in bars has gone on increasing at the same time. Thirteen millions sterling worth of new gold coin in 1885, added to the existing gold circulation of the above countries, amounting at the very least to 650 millions, is an increase of about 2 per cent., and exceeds the year's growth either as expressed by

NOTE TO PAGE 250 LINE 21.

Since this book was printed, an article in the *Economist* of June 4th, 1887, strongly confirms the opinion, that gold has not been scarce during the years that prices have fallen the most : it appears that during the six years 1881 to 1887, there has been an increase of 60 millions £ in the gold held by four great institutions taken together; viz., the United States Treasury, the Bank of France, the Bank of Germany, and the Bank of England.

This addition has not been caused by the substitution of gold for silver, since the silver itself in the same four institutions has grown by 31 millions £.

Nor can the gold have been squeezed out of the other 34 of the 38 banks I have mentioned; because if this were so, the rate of interest at those 34 banks would have risen, and this rise, by acting on the foreign exchanges, would have brought the gold back.

Since 1881 therefore, gold has been plentiful.

I conclude that prices have not fallen because gold has been scarce, but that the fall of prices from other causes has reduced the quantity of gold required for the circulation of commodities.

Probable increase of the population of the gold-using nations in 15 years (the estimate is my own), 19 to 23%.

If these estimates are correct, it is evident that the stock of gold has more than kept pace with the population.

There are two other facts rather inconsistent with the existence of scarcity: the first that exclusive of £1,310,371 of light coinage reintegrated to its full weight, does not argue any dearth of gold, seeing that the world's supply of gold bullion in bars has gone on increasing at the same time. Thirteen millions sterling worth of new gold coin in 1885, added to the existing gold circulation of the above countries, amounting at the very least to 650 millions, is an increase of about 2 per cent., and exceeds the year's growth either as expressed by the increase of population or of trade."

IX.

OUR PROSPECTS.

I BELIEVE therefore, that the general fall of prices is not caused by a scarcity of gold, but by a lessened demand for commodities and labour; *i.e.* by depression of trade; I believe that the fall of prices and the depression of trade are caused by the want of a field for employment, or rather for profitable employment. The orthodox economists indeed say that where capital and labour are abundant, employment cannot be wanting. Granted, if this be taken literally: for suppose that I have £1,000 at my banker's, I can draw it out gradually, and pay it to men set to work to reclaim a piece of waste ground: but if this operation ends with giving me only £10 a year or 1 per cent., my neighbours will not follow my example, but will await a better opportunity. We must modify the orthodox assertion, and say that given abundant capital and labour, even then *profitable* employment *may* be wanting.

What remedies can be found? After the depression of 1842, a series of remedies occurred: first, a vast construction of railways, leading to an excessive demand for capital and labour, followed in 1847 by revulsion and panic; then the adoption of free-trade made easy by the Irish famine of 1846, with a final abandonment in 1849 of taxes on food; again, in 1848 and 1851, the gold discoveries in California and Australia. These were heroic remedies, not to be found by science, but arising spontaneously.

One remedy indeed is within our reach, but we are too stupid or too apathetic to seize it: I mean the adoption by foreigners of reasonable tariffs on our productions. This I say is within our reach. We have only to practise retaliation, *as Adam Smith recommends*, and the thing is done. I say this as a veteran free-trader: I even claim to be more a free-trader than the members of the Cobden-club: for they only preach free-trade; I would *compel* it. They sigh and lament over the unwise foreigners; I would blow the trumpet and make war upon them with their own weapons:—tax us if you like, but we will tax you in return; we will have fair play, for we do not, like Tartuffe, love to be spit upon.

After all, the most interesting question is:—what are our prospects for the future? Let us try to judge by the past.

After the long war, ended by the peace of 1815, we had a period of bitter adversity: "War our great customer, was dead," and it required some years to open new channels of trade; besides that we were embarrassed by our depreciated paper currency, by political discontent, and by the severe fall in prices of·land and its produce.

During the nine following years there was slow, steady improvement, until at last mercantile transactions were so unduly extended that in 1825 there came a· Revulsion and a Panic. The country soon rallied from these, and again there was overtrading, resulting in the Panic of 1837.

We then entered on a new era. The school of Loyd Jones (Lord Overstone) attributed the violent fluctuations of 1825 and 1837 to flaws in the constitution of the Bank of England and of the currency: alter these, they said, and trade will be steady. Sir Robert Peel was converted, and gave us the Act of 1844. Yet there was a Panic again within three years (1847) and another in 1857. The Act therefore, failed to do what it was intended for; though during forty years it has been found so useful for enforcing caution on the Bank of England and other capitalists, that it has remained unaltered.

The Panic of 1847 arose from the too hasty construction of railways: that of 1857 from overtrading, and especially with the United States. Then came that of 1866, which was caused mainly by an undue extension of joint stock companies, and directly by the failure of one of them, Overend Gurney and Co. (limited).

Since 1866 there has been no Panic, but there have been two Revulsions, viz. in 1875 and 1884: these might have culminated in panics, but that the nation is saturated with capital, accumulated during the twenty-five prosperous though chequered years that succeeded our adoption of free-trade.

Can we on this short history build hopes of future prosperity? I am afraid not unless some wide field for employment should offer itself: some vast railway construction in the East, or a spirited resolve to improve our lands. The construction of railways in the East, and especially in China, must be left to arise naturally. The improvement of our lands by the application of abundant capital, will scarcely be general unless we can cure the madness which denies the right of individual property in land: Mr. Henry George and the extravagant Irish Nationalists are impoverishing our people by destroying the sense of security, and thus retarding the application of capital: for what sane persons will improve land which may be taken from them without compensation?

But the socialistic gabble about the wickedness of

private property in land, will be silenced: the sense of security will slowly return: landowners and a new race of farmers will by machinery and improved management multiply the annual productiveness of the soil; so that instead of the 28 bushels of wheat per acre we now reap against the poor 14 to 20 of other countries, we may rise generally to the 35 bushels of Cambridgeshire or the 37 bushels of Aberdeenshire; and this by the application of coal and iron which do not consume food. No one can prophesy what other wonders are in store for us under the pressure of the low prices of imported food.

Such improvements would add much to the resources of the country and to the means of living distributed among the people. But apparently they will not come speedily enough to give us that prosperity which prevailed on the whole from 1850 to 1875. On the other hand, we may so far come to our senses as, by means of retaliation under the guidance of Adam Smith, to enlarge the markets for our manufactures. Probably in that case we shall have our ebbs and flows of the commercial tide: excessive foreign demands for goods at one time, followed by reaction and revulsion at another.

What is wanted is such a change in other respects as shall moderate the ill results of these fluctuations. Many persons have always been found who escaped bad consequences, and some who have even profited by the periodical changes: keeping available funds in prosperous times ready to be profitably invested when revulsion and low prices come upon us.

The desideratum is human resolution, shown by moderation during prosperity and patience in adversity: we want in daily life more philosophy, that is a greater predominance of reason over passion.

X.

SUMMARY OF THE WHOLE.

1. THERE can be no doubt that trade is depressed, whatever may be said to the contrary here and there by one of the dilettanti politicians: neither can we dispute the general opinion that the depression of manufactures is closely connected with the condition of our exports, and that the depression of farming is closely connected with the condition of our imports. Why our exports have ceased to grow and have even fallen in value, is another question. The figures however are these: having multiplied fivefold between 1850 and 1875, that is from 50 to 250 millions £, they then fell steadily till in 1879 they were so low as 192 millions £, and though they rallied a little, were in 1885 only 213 millions £, a considerably smaller amount than that of 1871 (14 years earlier). Taking into account the increase of population by 5 millions (or one-sixth) the exports

in 1885 were greatly lessened, to the grievous injury of capitalists and workmen.

2. This adversity is unequally distributed, being felt most by the iron and coal trades, much by the hardware trades, less by the cotton manufacturers, and least of all by the woollen manufacturers.

Farming also, is in a very depressed condition.

3. We cannot learn much from the varying amounts in savings-banks, because in good times savings are profitably used in business, and in bad times, prices of maintenance being low as at present, people of small fixed incomes are able to lay by something against a rainy day, and naturally resort to savings-banks. The moderation of pauperism proves little, because the very low prices of food both enable the very poor to rub on without assistance, and materially lessen the cost of parish relief.

4. So far we have as our evidence of the actual depression, only the bad condition of our exports; but that evidence is irresistible.

5. Against it however, are adduced the returns of the income-tax. It is pointed out that between 1876 and 1884 the assessments grew by 50 millions £, viz. from about 580 to 630 millions £. But during those 8 years population grew by 3 millions, viz. from 33 to 36 millions. Both of them grew by about 9 per cent. Therefore in proportion to population the assessments to the income-tax were about stationary.

6. At first sight this appears inconsistent with

the alleged depression of trade. But it must be remembered that trade, and even trade and farming taken together, are not the only sources of the incomes assessed. Besides minor ones there are two other copious sources:—railways and houses (including shops and places of wholesale business).

7. Between 1876 and 1884, the assessments of railways increased by 9 millions £ (from 28 to 37 millions £).

8. During the same period the assessments of houses of the three kingdoms, increased by the extraordinary amount of 30 millions £ (from 97 to 127 millions £).

9. Thus, railways and houses account for 40 out of the 50 millions £ of increase; and these incomes are derived from investments and not from trade-profits. Since then, population considered, the increase of 50 millions £ only made the income-tax stationary, the incomes from sources other than railways and houses fell off greatly.

10. Thus we must believe that between 1876 and 1884, the profits of business both in town and country were much reduced, population considered. But the adversity may have been severer in some departments than in others: nay, some traders and classes of them may be prosperous; just as in a calamitous war, the government contractors may earn large incomes while their neighbours are ruined.

11. It is believed that in fact retail traders have been in many branches doing better than usual,

because they have bought at reduced rates, without lowering their selling prices proportionately. I appeal for proof to the marvellous outlay in recent years on huge and splendid shops, built no doubt, with previous savings, but which would not have been built unless the retailers found that their business was extensive enough and profitable enough to defray the vastly enlarged rental. I appeal also to experienced men of business to say whether a fall in cost price at once causes an equal reduction of selling prices. In a wholesale business this inconsistency is short-lived, but retailers may reap the advantage for years. I confirm my opinion by the reports of the Civil Service Stores, that immense retail business, which since the fall of wholesale prices has yielded an unusual rate of profit. The same lesson is taught by the coöperative associations, which have earned increased profits in their sales of commodities.

But since the profits wholesale and retail, are all thrown together in Schedule D, a serious diminution of incomes must have occurred in the wholesale trades.

12. This diminution is felt the more because of the extraordinary prosperity between 1850 and 1875, arising partly from the vast construction of railways, partly from the gold-discoveries, and above all from our adoption of free-trade. Men accustomed for 25 years to make money easily and abundantly, felt it hard that they should now have to toil and moil in order to scrape together moderate incomes.

13. What are the Causes of the depression?

Not foreign protective duties, for these were levied when our trade was prosperous: to remove them would be advantageous to us, but they cannot alone have caused the depression since 1875. Besides: the European countries generally and the United States have suffered as much as we have.

14. Orthodox political economy says that there cannot be gluts, and that the fault is not in over-production but in wrong production. This dogma is absurd. The study of Capital and Self-Maintenance will show how the fallacy has arisen.

15. We want occupations for labour and capital; *i.e.* we want a Field for Employment. If China adopted the imitative policy of Japan and therefore set earnestly to work in constructing railways, that might swallow up the spare capital of the world. If Great Britain found it possible to boldly meet agricultural distress by rapidly laying out £20 an acre in improvements, that would swallow up our British spare capital.

16. A serious narrowing of the field for employment through the world has arisen from diminution of railway construction. If by new inventions the cost of constructing and working railways were suddenly reduced by one-half, the rush for new lines might relieve for a generation the universal glut.

17. The two great wars, the one the American in 1861-65, the other the Franco-German in 1870-71, exhausted hundreds of millions sterling of capital:

new wars, lamentable as they would be, would relieve our financial plethora: the greater evil would swallow up the less.

18. Many persons seriously believe that an imperfect currency is at the bottom of our distress: give us a legal-tender coinage of silver as well as gold and distress will cease. It takes a long search to discover the fundamental notions of bi-metallism, and when they are found they are mostly valueless: mostly I say, not altogether.

19. The dearness of gold is the cause of the mischief, say eminent men. I do not believe that gold is scarce or dear.

20. The loss of gold by the wear of coin has been much overestimated. The loss throughout the world instead of being 5 or 10 millions £ a year, is probably not anything approaching one million. Then again, in reckoning the quantity consumed by manufactures, it is forgotten that a considerable proportion of this is supplied by broken jewellery, and scraps and dust from various sources, going down so low as a butler's leathers.

21. We are told on fair authority that the stocks of unused gold bear a heavy proportion to the quantity in use.

22. As to Remedies for our trade depression there is but little we can do. We ought indeed to resort to Retaliation to compel foreigners to receive

our manufactures on reasonable terms: our manufactures are our international currency which we pay for the wheat, sugar, coffee, tea, that we import; that currency is depreciated throughout the greater part of the world by the duties levelled upon it; as reasoning beings we should disregard the jabber about free-trade and should compel other nations to adopt it wholly or partially so far as we are concerned.

23. We cannot find such remedies as will restore the prosperity of 1850 to 1875: but we might hope to regain our strength as we did after the peace of 1815, and after the revulsions or panics of 1825, 1837, 1847, 1857, 1866, 1875.

24. One change for the better may be expected. During the last twenty years the sense of security of property has been terribly shaken. I will not trespass on the domain of politics by asking whether the Irish Land Acts were necessary, well contrived or successful; but however useful or necessary they might be thought, they have certainly helped to disturb our old notions of the sacredness of property, and have thus discouraged us from setting our capital to work to improve our fields and employ our labourers. Gradually, it may be hoped, the sense of security will return and capital will be laid out on promising enterprises. The thorough Conservatism of Jeremy Bentham as to the sense of security, will regain its influence.

---

25. After all, the true effectual unfailing permanent

SECT. X.   DEPRESSION OF TRADE.   263

remedy is in ourselves. The British race is not exhausted or weakened: it is that race which has formed our institutions and adapted them to the changes of time and circumstance. More than a hundred years ago (in 1776) Adam Smith ended the first edition of his great work with the words:—
"If any of the provinces of the British Empire cannot be made to contribute towards the support of the whole empire, it is surely time that Great Britain should . . . endeavour to accommodate her future views and designs to the real mediocrity of her circumstances." Seventeen years after this gloomy advice, Great Britain entered on that tedious and exhausting war which was concluded in 1815 by Waterloo and the Peace of Paris, and which placed our country at the head of civilized nations. Seventy years of comparative peace have since given to our arms and to our faculty of government, the secure possession of an empire the greatest, the most humane, and the most glorious the world has seen. The British race has done great things and will continue to do them; bearing prosperity with some moderation, and adversity with stubborn courage.

NOTE.—The *Economist's* comparison of 1885 and 1886.

	Quantities have increased.	Gross Values have diminisued.
In 1886.		
Exports and Imports taken together	3 per cent.	6 per cent.
Imports: manufactures and materials	5 ,,	6 to 7 ,,
The quantities of food imported have fallen 4 to 5%		
Exports: Textiles	7 ,,	5 ,,
,, Minerals and metals	4 ,,	7 ,,

Chapter V.

RETALIATION NECESSARY TO FREE TRADE.

I.

ADAM SMITH'S DOCTRINE.

THIRTY years ago, in *The Science of Social Opulence*, I avowed myself a Free-Trader: I am as ardent a Free-Trader now as I was then. But a great change has taken place: thirty years ago it was hoped that our brilliant example would make converts of the nations: now we find that our example has gone for nothing, and that in both hemispheres Protection reigns supreme. Peel and Cobden were confident that six years would convert the world: six times six years have passed and not one nation has been regenerated.

What next? Shall we sit down with folded hands and leave the world to its economic barbarism? By all means, if we have no interest in the matter: but we have the most pressing interest; for while Americans and Frenchmen punish themselves by using dear manufactures, they punish us by robbing our workmen of the means of living.

I say that having this surpassing interest in effecting conversions, we are idiots if we recline on the bank in hopes that the river of human folly will run itself dry.

We have in fact used example and preaching: since both have failed, what remains?

The simplest of remedies:—RETALIATION.

I know what follows from the mouths of ignorant and besotted politicians:—" No Protection! Free-trade for ever!" The shouts are just as idiotic as those of old:—" The Plot! No Popery! Church and King! Down with the Lords!" It is with such parrot cries that knaves and fanatics govern fools; and they are worthy of the leaders and the followers; for parrots do not reason, they only screech.

Yet, it will be said, you also have your cry, Retaliation. But this cry is founded on authority and reason. First as to authority: I will quote the words of the venerable and sagacious Adam Smith. In book iv., chapter 2, he says:—

" The case in which it may sometimes be *a matter of deliberation* how far it is proper to continue the free importation of certain foreign goods, is, when some foreign nation restrains by high duties or prohibitions the importation of some of our manufactures into their country. Revenge in this case naturally dictates retaliation. . . . Nations, accordingly, seldom fail to retaliate in this manner. The French have been particularly forward to favour their own manufactures by restraining the importation of such foreign goods as could come into competition with them. . . . Colbert, by the tarif of 1667, imposed very high duties upon a great number of foreign manufactures. Upon his refusing to moderate them in favour of the Dutch, they in 1671 prohibited the importation of the wines, brandies, and manufactures of France. . . . It was about the same time that the French and English began mutually to oppress each other's industry, by the like duties and prohibitions, of which the French, however, seem to have set the first example." Again :—" In 1697 the English prohibited the importation of bonelace, the manufacture of Flanders. The Government of that country prohibited in return the importation of English woollens. In 1700, the prohibition of importing bonelace into England, was taken off upon condition that the importation of English woollens into Flanders should be put on the same footing as before."

So far, we have a history and a mild approbation: now let us see Adam Smith's deliberate opinion. "*There may be good policy in retaliations of this kind*, when there is a probability that they will procure the repeal of the high duties or prohibitions complained of. The recovery of a great foreign market will generally more than compensate the transitory inconveniency of paying dearer during a short time for some sorts of goods. To judge whether such retaliations are likely to produce such an effect, does not, perhaps, belong so much to the science of a legislator, . . . as to the skill of that insidious and crafty animal, vulgarly called a statesman or politician."

I have produced my authority, and that of the highest possible character. I would almost rather go wrong with Adam Smith than right with the hollow, worn-out Cobden Club, the laughing-stock of nations.

Let no one, after reading Adam Smith, dare to say that my cry of Retaliation, is ignorant, besotted, or parrot-like, as are "Free Trade!"—"No Protection!"

II.

APPLICATION TO US.

I HAVE said that my demand for Retaliation is not thoughtless and parrot-like, but is founded on both authority and reason. I have given an authority which seems beyond all dispute. I now appeal to reason, to show that Adam Smith's doctrine is applicable to us.

The doctrine is that "there may be good policy in retaliations of this kind, when there is a probability that they will procure the repeal of the high duties or prohibitions complained of. The recovery of a great foreign market will generally more than compensate the transitory inconveniency of paying dearer during a short time for some sorts of goods."

The foreign markets we desire to recover are great ones: that of the United States with more than 50 millions of people: that of Germany with more than 40 millions: that of France with a population larger than our own: that of Russia huge though poor: those of Austria, Spain, Italy, Brazil.

It is notorious that the duties on our goods levied by these States are many of them exorbitant. If indeed, these duties were only as high as the average duties levied on all their imports, we should in many cases have little to complain of: for the average import duties, as we are told, are only

1% $1\frac{1}{2}\%$ 5% 6% $6\frac{1}{2}\%$ 9%
in Holland, Belgium, Austria, Germany, France, Denmark.

But the case is far different with other States, the average import duties being

28% 26% 24% 44%
in the United States, Portugal, Spain, Brazil.

These averages too, tell us only a part of our own ill-treatment. France imposes an average duty of only $6\frac{1}{2}$ per cent.: but the lowness of this average is caused by her imposing no duty at all on some goods, as silk for instance, and very little on raw produce; our goods on the contrary are heavily taxed, and until 1860 were prohibited.

Now look at the United States where the average is 28 per cent. This high rate is moderate as compared with what we are made to pay. In 1884 a bill was introduced at Washington, proposing a reduction of 20 per cent. on a large number of articles. In future the duty on cottons (calico and yarn for example) was not to exceed 40 per cent. : this was *after* the reduction : on hardware, *after* the reduction, it was not to exceed 50 per cent. : on wool, woollen goods, and glass it was not to exceed 60 per cent. These extravagant rates were to be levied under the *new* tariff.

The foreign markets then, which we want to recover are vast; the import duties we suffer under are monstrous. Is there any probability that we should right ourselves by means of Retaliation? If so, at what cost to ourselves? I propose to show that we could easily right ourselves, and this at little cost.

If our commerce with the United States were small, it might be difficult to make an impression on the nation with more than 50 millions of people. But the commerce is really of vast dimensions. So late as 1883, *half* of the American foreign trade was carried on with Great Britain and her colonies, while that with France was only one-tenth, and that with Germany one-twelfth. The Americans may well tremble lest the English should open their eyes and adopt retaliation.

Other figures may cause a still greater tremor.

The American exports to Great Britain were £84,000,000
The imports from Great Britain were only £38,000,000
or less than half the exports.

It must alarm the Americans to see that we English are by far their best customers, and that we have strong reasons for dissatisfaction and anger. They may anxiously inquire what means we have of punishment and redress. The means are easy and efficacious.

Cotton-wool we must not touch; for if we levied a duty on it, we should raise the prices of our yarn and calico to the injury of our foreign trade. But the same objection does not apply to corn, pork, or cattle. The Americans send us much wheat, and this is raised over the greater part of the Union, from New York to California. Some of it is grown near the Atlantic coast, and the producers get for this we may suppose 20s. a quarter: another portion has to be brought down the rivers, and the cost of this conveyance may reduce the growers' receipts to 15s. a quarter: the growers more distant from the coast may get only 10s. a quarter, and others so little as 5s., leaving a certain number of distant settlers to burn their crops for cooking.

Now if we imposed a duty of 5s., whilst admitting without charge the wheat of the free-trading India and New South Wales, that would tend to lower the American receipts by 5s. a quarter; leaving nothing for the most distant farmers, and reducing the 10s. to 5s., the 15s. to 10s., and the 20s. to 15s.

This would be a heavy blow to the growers. That it would be effectual we know from the Americans themselves: a member of the New York Chamber of Commerce lately made the extravagant assertion, that a differential duty, not of 5s. but of 1s. a quarter, would do more to bring about free-trade than all the publications of the Cobden Club. As a threat and suggestion of higher punishment impending it might do something. A more reasonable person, after describing the immense newly opened region in Canada, with a greater capacity for growing wheat and rearing cattle than all the land on the Baltic, the Black Sea, and the Mediterranean taken together, declares that if we should impose on American wheat a duty of 3s. 4d. a quarter, while accepting Canadian wheat without duty; and if we should treat in the same way, cattle, beef, pork, cheese, and butter, we "should cripple, if not ruin all the farmers of the United States."

A simple, cheap, and effective remedy then, is within our reach.

It seldom happens that an economical truth is so manifest as this; that retaliation is necessary and easy. I sympathise with Sydney Smith, who in the earlier days of the Edinburgh reviewers, said:—" I wish I were as cock-sure of any one thing as Tom Macaulay is of everything." But I have the happiness of being cock-sure of one truth:—That retaliation is necessary to Free Trade.

III.

ALLEGED DEAR BREAD: MR. BRIGHT: SPAIN.

HERE we shall be met with the discordant screeching of the brainless birds: this is just the opportunity for the parrots to make night hideous with "No Jews! Church and King! Cheap bread!"

Do I propose to make bread dear? The price of the 4lb. loaf of late has been 4½d. to 5d.; this is with wheat at 32s. to 40s.: a rise in wheat of 5s. a quarter till America had given way, might add to the price of bread for a short time about ½d. a loaf: a man with a numerous family, consuming twelve loaves a week, would have to pay sixpence a week additional; but if he got more employment through a reduction of the American import duties, he might add to his income ten or twenty times the 6d. Such is the "dear bread!" with which our ears are dinned. It is even probable that wheat would not rise 5s. a quarter even for a time. At any rate since a rise of 1s. would increase the supplies from various countries: that of 2s. still further supplies, and so on, we may use Adam Smith's language, and say that "the recovery of a great foreign market will more than compensate the *transitory* inconvenience of paying" an additional ½d. a loaf.

Certain thoughtless scribes pretend that in levying a duty of 5s. a quarter we should be restoring the corn laws: they do not know that those laws imposed duties on a sliding scale; generally shutting corn out, and admitting it only when the price was twice its present average, whereas I only propose to levy a small duty in some cases, and for a time. A "restoration of the corn laws" forsooth!

An incidental advantage of our taking less wheat from America would be that we should get more from India, which already sends us millions of quarters annually. Anything which binds us more closely to India is an occasion for rejoicing to a true Englishman. And our interest coincides with our patriotism; for India takes our goods freely, and to the amount of 30 millions sterling a year; nearly as much as is taken by the United States, and one-eighth of our whole exportations.

With regard to our joy in the possession of India and in the greatness of England, that, say Quaker statesmen, is foolish if not wicked; for patriotism is a heathen virtue. It seems to me strange that Mr. Bright, whose memory is crowded with English poetry, should have imbibed so little of its spirit as not to understand the ardour of Scott's Minstrel :—

> Breathes there the man with soul so dead,
> Who never to himself hath said
> This is my own, my native land?
> Whose heart hath ne'er within him burned,
> As home his footsteps he hath turned,
> From wandering on a foreign strand?

But Mr. Bright goes farther: he denies that we gain any advantage by our possession. Yet he knows that if India fell into the hands of Russia or France, or had a Government of her own, our goods would be at once heavily taxed or prohibited. Despite this he has the audacity to say falsely:—"You have Gibraltar, Malta, the Suez Canal, Perim, and Aden; you have all these stepping-stones to India, and you have India; but excepting the thirty young gentlemen who find places there every year, and a profit of £10,000,000, there is not a single result which is beneficial to the thirty-four millions of the United Kingdom." Pity that Mr. Bright's statuesque oratory should not have a substratum of ordinary sense!

Again; What is gone with the old philanthropy of the Quakers? A hundred years ago and for half a century afterwards, they were the ardent supporters of the abolition of the African slave-trade, when our efforts to suppress it nearly involved us in war with France and America. But there are in India, millions (two at least) of girls and women in worse than negro slavery: I mean the widows of all ages from infancy upwards: children and mature women condemned either to vice or to the most shameful drudgery, all the more galling because they see their sisters wives and mothers. The only hope of relieving these wretched millions, is in the continued predominance of Great Britain. We may in the end accomplish this heroic task, just as we have put an end to the burning of widows and the murder of Rajpoot female children. What recks Mr. Bright? Perish the widows rather than that we should have the burden of greatness! Where I say, is Quaker philanthropy? I would not impose a duty of 5s. on American wheat in order to benefit India, but I am glad that as it happens we should thus morally benefit India by imposing the duty. Another incidental advantage is one in the case of war: for now that more than half the bread we eat comes from abroad, it is well that our supplies should be obtained from all quarters of the earth. We formerly got too much from Russia, then from Russia and the United States taken together: now, half comes from America, including California. We may fairly wish that the competition of India and Canada should reduce this to a more reasonable amount. But not even for this would I impose a differential duty on the wheat of the United States: let our goods be freely admitted and theirs should be freely admitted by us.

Now look at Spain; as to which country Lord Salisbury lately said, that it seemed fair and reasonable that by an increased import duty on her wines, we should retaliate for her shameful treatment of us.

Note these facts. A quarter of a century ago, Spain found herself injured by the treaty that Cobden negotiated, under which France admitted our goods, and at comparatively moderate duties, in consideration of concessions on our part as to French productions. Spain retaliated by raising her duties on

French and on English goods. France at once gave notice that if the surcharges were continued as to her goods, Spain should also pay higher duties in France. Spain had to yield and withdraw her surcharges.

England did not even threaten to retaliate, and the surcharges on her goods were continued. Not content with this, "in 1877 Spain remodelled her Customs duties, establishing a higher and a lower tariff, the lower to apply to those countries with which she had negotiated treaties, the higher to those with which she had no commercial undertaking." We see the result in the following extract from a Liverpool newspaper :—

Mr. Ralph Heaton, of Birmingham, lately had a contract for the supply of brass to Spain. And where was he compelled to purchase it? Why, from Germany, and simply because the import duty on brass from Germany into Spain was £7 a ton whilst from England it was £14 a ton.

The Spaniards themselves are trembling with the fear that we may recover from our fatuity. One of them says :—Besides the tariff against us after the Anglo-French treaty of 1860, "in 1877 a Spanish differential tariff was made against the English, with the avowed object of obliging them to make concessions as to Spanish wines. When at last they consented, Spain repelled them: now there are indications of a tendency on the part of England to use the same means which we were the first to employ. . . . . Last month the Birmingham

Chamber of Commerce defeated a motion in favour of reciprocity by only 62 votes against 49; and the Nottingham Chamber is altogether in favour of reciprocity or something more. . . . . . The most absurd part of the business is, what we refuse to England, which takes from us to the extent of nearly 10 millions sterling a year, we benevolently concede to Germany which takes from us only one-thirteenth part of *one* million."

Is not Lord Salisbury amply justified in suggesting retaliation? The most hare-brained and impudent of birds cannot here get up a chorus of "No taxes on wine! Cheap sherry for ever!"

IV.

THE COBDEN CLUB: DEMOCRACY: TREATIES.

TO me then, the case of Retaliation *v.* Laissez-faire is so clear that I am at a loss to know what plausible reply can be given. It was not so forty years ago, when Peel and Cobden confidently foretold that within six years the world would be converted to the true economical faith. They trusted to persuasion, and to the best of all persuasion, example. Our example has been preëminent during a generation and a half, and yet the hearts of the nations are as hard as the nether millstone. Example has failed.

But direct persuasion has been added. Our newspapers and periodicals have sung pæans to free-trade. The Cobden Club, with riches at command, have poured their money into the laps of paper-makers, printers, and paid agents; they have sent shiploads of pamphlets and leaflets to the United States; and my friend, the late Mr. Dixwell, of Boston, a subtle and able Protectionist writer, complained to me of the nuisance which, like a cloud of house-flies, irritated without wounding. This is what has made the Cobden Club the laughing-stock of foreigners, who feel as we should feel, if the French blocked our post offices with circulars in favour of peasant proprietorship, equal division of property at death, and liberty, equality, fraternity.

Even if we could induce a nation to try free-trade, there would remain an insuperable difficulty in making the practice permanent. We have got used to it, and yet our workmen complain that it is a shame to allow the importation of German hardware and French silks, while Englishmen want employment.

We are told by Horace Greeley, a trustworthy American writer, who once hoped to be President of the United States, that the demand for protection there arose thus: the tariff had been lowered, and English goods were coming in freely: bad times followed; the manufacturers and their people complained that the bread was taken out of their mouths by British competition; then came new protective import duties. The present very high tariff, no doubt, resulted from the civil war; but why has it not been duly lowered during twenty years of peace? If it had been so, then during the last few years of American distress there would have been a successful clamour for a new rise.

Democracies seem naturally protectionist, because the workmen are predominant and feel the pinch of foreign rivalry. In 1848, after the revolution in France, one of the first things the democracy did was to insist upon banishing English competition: this was not felt by French artizans, for British goods were then shut out of France: but by the labourers, who bitterly complained that in constructing railways English navvies were employed. The English contractors had to send their countrymen home. Our Colonies have democratic governments: one of them lately, South Australia, had a want of employment for the artizans in the manufactures which had been established under the protective system: the unemployed loudly demanded higher import duties.

Even therefore, if by example and persuasion we could induce foreigners to try free-trade, we might be sure that this would be abandoned on the first smart of national distress.

Some persons will say that since example and argument have failed to make foreign converts, we must resort to treaties. Adam Smith however, whose authority is justly supreme, condemns commercial treaties. He says that "though they may be advantageous to the merchants and manufacturers of the favoured, they are necessarily disadvantageous to those of the favouring country. A monopoly is thus granted against them to a foreign nation; and they must frequently buy the foreign goods they have occasion for, dearer than if the free competition of other nations was admitted."

Since our adoption of free-trade, we have entered into one commercial treaty of importance, that with France in 1860, negotiated by Cobden himself. Before that time British goods were not merely taxed in France, but were absolutely prohibited, as they had been for seventy years, *i.e.* since the law of the 10 Brumaire, an. V. (1797). At the Paris Exhibition of 1855 it was seen that French manufactures had made sufficient progress to allow a relaxation of this rigorous system. The Emperor resolved that prohibitions should cease, and laid a bill to that effect before the Corps Législatif; but that usually submissive body received the proposal so roughly that it was withdrawn, with a promise not to interfere with the prohibitions for five years.

This period would expire in 1860. The year before this it occurred to Lord Palmerston, that it would strengthen his party in the House of Commons, if he could get a relaxation of the rigid French system. Louis Napoleon was confirmed in his desire of accomplishing this by his sympathy with

Palmerston, who at the *coup d'état* of 1851 and ever since had been friendly to him. Cobden, who had refused a high seat in the Ministry, accepted the charge of negotiating a treaty.

The terms agreed on were one-sided. It is true that we were still to levy a considerable duty on light wines, but this was for the sake of revenue, and was by no means protective, since we do not ourselves make wine, and do levy a duty on the substitutes, malt or beer, and British spirits. On the other hand, the French were still to impose heavy protective duties on our manufactures, although they ceased to prohibit them, while we undertook to admit without duty the gloves, ribbons, and other productions of France.

This treaty is in one respect an eternal disgrace to Lord Palmerston, though he only followed the pernicious example of previous ministers. Sir Robert Peel, despite his enthusiasm for free-trade, abstained from the repeal of the duties on French articles, perhaps because he resented the prohibition of English goods in France, probably also because he trembled at the thought of reducing to pauperism the large population of Coventry and its neighbourhood. But Palmerston and Cobden bestowed not a thought on these unfortunates: with a light heart they took away their employment and their bread, that ladies might get at a reduced price their gloves and their ribbons.

I blush when I turn to this page of our history.

The treaty, by suddenly bringing French articles into competition with ours, inflicted ruin, absolute ruin, on thousands of the artizans of Coventry and Nuneaton and their environs: so long did the depression of trade continue that the workmen, hitherto industrious, were taught to live on charity and idleness, a habit resulting, as I was assured by the vicar of Nuneaton, in the destruction of thrift and morality.

Huskisson had formerly lowered the duties on silks, but he had not removed the whole of them at a stroke. Palmerston did remove them at a stroke, and must have known what fatal consequences would follow: at any rate he soon did know, for so crying was the misery that a national subscription was set on foot to mitigate it. But why should this have been left to private benevolence? If one man falls into impotence through accident, or even by his own fault, he is legally entitled to relief; but when a whole city and its neighbours were deprived of their means of living in order to strengthen a political party, not a finger was raised by the Ministry to anticipate and provide against the approaching distress. Such is the distortion of the true doctrine of laissez-faire.

Besides; treaties are no more permanent than are voluntary reductions of duties; the French Treaty of 1860 soon expired, and then the French seized the opportunity of raising their import duties on our goods. They knew that we should lie down and allow them to beat us, and that we should not dream of resenting their ill-usage by returning blow for blow. Yet in commerce as in war, defensive fighting is not merely justifiable, it is necessary, and in commerce defensive fighting is Retaliation.

On the whole I have no love of commercial treaties, which are often one-sided and generally temporary, and are far inferior to that other remedy, Retaliation.

To all this reasoning the reply will be:—" Great is Diana of the Ephesians!"

The world cannot live without a superstition: the Romans sought the will of the gods in the entrails of victims and the flight of birds; the Christians of the middle-ages had their scapularies and periapts and spells; the Hindoo will bend and kiss the hem of the garment of the meanest Brahmin, and must needs purify his house if a European foot has crossed the threshold. The Brahmin is debarred from practising the beneficent European surgery, because he is forbidden to touch a dead body; and can therefore neither study the human frame by dissection nor examine the corpse of his patient. The English superstition of to-day is free-trade: if any stranger utters a word against the divinity, the votaries yell out, "Blasphemy! Sacrilege! Great is Diana of the Ephesians!"

V.

THREATS SUFFICIENT: EXISTING TREATIES.

RETALIATION is effective because it falls heavily on a particular class of a nation, and is felt at once. If we demonstrate to the South Australians generally, that by raising their import duties on manufactures they condemn themselves to pay too much for their saucepans and fenders, their calico and broadcloth, they will grumble, but they will bear it for the sake of preventing distress and discontent among the artizans: if however, the English retaliated by laying a duty on South Australian corn, that would be so injurious to all wheat growers and so fatal to many, that the high tariff on British productions would be cancelled.

We have seen the United States acknowledging that a trifling differential duty on American wheat, cattle, and pork, would ruin tens of thousands of farmers: no Congress could resist their demand for better treatment of British manufactures, in order to secure free entry of American produce into England.

Actual retaliation would seldom be necessary: threats on our part would be sufficient. After 1860, when the Spaniards were about to levy increased duties on French products, the French were going to retaliate, but the Spaniards withdrew their surcharge: no mercy was shown to us because we did not even threaten to retaliate.

One difficulty may be anticipated: we have treaties with certain nations, providing that they shall be put on the footing of the most favoured nation; how then, can we retaliate in a particular case? We evaded this difficulty in 1860: we wanted to favour light French wines; but instead of enacting that these should come in at a low duty, we enacted that *all* light wines should be so admitted: since there was but little light wine besides the French that could come in, this general regulation did what was wanted. In the same way, we might in general terms give notice, that all nations which charged certain duties on our goods, should pay on importation 2s. or 5s. a quarter on their wheat and 10s. or 20s. on every ox. This might be afterwards extended to other commodities, such as strong wine. No one nation could reasonably complain of a rule applied to the whole world.

Ought this retaliation to apply to our Colonies? I say in principle, yes! though I am aware that the contrary opinion is maintained by statesmen of much weight.

If there are two brothers, A and B, the one a maker of iron and the other a buyer, B will give a preference to A as against other makers: but he will give only a preference; he will not pay A a higher price than he pays to his competitors. If A says, you might give me 5s. a ton over the market price,

B will reply, you might sell to me at 5s. under the market price. So, if the Victorians say, you might give us 3d. a pound more for wool than you give to foreigners, we reply, you might (by means of bounties) sell wool to us at 3d. less than you get from foreigners. Let brothers be content to give and take the market price: let England and her Colonies also give and take the market price of the world. Yet it might be well for a time to admit all Colonial produce free: partly to aggravate the punishments of foreign protectionists; and also to make sure of ample supplies.

VI.

FAIR-TRADE: MR. BRIGHT: REPEAL 1846.

FINALLY, I desire to call attention to three facts.

First, I am not a Protectionist under the guise of a Fair-Trader. When my neighbours see in England plyers and screws made in Germany, they ask why we should not be contented with our own make, and imitate foreigners by putting a duty on the imported articles: I reply that such a practice carried out as to commodities generally, would raise our cost of living and thus impoverish us. "But the Germans deprive our workmen of employment:" I reply that they really deprive our hardware-workmen of employment, but on the other hand give employment to the makers of cottons, linen, and woollens, which the Germans receive in payment for the hardware. "But they take our money:" I reply that the silver and gold of which our money consists, are foreign commodities which we pay for with manufactures resulting from the employment of artizans. It is found by experience that the safest plan is to bear the evil of foreign interference and let the course of trade alone, rather than build up a wall of Protection which sooner or later will come down with a run: a gradual displacement is a far less evil. Holding these opinions I am not a Fair-Trader. Nay, I contend that I am more a *Free*-Trader than are the members of the Cobden Club: they are satisfied with practising and preaching free-trade, whereas I would not only practice and preach it but would also by retaliation compel others to adopt it: the Cobden Club are apathetic, I am aggressive: they are peaceable, I am warlike.

The second fact is Mr. Bright's claim to be considered the apostle, the St. Paul, of free-trade. That he was a minor apostle I grant, but I maintain that Cobden was *the* Apostle, overtopping Mr. Bright by a head and shoulders. If this be not so, how was it that the northern manufacturers, having raised a sum of 50 or 60,000 £, presented it all to Cobden? How was it again, that the associated free-traders took the name of the Cobden Club:

why did not they call themselves the Bright Club, or the Bright-and-Cobden Club, or the Cobden-and-Bright Club? Why did Mr. Bright's name find no place? It was because they recognised Cobden and not Bright as the apostle of repeal of the corn-laws.

The third fact is that Mr. Bright misunderstands and shamefully misrepresents the results of Peel's Act of 1846 respecting the corn-laws. The first result was a steadiness in the prices of corn and bread: before 1846 wheat varied rapidly from 50 to 80s., and even the year after the repeal (1847) it actually reached 100s., nearly twice its ordinary price: now it varies slowly. But it was a great mischief formerly that those who lived mainly on bread never knew what it would cost them. The second result of the repeal, and a very great one, was the increase of our foreign trade; our exports growing from 50 up to 250 millions £ in 25 years. Now Mr. Bright disregards these changes, though he can scarcely be ignorant of them; he prefers to harp on one string and to harp falsely, uttering the monotonous strain "I gave you cheap bread, and but for me you would have been paying during 30 years 7d. to 9d. a loaf instead of 5d. to 6d." It is Mr. Bright's pleasure to forget that comparing the 20 years before the repeal of the corn-laws with the twenty years after it, the quartern loaf was about ½d. cheaper in the second period and not 2d. or 3d. cheaper. But figures like facts are caviare to the rhetorician.

VII.

SUMMARY.

I HAVE thus tried to show that after forty years' experience, we know it a hopeless attempt to convert the world to Free-trade by example and persuasion: that this is to us a matter of supreme importance: that nothing remains to us but to adopt Retaliation. I have ridiculed the ordinary parrot-screeches uttered in reply. As to my own cry of Retaliation, I have on my side both authority and reason.

My authority is the highest possible, that of Adam Smith; who says that there may be good policy in retaliation when it is likely to succeed.

As to reason, I have shown that retaliation is likely to succeed: that we are at present shut out of vast foreign markets, and this by extravagant import duties. I have added that in the case of the considerable market of Spain, duties are levied on our goods which are not levied on German goods of the same kind. I have quoted the opinions of foreigners: of the United States, where it is conceded that a trifling differential duty put by us on their raw produce, would ruin half their farmers: of Spain where similar alarm is felt. I would not tax cotton wool, but I would begin with a duty of 2s. 6d. or 5s. on wheat from all protective countries, while admitting it without duty from free-trading countries and colonies, such as India and New South Wales.

What other means are open to us? Example and persuasion have failed: even if they succeeded for a time they would probably be not permanent: we know from Horace Greeley that in America, bad times bring irresistible demands for renewed or increased Protection; South Australia has lately followed this example; even among ourselves the artizans mutter that we ought not to import German goods while our own people are walking the streets. Treaties are equally uncertain as to duration, while they are only partially efficacious, are very troublesome, and are more or less humiliating.

Nothing is left but retaliation; a remedy advised by Adam Smith, based on common sense, and found in the highest degree efficacious.

For these forty years we have been playing the part of the sluggish giant, who allows the dwarfs to pick his pockets. Let us up and shake off this indolence, and apply the great powers we possess, not to damaging others but to righting ourselves.

The Cobden Club and its abettors, some of them among the greatest men of the nation, but as ignorant of true political economy as are the waiters at the attractive annual dinner, imagine that the rulers of Great Britain display magnanimity in shutting their eyes against the injuries done to our commerce. Magnanimity! and at whose expense? At the expense of the half-employed millions. The well-born and wealthy men wrap themselves around with their vicarious generosity as with a cloak, and sleep the sleep of the just; neglecting in their egotism or selfishness the artizans pale and moody, their wives half-clothed and pinched, and their children demoralized with hunger.

Chapter VI.

THE PURSE AND THE CASHBOX.

I.

A HUNDRED SOVEREIGNS AND TEN: CAPITAL AND SELF-MAINTENANCE.

I FEEL some confidence in reprinting this Essay, because it had the approval of the late Dr. W. B. Hodgson, the distinguished lecturer, and Professor of Political Economy in Edinburgh University. He wrote me word that he regularly taught the Essay to his students: not long before his death, he visited me, and suggested a few verbal amendments, all of which I have adopted. I have also made independently some alterations, and especially in the terms I employ, though not in substance.

You are a manufacturer, carrying in your purse ten sovereigns for household purposes, and having

THE PURSE AND THE CASHBOX.

in your cashbox at your factory, a hundred sovereigns for the purchase of wood and iron and for paying wages. What do political economists call the ten sovereigns and the hundred sovereigns?

Many if not most political economists call the ten and the hundred by the same name:—Capital. For the ten like the hundred are the results of labour and saving, the ten like the hundred are to be used in the purchase of commodities and in the paying of wages.

But perhaps we may find reasons for requiring different names for these two sums of money: we may say that though they have the same origin, and are both of them used in paying for commodities and services, yet there is a distinction which forbids the application of the same name to both of them.

All agree that the hundred sovereigns are Capital: what shall we call the ten?

But first, what is the distinction between the ten and the hundred sovereigns?

Suppose that in a fit of extravagance, you alter the proportions of your purse and your cashbox: that every week you put fifty instead of ten into the purse, and only sixty instead of a hundred into the cashbox.

Former division, Purse 10, Cashbox 100, Total 110
Latter   ,,   ,, 50,   ,,   60, ,, same

Let this extravagance continue from the 1st January

to the 31st December. In a previous year you had spent on your household in fifty-two weeks £520. In this extravagant year you have spent £2,600. Two years ago the Capital invested in your business was . . . . . £10,000. A year ago (if you had during the first year just spent the profits) it continued to be . . . . £10,000. But now, at the close of the extravagant year it is only . . . . . £7,920.

Your capital in your business is £2,080 less than it was at first. If your new household expenditure of £2,080 has been incurred in keeping horses and servants, in feasting, in travelling, in gambling, then the money is irrecoverably gone: you have had your pleasures and nothing remains but the memory of them.

But if instead of this, the £2,080 had been laid out at the factory on wood and iron and as wages to artizans, the £2,080 would have been returned to you in the form of hardware which you could sell for at least the cost.

Here then is the required distinction between the purse and the cashbox: the contents of the purse perish in the using, the contents of the cashbox are reproduced.

Let us go back to the first year: you put £10 into the purse, and £100 into the cashbox. We see that the ten sovereigns and the hundred are equally produced by labour and accumulated by saving, and are equally applied to buying commodities and services: we see on the other hand that the commodities and services bought with the ten sovereigns are essentially different from those bought by the hundred: that those bought with the ten disappear once for all, while those bought with the hundred, reappear in the form of hardware.

What names shall we apply to the two sums? Ordinary Political Economists call them both Capital, because they have an origin in common, and are both of them used in buying commodities and labour: they disregard the distinction I have pointed out, that the ten sovereigns disappear in the using, while the hundred are reproduced.

I concede that we may usefully have *a* name for both sums taken together.

I only say that Capital is not the name: that this word is fitly applied to the hundred sovereigns in the cashbox, but not to the ten sovereigns in the purse. To call these ten sovereigns capital tends to error. Capital is a word in common and frequent use: if a man saves part of his income and applies it to his business, we say he capitalizes it: if a man takes money out of business beyond his profits, and lays it out in furniture and horses, we say that he has trenched on his capital. Capital is thus, money or money's worth employed in earning an income, and further in earning an income by carrying on a business.

We want another general name then, for the ten and the hundred sovereigns taken together. Adam Smith used the word Stock: what he in the end called Capital, he at first called Capital-Stock, following the example of his predecessors; indicating that Stock was a wider name than Capital, and that Capital-Stock or Capital was a part of Stock.

According to Adam Smith, a farmer's cows are stock, a manufacturer's materials are stock; and this is in accordance with general usage. But there are other things produced by labour and accumulated by saving, to which the word is not applicable: such things as farm-buildings, factories, canals, railways.

I formerly suggested that in the absence of a better word, we might extend the meaning of Stock when writing on Political Economy, to the immoveable things, farm-buildings, factories, canals, railways: but only in the absence of a better word; for I object to using a word in a sense different from that of common life, and would do so only under the stress of necessity.

I now propose a new term which is free from this objection, and which has the advantage of being connotative (denoting its own meaning). That new term is Human Productions.

In the "Terms and Definitions" at the beginning of this volume, I divide all property, into "Gifts-of-Nature" and "Human-Productions:" the Gifts-of-Nature consisting of such things as unimproved land and streams, natural forests, hills of coal: while

Human-Productions consist of such things as the improvements of land and of streams, roads, manufacturing stock and machinery, dwelling-houses, furniture, food, clothing. Services must not be called Human-Productions, because they are not Property.

Now then, we have the general name for the 100 sovereigns and the 10 sovereigns taken together; viz. Human Production: we also have the name for the 100 sovereigns alone; viz. Capital: we still want a name for the 10 sovereigns alone.

Thirty years ago, in my "Science of Social Opulence," I proposed to call the ten sovereigns and the things they buy, Self-Maintenance; and some years later I again formally proposed the use of that term: fifteen years after my first publication I had to say that I had made no converts to the use of the term, or to the importance of using any specific term: I am now more fortunate, since I can appeal to the authority of the late Dr. W. B. Hodgson. Even without this encouragement I should have continued to use and recommend the distinction between Capital and Not-Capital, and to call the Not-Capital Self-Maintenance, until a better term is found. I insist on the distinction because I find that it solves certain difficult problems, and especially the questions about over-production, a thing generally pronounced by Political Economists to be impossible.

If I am asked whether, while adopting the distinction between the 100 sovereigns and the 10, we might not find a better term for the 10 than Self-Maintenance, I concede that probably a better term might be found. "Not-Capital" may be suggested: It may be defended on the ground that we should as far as possible use terms translatable into foreign languages. But this cannot be said of Self-Maintenance: for taking the French language, all words compounded with self are impossible: our self-government becomes "le gouvernement de soi par soi-même." Not-Capital would suit the French better.

We have an example of this compounding of a term with the word Not. Carew, quoted by Johnson, says:—"Of wheat there are two sorts: French, which is bearded, and requireth the best soil; and *not-wheat*, so termed because it is unbearded, being contented with a meaner earth."

"Not-Capital" has another advantage over "Self-Maintenance," that it does not suggest an inaccuracy. For whereas Self-Maintenance does suggest that the Maintenance is destined for a man only, and not for his wife and children as well, Not-Capital is free from this defect. The maintenance of servants also has to be decided, as included or not in the term: I include it, and I will afterwards show why.

On the other hand "Not-Capital" has its ambiguity. It would naturally be taken to mean all Property that is not capital: it would thus include land: but it is intended only for the 10 sovereigns and the things proposed to be bought with them and consumed. The division of Property is into

Gifts of Nature, and

Human Productions, subdivided into Capital and Not-Capital (or Self-Maintenance).

A Frenchman may therefore prefer Not-Capital; an Englishman, Self-Maintenance.

The 10 sovereigns in my purse then, are Not-Capital (or Self-Maintenance). I spend part of them on the necessaries of life, as bread, meat, clothes, shelter: part on superfluities, as wine, broadcloth, travelling: part on luxuries, as Château Lafite and high-stepping horses. All these disappear without reproducing themselves.

Again; I share with wife and children, the necessaries, the superfluities, and the luxuries I buy: these things consumed by my family are Not-Capital. I give half a crown to a destitute person or a guinea to a dispensary: these things like the last, are Not-Capital.

Servants also I say, are maintained by Not-Capital. This will be seen at once in the case of housemaids and butlers, who only render services and reproduce nothing: but as to cooks and gardeners doubts may be felt, since they prepare or produce food: I will soon give my reasons for holding that they are maintained with Not-Capital.

II.

USE OF THE DISTINCTION.

WE have got thus far then: that the results of labour may be called Human Productions, as distinguished from unimproved land, streams, and other things, which are Gifts of Nature: that Human Productions, represented by my 110 sovereigns, may be divided into Capital (the 100 sovereigns in my cashbox) and Self-Maintenance or Not-Capital (the 10 sovereigns in my purse).

But is there any use in this distinction? I believe it will be found to lie at the root of many considerable doctrines.

For example: we are told that the employment of labour is immediately dependent upon the existence of capital; that it is only as capital grows that the demand for labour grows.

It is seen that when there is abundance of food and other means of subsistence, the holders are willing to employ labourers, who are required to work in payment. Substitute "capital" for "food and other means of subsistence," and you may say that the employment of labour grows with the growth of capital.

But is this substitution to be defended? Certainly not. There may be a growth of Capital without an immediate growth of labourers' maintenance. Railways are Capital: for they are Human Productions used in a business, that of conveyance. Now in 1848, there had been a vast construction of railways during the previous years: while the railways were being made there was an unusual demand for labour: but in 1848 and 1849, there was a great depression of trade, following the fever and Panic of 1847, and little demand for labour. The capital of the country had not been diminished, but it had changed its form: it had to a great extent become fixed: while it is Circulating (Unfixed) Capital that sets labour to work.

All that can be truly said is, that an augmentation of Circulating (or Unfixed) Capital favours a demand for labour.

Working men know too well that the immediate effect of additional machinery (Fixed Capital) is to supersede labour: therefore they formerly violently destroyed machines for threshing and lace-making.

Men then, are set to work by Circulating (or Unfixed) Capital, or rather by its possessors. But these traders will not set them to work unless they have some profitable task for them. A Field for Employment is necessary, as is conceded by Mr. J. S. Mill. But this I will not insist on at present.

Then again, it is erroneous to say even that labour is dependent upon unfixed capital; for this means that it is altogether so dependent; while the truth is that it is only partly so dependent.

Without unfixed capital indeed, the human race would cease to exist, or at any rate would be reduced to a few wanderers poorly subsisting on wild fruits, honey, and wild animals: for a man cannot have his herd of cattle, much less can he till the ground, without unfixed capital to carry on his business.

What I am contending for is, that the world being constituted as it is, with quantities of unfixed capital, and labourers maintained with it, many other labourers are maintained with a different fund.

Take the case of a gentleman with a large income derived from land or consols, or foreign funds. He employs ten women servants and five men: his income is suddenly and greatly increased; he doubles the number of his servants: the demand for this kind of labour grows as the income grows.

I do not mean that the gentleman must of necessity add to the number of his servants. On the contrary; when he receives £1000, the first instalment of his augmented income, he will have to determine whether he will spend it as Self-Maintenance, or whether he will use it as Capital in some business. What I mean is, that if he resolves to spend it, and to do this partly by multiplying his servants, then the demand for servants increases. This labour is employed and paid by Self-Maintenance.

You may object that the demand for labour caused

by capital is permanent, because the capital reproduces itself: in the case of a farmer by his crops, milk, and fat cattle; in the case of a manufacturer by finished goods; in the case of foreign trade by the products imported; whereas, you say, the demand for labour caused by self-maintenance is temporary, because the fund does not reproduce itself. I reply that though the fund does not reproduce itself it may be reproduced otherwise: for the gentleman's income may consist of the rent of land, and both the land and the average rent are more permanent than capital and profit; or it may consist of interest well secured, and this is more permanent than capital and profit.

Self-maintenance then, supplied from a permanent source, causes a direct demand for labour just as capital does. Nor must this be regarded as a trifling exception to the supposed law that labour is dependent upon capital. It is a wonderful fact that throughout England and Wales, the female domestic servants are as numerous as the farm-labourers' wives. True, the farm-labourers and their wives commonly have families dependent upon them, while domestic female servants are for the most part single (*i.e.* in England as distinguished from Ireland). Therefore the number of persons maintained by farm-labour is far greater than the number maintained by domestic service.

The case is more strongly in my favour, if we consider the money paid to each of the two classes.

The average earnings of farm-labourers, after deducting for loss of time through bad weather, and for the low wages of mere youths, cannot much exceed £30 a year. Mr. Porter calls £35 a year the cost of a female domestic, but I should think £25 nearer the mark for women, girls, and mere children taken together: £30 a year, the same amount as farm earnings, may perhaps be taken as the average cost of all domestics male and female: and since the domestics are about as many as the married farm-labourers their cost is as great: *i.e.* the self-maintenance thus employed equals the capital thus employed.

Labour therefore, is not directly dependent on capital only: it is to a large extent directly dependent on self-maintenance: *i.e.* on that Not-Capital represented by the 10 sovereigns in my purse.

This is a matter of such importance that I will give another illustration. An American migrates to the West, becomes a farmer, and employs a little capital: he has no labourer to help him. For several years his gains are no more than he would have earned by working for another settler, and at the end of each year his unfixed capital is just what he began with. But a change occurs: his crops prove larger than before: he has a surplus beyond what he has hitherto consumed annually; suppose 20 quarters of corn.

He has now to determine what he shall do with the 20 quarters; whether he shall extend his cultivation and thus use the 20 quarters as capital; or whether he shall apply them to improve his mode of living. He decides on keeping a female servant, and he thus uses the 20 quarters (or what they buy) as Self-Maintenance or Not-Capital (like the 10 sovereigns in my purse).

This surplus we may suppose to be the result of not merely a fine season, but of improved farming: it will therefore occur after each future harvest (unequally of course, varying from 40 quarters one year to nothing another year). This surplus, like any other profit on capital is permanent; for capital is not commonly employed unless it yield a profit.

We see that capital is at the root of the matter: that without it there can be no production. We see also that where capital is employed it will yield a profit on the average; and that this profit may be used as self-maintenance: farther, that the employment given by self-maintenance may be permanent, just as for example the employment of domestic servants among ourselves is permanent.

But we must go a step farther. You are a manufacturer of silks, and you employ a thousand pair of hands. For a time you sell all the goods you make: but after a bad harvest or two, your richer customers find their rents ill paid, and so they buy and you sell fewer silks. You have now a stock of silks unsaleable for the time: your capital is safe, but much of it is in the form of silks instead of money: you are obliged to cut down your workpeople's employment to three days a week. Your demand for labour is diminished by one-half. Why? By a diminution of capital? Not at all. Your demand for labour is diminished because the demand for its productions is diminished; and the demand for its productions is diminished because the buyers' self-maintenance is diminished.

A manufacturer's capital directly employs labour: but it is self-maintenance which periodically replaces the capital and enables it to continue the employment of labour. It is self-maintenance therefore, which here sets labour to work and pays, the silk-manufacture being the channel through which the self-maintenance flows from the landlord to the artizan. I will show elsewhere that you, the silk-manufacturer, are not *necessary* to the exchange of the landlord's rent for silks: that the landlord *might* directly employ the artizans, and that your factory exists only because it can supply silks cheaper than they could be obtained otherwise.

I will show also that if the landlord did employ the artizans on his own premises, he would not be carrying on a business, any more than he carries on a business when he employs a cook or a sempstress.

The landlord's rents no doubt, arise from the farmer's capital on the land: the rents are paid out of the farmer's gross profits: without capital there could be no profits and no rent: capital is at the root. But capital generally yields profit, and this profit supplies the rent which is commonly used by the landlord as self-maintenance, and which buys your silks and through you pays your artizans.

We are met at this point with the dogma, that where there is capital there will be employment: that if silks cease to be wanted the capitalist will turn to some other employment. Suppose he turns to the manufacture of furniture and finds that less of this is being bought since the falling away of rents: he sees that the upholsterer's warehouses are crowded with goods, and that there is no place for an additional manufacturer.

All production takes place with a view to consumption, and consumption is the same thing as using for self-maintenance. When consumption, when self-maintenance, are reduced, production must be diminished.

Other objections will be made to these views, because they seem inconsistent with the dogmas of orthodox political economy; one of which as we have seen is that capital can always give employment to labour; and another that overproduction is impossible, since what is called overproduction is really wrong production. At present however, we are concerned only with the division of Human

Productions into Capital and Self-Maintenance (or Not-Capital): we have discussed a certain doctrine only as a means of fully considering this division.

III.

WHEAT IN THE HANDS OF FARMER, DEALER, CONSUMER: SPENDING AND SAVING.

VETERAN political economists will go on teaching that the bread they eat is capital. Wheat no doubt, is capital in the hands of the farmer, so long as it is growing, and even till it is threshed out: at this last stage he may divide it, or divide the money he gets for it; setting aside the greater part to be employed on further production, and the smaller part for his household expenses: *i.e.* the greater part as capital and the smaller as maintenance.

Wheat is also capital in the hands of the corn-dealer, who buys and sells it: the profit he makes by the buying and selling is a fund which he can either add to his capital or use as self-maintenance. The case is the same with the miller and the baker: the corn, the flour, the bread, are capital to them, and the profit they earn is at their disposal.

But the bread in my pantry is not capital: I do not carry on a business with it: I do not earn money by using it. It is true that I cannot earn money without using it, but the using it does not of itself bring money. I may lead an entirely idle life; I may addict myself to literature or science as an amateur; I may earn no money; yet I shall eat bread just as a money-getter eats it. Therefore, the bread in my pantry, not being used in carrying on a business is not capital: it is self-maintenance: when I am filled with it I may or may not go and earn money.

But with part of this bread I feed domestics, and they render services: a sempstress and a gardener even produce commodities: surely this portion of the bread is capital, and especially in the cases of sempstress and gardener.

The most difficult question is whether in employing these two to produce commodities, I carry on a business, and therefore earn a profit in money or money's worth.

Let us take the sempstress first.

A manufacturer at Belfast produces 100 pieces of linen, and sells them at a profit to a warehouseman in Leeds: the warehouseman sells them in smaller quantities and makes his profit. So far the 100 pieces are capital. Wanting shirts, you buy one of these pieces, and set a sempstress to cut it up into smaller pieces of various forms, and to sew these into shirts: these are more valuable to you than the uncut linen was.

It is contended that you are acting here as a capitalist: that your piece of linen is capital and the maintenance and wages given to the sempstress are capital: that the shirts are more valuable to you than the linen together with the cost of making the shirts: that you carry on the business of shirtmaking, supplying materials and paying wages.

There is however, another view of the question, and it rests on the meaning of the word valuable. The sempstress cuts your piece of linen into strips, squares, and trapeziums: these curious figures are worth more to you than the original roll. I say they are worth more *to you*: but try to sell them, and see if they are worth more in the market. Most of your neighbours use calico and not linen: of those who use linen one finds that yours is too fine, and another that it is too coarse; a third person is taller than you are and a fourth is shorter. A dealer accommodates you by giving you half what you paid.

If instead of selling your roll or its shreds, you go on with the getting of shirts, the strips and gussets are more valuable to you than the roll was: they are more valuable because you are a stage nearer to the shirts you want. The additional value is a value in use and not a value in exchange: but the business of a capitalist is to add to the value in exchange.

I conclude that your roll of linen, and the money you lay out on it, are self-maintenance and not capital.

The same is true of a cook. The joint she roasts for you is not so saleable as the same joint before it was roasted: the butcher would take it back before it was cooked, but not afterwards: after the roasting, it is worth more to you for your use but not for exchange. To a capitalist who keeps an eating-house, a joint is worth more money after it is cooked: the money he has expended on buying and cooking it is capital.

Your gardener comes into the same category with the cook: the vegetables and fruit and flowers he sends into the house might be bought for half the money they cost you: yet you go on employing him to produce potatoes and calceolarias and grapes, because you find a satisfaction in doing this. If you spend £100 a year on your garden and the products are worth £110, then your outlay comes back to you with a profit, and the £100 may be called capital: but in fact if you try to sell the produce you will be fortunate if you are offered £50 for it: you get a value in use and not in exchange, the wages you pay are not capital but self-maintenance.

All domestic servants then, are maintained and employed with self-maintenance.

We now come to the important division into two classes, of self-maintenance itself.

When you bring home 10 sovereigns, you do not propose to eat or drink them: you propose to exchange them for food, clothes, shelter, domestic services. These Human Productions and services may be called Final-Self-Maintenance, while the 10 sovereigns may be called Mediate-Self-Maintenance.

The Final-Self-Maintenance consists of the very articles you eat, drink, and otherwise consume; also of the very domestic services you receive. The Mediate-Self-Maintenance consists of the 10 sovereigns.

In Ireland, where married women are employed as house servants, and these find their own provisions, a sovereign a week may be given to them for this purpose, and this sovereign is of course Mediate-Self-Maintenance: in England, where the servants are generally unmarried, the sovereign or the greater part of it will be used in buying bread, meat, tea, for the servants' use; and these provisions are (in the hands of the master) Mediate-Self-Maintenance.

Hitherto I have divided all property into Gifts of Nature (Land &c.) and Human Productions (Money &c.): these Human Productions I have divided into Capital and Self-Maintenance. But assume now, that at the end of a year you find yourself with £500 which you can spare from your business, and which you will not spend, *i.e.* which you will not use as self-maintenance. You determine to invest this sum as a present reserve and as a future provision for your family: you may lend it to your neighbour, to use as capital in his business.

How shall this sum be classed in the schedule of

your possessions? It is not capital to you, nor is it self-maintenance. It is a loan. If you have bought Consols with the £500, you have bought a right to receive every year £15 or £16. Writers often speak loosely of the capital of the national debt, and of the interest; your £500 they call capital and your £15 or £16 they call interest. Political Economy requires more exactness.

If Government next year borrowed 100 millions £, and spent that sum on a war, the whole sum would be dissipated: there would be nothing left with which a business could be carried on: there would remain only a debt, or rather a promise of a perpetual annuity of 3 or 4 millions £. Still it is necessary to distinguish between the sum lent and the interest: if we must not say capital, some other word must be found. Lawyers call it the Corpus, the body: if that is too technical or pedantic, we may adopt the good vernacular word Principal. We will say the Principal and the Interest of the National Debt: and when we speak of the debt owing to you by your neighbour, we will say that the *Principal* is £500.

We ought now to see clearly the meaning of the verbs, *to spend* and *to save*. To spend is to use as self-maintenance. You bring home in your purse 10 sovereigns, and you use them in buying food, clothes, shelter, services, for yourself, your wife and your children. You use them as self-maintenance, *i.e.* you spend them.

But instead of 110 sovereigns you may have 130 at command: 100 you put into the cashbox, to replace your previous outlay of capital on materials and wages; 10 you bring home to spend; 20 remain and these you resolve to save. You may do this by adding them to the capital in your business; or by lending them on security; or by burying them in your cellar; by any operation which secures the principal with or without interest.

It is commonly said that the capitalist spends his money as much as the prodigal; but in a different way. He pays his capital of 100 sovereigns to the ironmaster and the artizan; he pays his self-maintenance of 10 sovereigns to the baker, the gardener and the cook. It is better, I think, to say that the 100 sovereigns are *expended* or laid out, and that the 10 sovereigns are *spent*. Capital is expended or laid out, self-maintenance is spent.

We may also see the meaning of "Income." In ordinary language, it is what a man may spend in a year, without lessening his property: on the 1st January you are worth £10,000, and on the 31st December you are worth the same: during the year you have spent £400, the interest on the £10,000: therefore your income has been £400. You may have received a legacy of £500 and spent it, making your expenditure £900; but you would say that your income was not £900 but £400.

Income then may be defined, as the human productions a man may apply periodically as self-maintenance, without lessening his property: may apply, not once but periodically.

IV.

WORKMEN: PRODUCTIVE FORCES.

THE laws I have tried to develop, have as yet applied to employers and unoccupied men but not to workmen; and as workmen with their families are six-sevenths of the population, these laws if they do not apply to workmen are of limited extent.

It may seem that though your weekly expenditure at home is a consumption of self-maintenance, the workman's expenditure at home is a consumption of capital: for out of the money in your cashbox, you pay 27s. to a smith for a week's labour: this sum is part of your capital, and if the smith buys food and beer with it, eats the food and drinks the beer, he appears to consume your capital.

The money in your hands was capital: the question is, what it is in the smith's hands. Observe that the smith does not necessarily consume it: he may do what is often done by workmen, apply part of it to carrying on a little business at home, he may buy twine and children's toys to sell again: *i.e.* he may use part of the money as capital in carrying on a business.

But though the smith may apply this particular money to carrying on a business, he cannot do the same with all he receives, since he must needs live. Say that he is a bachelor and spends only 1s. a day or 7s. a week: what character has this 1s.?

The 1s. is laid out on the mere necessaries of life; on such food, clothes, and lodging as are necessary to keep up the man's strength. The expenditure of the 1s. is required for production by the factory: since without that expenditure the man cannot work, and without his work the factory cannot go on. Therefore the 1s. the man spends is so employed as to help in carrying on business. Is it therefore capital?

I maintain here as elsewhere, that the smith's strength and skill are *productive forces:* therefore I say that in maintaining himself he is keeping up those forces; and that this maintenance of himself and of his productive forces is self-maintenance. The factory cannot go on without productive forces; but these are not capital: nor can we class as capital the 1s. a day employed by the smith in keeping them up.

You say that the 1s. a day is used in maintaining a man whose labour is necessary to carry on your business. I grant that the 1s. while in your hands was capital: but what does it become when it has passed into the workman's hands and he applies it to buying necessary sustenance?

Your classification treats a man as it treats a horse: it sets man and horse down as your property; as your animated instruments. Now when you lay out 7s. on hay and oats for a horse employed in your business, you certainly use the 7s. as capital, just as you do if you use 7s. in repairing a machine: the horse after each meal is worth more by the money the meal has cost; and the machine after the repairs is worth more by the money the repairs have cost. You may say plausibly but untruly, that just as the hay and oats, after they are eaten and become part of the horse, are still your capital, so the bread and meat eaten by the workman are part of your capital. But there is this difference: the horse is your property; the man is not your property: the hay and oats after they are eaten, are your property in the form of animated horse-flesh; the bread and meat consumed by the man are his and not yours. If the bread and meat are capital at all, they are his capital and not yours. But they are not capital, since capital is used for earning a money-profit, whereas the workman is bent on earning, not profit but wages.

Again; say, that I was a Southern planter before the American civil war twenty years ago (1861 to 1865). I spent a dollar on the necessaries of life for a slave: the maize and rum I bought were my capital, and after they were consumed continued to be my capital in the form of living human flesh. But they were my capital, not his: they were part of the slave, who was my property: the slave himself being, like a horse, a chattel. This notion of a slave being a chattel is handed down from the ancients. A Roman lawyer said that all persons have rights. An objector replied:—what about slaves?—Answer: a slave is not a person but a thing.

A free workman differs from a slave and a horse: he is not a chattel: I have not bought or reared the free man; I cannot sell him or hire him out: his clothes and furniture are his own. The money he earns is at his disposal: he spends part on the necessaries of life: and for what purposes? First of all, he intends to satisfy his desires for food, drink, warmth, sleep; so far he uses his money as self-maintenance. Secondly, he intends to restore his capacity for work; *i.e.* his productive force. But this productive force is not of itself capital and not even property: it is much better than property.

If you object that his aim is by means of this productive force, to earn money and money's-worth, I reply that he purposes to earn wages. Now when you and I use money as capital, we propose to earn profit and not wages. The workman's money then, is not capital, because it is not used for earning profit.

You may choose to deny this distinction: you may say that money used for gaining further money is the same thing whether it is in the hands of masters or of workmen. That is simply a higher generalization; you may find a name applicable to both kinds; you may call them productive money. But your new class contains two sub-classes, capital and self-maintenance; applied, the one to produce profit and the other to produce wages.

You cannot pretend that profit and wages are the same; for if so, what mean the maxims that profit and wages are antagonistic? that as nations advance, the rate of farm wages rises while the rate of profit falls? that the profits of the manufacturer at times are too high and the wages of labour are too low?

The smith earning 27s. a week, applies 7s. of it or the whole to his weekly support. He uses it first to satisfy his hunger, thirst, and desire for warmth: secondly, to fit himself for earning wages. This, as I contend, is self-maintenance.

It must be conceded that if we compare the smith's expenditure with the expenditure by an idle annuitant, who has not earned his pension by previous work, the result of the two expenditures is different. The smith, by his labour, adds to the Human Productions of the nation, but the annuitant adds nothing. The smith is a productive member of society, the annuitant is an unproductive one. If it were desirable to multiply distinctions, we might call the smith's expenditure productive self-maintenance, and the annuitant's unproductive self-maintenance.

To prevent misapprehension, it must be remembered that I assume an annuitant who has not earned his annuity. But pensions generally have been earned by previous services, and the pension in this case has been well called deferred pay: a military or civil servant is content with smaller present pay, in consideration of the prospect of an income for his declining years. Such pensions are as much productive as was the pay for active service.

What is true of the smith is true also of his employer. You, a capitalist, cannot continue to superintend your business and earn a profit, unless your health and vigour are kept up: in keeping these up, a small part of your expenditure is necessary; if 1s. a day suffices for the smith, 1s. a day may suffice for you. We will say then, that out of your whole expenditure of £1 a day, or £10 a day, 1s. a day goes to keep up your health and vigour, and is productive self-maintenance; and that 19s. a day or £9. 19s. a day must go to the gratification of your desires, reasonable or unreasonable, and that this expenditure is unproductive self-maintenance.

We must advance another step. I have assumed that you and your smith are both of you unmarried, and are therefore able to limit your expenses to 1s. a day: most men however, are married and have children. Let us say that the smith, to keep himself and his wife and children in health and vigour, has to spend 21s. a week, and is able to save only 6s.;

that in fact, he uses 21s. as self-maintenance, and applies the 6s. to a little business, or deposits it for safe keeping.

The smith spends weekly, 7s. on himself and 14s. on his wife and children. The 7s. are productive self-maintenance, because they maintain a productive member of society: what shall we say of the 21s.? If there were no wives and families, the succession of labourers and artizans would cease; production would be at an end for want of hands: wives and families therefore, are necessary at one remove to the production of commodities; and the 14s. a week spent on the wife and family may be called productive self-maintenance.

I say therefore, that the 27s. you have in your hand ready to give to your workman are capital: that when you have given them to him, they become in his hands, according to the use he makes of them, self-maintenance, capital, or principal: self-maintenance, if he spend them all in maintaining himself and his wife and children; capital, so far as he employs them in carrying on a business; principal, so far as he deposits them for safe keeping.

The 27s. then, are constantly changing their character. In your hands they are capital: in the workman's hands they may be all spent as self-maintenance. From him they pass to the shopkeepers, of whom one uses his share as capital; another, his share as self-maintenance; a third deposits his share as principal. From the retail dealers they pass to the wholesale dealers, who may appropriate them just as the retailers have done.

This is true of mediate self-maintenance: but the final self-maintenance, the bread and beer and cloth you buy for yourself, your wife and children, do not again change their character: they are consumed and disappear. The bread and beer and tea which you buy for your domestic servants, are mediate self-maintenance in your hands, but become final self-maintenance in their hands and when consumed by them finally disappear.

V.

RECONSIDERATION: IF WITHOUT MONEY: SUMMARY.

THERE will still linger in the mind, the notion that what I have called self-maintenance is in one sense capital. The 27s. you have paid to the smith, have passed from your hands and are no longer capital to you: the smith has, with 7s. out of the 27s. bought bread, beef, and beer wherewith to maintain his strength. The community, after these commodities are consumed, possesses less of them than before, but it possesses instead of them the additional vigour of the smith. Must not this vigour be reckoned a part of the national capital? I say no: I say that it possesses additional productive force.

Take a larger scale. Here are two countries similarly situated and equally well endowed by nature. Each contains 5 millions of men: but in the one country there are 4 millions of vigorous labourers, and in the other only 3 millions of labourers and these equally vigorous. Will not the country with the 4 millions produce far more (a third more) than the country with the 3 millions? Now this additional million of vigorous labourers has been formed by an outlay on food and shelter, just as oxen and sheep have been formed: the million labourers are productive to the nation just as the oxen and sheep are productive to the farmer. Must not the vigorous labourers be reckoned part of the capital of the nation, just as the oxen and sheep are reckoned part of the capital of the farmer?

I reply that if the nation, represented by its government, possessed a million of slaves, saleable for money, and employed in a national business so as to yield an income, those slaves would be national capital, and their maintenance would be national capital.

"But slaves are less productive than free men: therefore, if a million slaves are capital, the million free men are still more capital."

By no means, I answer: the slaves are capital, the free men are much better than capital. The slaves are capital because they are property, and are that kind of property called Human Productions (reared by their masters like oxen) and employed in carrying on a business. The free men are not property but are better than property.

Slaves and free men are alike employed as productive forces, or for the productive forces they exert. But there are many other productive forces which are not capital either private or national: *e.g.* there are sunshine, rain, earthworms: these are not capital.

Let us recall our classification of possessions:—
Property,

divided into { Gifts of nature, (such as Land) / Human Productions, (such as farm produce and manufactures) }

Human Productions divided into Capital and Self-Maintenance.

Free men are not property and therefore are not capital: slaves are property; they are Human Productions; Capital (so far as they are employed in business). Free men are productive forces, just as land and streams are: or, if you prefer more exact statement, they possess productive forces at our command.

Of two nations equal in numbers, the aggregate revenue will belong to the one which has the greater productive forces: these forces reside partly in agents, partly in instruments; *i.e.* partly in the inhabitants, partly in their possessions. As to agents, one of the two nations may have such institutions and such hereditary customs that nearly all persons are producers: such was the case in Holland during our Stuart days, and such is the case in the United States now. The other nation may have a numerous leisure class and a numerous literary and scientific class; just as in France during our Stuart days and Great Britain now. Other things being equal, Holland and the United States would be the richer; France and England the more cultured.

Then as to instruments. One of the two nations may have more fertility in its land, richer coal-mines, rivers more numerous and more navigable: other things being equal and human capacities equal, the larger revenue will be found in that nation which has the greater productive forces.

These productive forces reside in material objects; and seem to be to the nation what the steam-engine, the smelting-furnace, the factory, are to the manufacturer: therefore, just as we call these manufacturing productive forces, capital, so it may seem we may call the Gifts of Nature and the capacities of the people, national capital.

I believe that this generalization, which classes all productive forces, or the things and persons they reside in, as national capital, is false. If land and men, or their productive qualities, are national capital, their earnings should follow the law of other earnings by capital, or at any rate should follow one and the same law. Now the special earnings of land and other Gifts of Nature are rent (differential rent): the earnings of capital are profit: the earnings of labour are wages: rent, profit, wages, do not follow one and the same law: on the contrary all three follow different laws.

Nations have a large aggregate income, not in proportion to something called national capital, but in proportion to national productive forces, residing in agents and in instruments.

I have said that nations have a large aggregate income in proportion to these: I have not said that they are *rich* in proportion to these; because they are partly rich by accumulated property which yields no income but only enjoyment: I mean such things as public buildings, public parks, picture galleries; of all which things old nations have far more than new nations.

Some readers may regard my reasoning as inconclusive, because it is founded principally on the use of money; and may be dissatisfied till they test the reasoning by applying it to a community in which money is unknown, and in which therefore, commodities are exchanged directly for commodities.

No doubt, the use of money does hide the operations of exchange: the farmer sells a flock of sheep for £100; takes the money to the bank; draws part of it out again to buy seed and implements. It seems to him that he exchanges sheep for money, and not sheep for commodities. The laws of production and distribution are hidden from him.

But we know what we are about when we assume the use of money: when I suppose that I have a cashbox and a purse, and use these the one in my business the other in my household, I suppose things familiar to me, and there is no conjecture in the case; but when I suppose a society without money I am left a good deal to imagination: in arguing about a fictitious society, we cannot be quite sure how production and exchange would go on.

However, let us try: let us imagine a settler in a district cut off from the world. Say that he has a store of corn: instead of dealing as you did with 110 sovereigns, he deals with 110 quarters of corn: 100 of these he sets aside for carrying on his farm, and 10 quarters he uses in maintaining his household. That is, he uses 100 quarters as capital, and 10 quarters as self-maintenance.

But next year, the settler is seized with a fit of extravagance, such as possessed you when you applied only 60 sovereigns a week instead of 100 to your business, and 50 instead of ten to your household: the settler now applies only 60 quarters instead of 100 to his business, and 50 instead of 10 to his household. If he repeated this process weekly, at the end of 50 weeks he would have laid out on his business only 3,000 quarters instead of 5,000; his harvest and other returns would be proportionately reduced: and he would have spent on his household 2,500 quarters instead of 500.

During the year of extravagance, the settler might

have paid for as much labour as in previous years: he might even have employed the same men, setting them to work at the house instead of the farm. The next year however, his outlay on his farm having been reduced as 60 to 100, *i.e.* to ⅗ths, his returns may be assumed to be reduced to ⅗ths of their original amount: he will have only 66 quarters to deal with instead of 110. Even if he pinches his household by reducing their weekly allowance to 6 quarters instead of 10, he will still have only 60 instead of 100 to employ on his farm. For here is the difference between capital and self-maintenance (or at any rate between unfixed capital and unfixed self-maintenance): the capital is reproduced and gives employment to labour year after year, but the self-maintenance perishes in the using.

Going back to the settler's original partition of his 110 quarters, by which he gave 100 quarters weekly to his business and 10 to his household, I call the whole 110 quarters Human Productions: I call the 100 applied to business, Capital; the 10 applied to the family, Self-Maintenance.

I have inquired further, whether this distinction has any importance. I tried the distinction by applying it to the common doctrine that labour is dependent upon capital for employment. Now we see that the settler, in his extravagant year, employed upon the support of labour the same 100 quarters of corn that he employed in the previous year; the difference being, that during the extravagant year, an unusual proportion of the labour was employed at the house, and a smaller proportion than usual at the business.

During the extravagant year then, self-maintenance acted just as capital had previously acted, in maintaining labour. But in the year following the extravagant year, the harvest being reduced from 110 quarters to 66, the employment of labour would be reduced to $\frac{3}{5}$ths of what it had been.

Self-maintenance then, so long as it continues, gives employment to labour. But in fact it does continue only so long as capital is applied to produce the self-maintenance: capital reproduces itself: self-maintenance does not.

Let us go a step further. Let us suppose that our settler is a manufacturer: that in the absence of money, he exchanges his goods for corn, which he stores in granaries. The goods are linen and cotton fabrics used by other settlers and their families. There comes an unprosperous season, and the demand for these fabrics is less than usual: the manufacturer sells fewer goods, and receives less corn: his business-warehouse is full, his granaries are half empty. He cannot now employ the usual amount of labour.

And why? Is it because his unfixed capital is lessened? By no means. Taking the warehouse and granaries together, the unfixed capital is as great as before. The manufacturer's demand for labour is lessened because his customers have bought less than usual; and the customers have bought less than usual because their self-maintenance is diminished by bad seasons.

If a prosperous season follows, the customers have self-maintenance at command, they flock in to buy the cotton and linen goods, they give corn in exchange, the manufacturer's granaries are filled, and his warehouse is emptied. Now he can employ the full quantity of labour.

Self-maintenance gives motion to capital and thus sets labour to work. Consumption is necessary to production. Without self-maintenance and consumpsumption, production and the demand for labour cease.

I stop here, and defer various questions which arise: such as the questions whether overproduction is possible, and what are the causes and cure of excessive competition. My object lately has been to show that whether with or without money in circulation, the same truths are apparent. I began with the ordinary capital in the form of money: I hope I have shown that the use of money only conceals the fact of exchanges and makes no difference in the doctrine of capital and self-maintenance.

I again copy some of my leading definitions.

Property is every possession which is saleable.

Gifts of Nature are things which men find existing and appropriate (land, streams).

Capital is Human Productions devoted to re-production: *i.e.* used in business or set apart to be so used.

Self-Maintenance is things set apart to be consumed by the owner, his wife and children, or things devoted to gratifications other than that of earning and saving. When it exists as money, it is Mediate Self-Maintenance, and when it exists as food, clothes, house-room, it is Final Self-Maintenance.

Chapter VII.

OVER-PRODUCTION: OVER-CAPITALIZATION: GLUTS.

I.

THIS subject grows naturally out of my last chapter (The Purse and the Cashbox), in which I have tried to establish the distinction between money used in carrying on a business, and money used at home in maintaining a family. I now propose to apply the distinction, and to show that on the due proportion between these two funds depends partly the well-being of the trading community.

All economists hold that if a nation lays out too much in its home expenditure, and thereby diminishes its capital, its productions will be lessened.

To Dr. Chalmers it seemed that if a nation lays out too little in its home expenditure, its capital will be unduly increased, and the result will be over-production and gluts.

It seemed to him that saving and spending required to be duly apportioned.

SECT. I. OVER-CAPITALIZATION : GLUTS.

In my last chapter on the Purse and the Cashbox it is assumed that out of £110 received every week as payment for goods sold, I at first put in my purse £10 for the use of the family, and £100 in my cashbox to be used in business: afterwards I determine to take home weekly only £5, and use £105 in business, thus saving £250 in the year. Since I now take home only £5 a week instead of £10, I spend less with the butcher, the baker, the grocer, the tailor, and employ fewer servants; and the tradesmen reduce their outlay on commodities for sale: there will therefore be to this extent a glut of these commodities. The result however is counterbalanced by another: an additional £5 a week is used in business, and in buying and in paying wages, as it would be if taken home. Yet there is this essential difference: at home the money would be used as self-maintenance, in the production (or purchase) of meat, fruits, flowers; or the rendering of services: all these are *consumed;* there is no reproduction, no production of a fund for next year's self-maintenance: whereas the additional money used in business does reproduce itself (with an increase or profit), and can be again used to carry on the business. But this reproduction is in the shape of more goods than were formerly produced, and unless the effectual demand for these has increased, the augmented produce will compete with the produce of my trade rivals: that is, there is over-production. No one denies that this may happen in any particular trade.

These troubles are caused by over-capitalization.

This doctrine is denied by many distinguished orthodox economists. M. J. B. Say in his *Économie Politique Pratique*, published in 1828, says (in one of the marginal contents), "Products *cannot* be all in excess at the same time." In the *Dictionnaire de l'Économie Politique* (1864), the ingenious and witty Bastiat, writing of the popular sayings "We are dying of plethora," "Consumption no longer equals production," "All markets are glutted, and all occupations are overcrowded," says that all these common statements are false. M. Michel Chevalier confesses that many objections have been made to the doctrine of M. Say; but yet, says he, it is true. Replying to these objections, M. Chevalier says: "The fundamental error is the arguing from the particular to the general, and treating an accident as a universal rule . . . It may certainly happen that an increase of production brings misfortune, but because an excess of production in one branch of manufactures must have unhappy consequences, we are not to condemn an increase of all branches, provided that it is gradual, and fitly arranged."

The fundamental notion of these French authors is, that the fault lies in *wrong production*, not in *over-production*.

Englishmen of the greatest note have held the same opinions. John Stuart Mill agrees with his father, and has no hesitation about the matter. Like the French authors quoted he holds that what appears to be over-production, is really *wrong* production. "The manufacturer has produced the wrong thing instead of the right . . . . He has produced a thing not wanted, instead of what was wanted."

There is an ambiguity in the word "*wanted*," and out of this ambiguity comes a fallacy. In every nation there are a thousand things *desired*. Adam Smith distinguishes between *desire* and *effective demand*. The famished desire food; the naked garments; the self-indulgent, luxuries. But these desires will not of themselves carry off commodities offered for sale: two other things are needful to cause an effective demand; (*a*) the means of payment and (*b*) the will to buy. The wholesale dealer will not buy unless the retailer will buy from him; and the retail dealer will not buy unless the consumer will buy from him; the consumer will not buy unless he has money, and resolves to spend it.

There is one desire which we have not yet taken into account: the desire of accumulation. John Stuart Mill indeed said that when a man has satisfied all his desires he will cease to produce: there is one desire, that of accumulation, which is never satisfied. Blind avarice causes no consumption of commodities: it adds to the capital and thus to the production of the country.

Let us look once more at the theory as given by the late Professor Fawcett, who abridged John Stuart Mill:—" The accumulation of capital . . never causes more commodities to be produced than can be consumed." No doubt the power of consumption is unlimited: there is no natural limit to what can be consumed, but there is an unfortunate ambiguity in the word "*can.*" Mr. Fawcett's sentence ought to be enlarged. "The accumulation of capital . . . never causes more commodities to be produced than *can* be consumed," *but often causes more than will be consumed.*

Here again is thought to be a ready answer to my doctrine:—a Lancashire manufacturer turns out yearly additional goods worth £250; B, a London manufacturer, does the same: A's goods may exchange for B's. May, I reply, but will they? not unless A and B have customers who are willing and able to buy them for consumption.

It must not be supposed however, that all political economists have denied the possibility of over-production. Malthus was an exception, so was Dr. Chalmers. Sismondi even believed that improvements in machinery permanently caused over-production. I must postpone the consideration of this interesting question to a future volume.

It was the excess of capital which was blamed by Malthus and Chalmers. The latter said, "Instead of spending my thousand guineas a year, it is certainly possible to stint myself to £50; and either directly, or through the medium of a loan (to others), I may spend (say *ex*pend) £1000 annually in the employment of labourers. . . . The things wanted by these new economists (Mill and others) is, that each man laying out as much as possible on productive expenditure, should lay out as little as possible on his own individual enjoyments."

Ricardo however, though he accepted in general terms the orthodox doctrine, yet conceded that a community acting as Chalmers suggested might suffer from over-production, since all demand for luxuries would cease, as would also the greater part of the demand for superfluities, and there would be a glut of everything but mere necessaries. Yet Ricardo did not see that this extreme case implies the principle Chalmers contended for.

Nothing is commoner in the trading world than to hear of excessive supply and gluts. At few periods have there been such general complaints as in 1884-5, of want of orders for both the home and the foreign trade. At the same time we also had an unusual supply of the products of both town and country.

Nor was this confined to Great Britain. The United States in 1884 had a serious revulsion, after the short-lived prosperity; the resistless impetus given to trade during the construction of vast stretches of new railways. France also was complaining of the flatness of trade: foreign importations were ruining her small proprietors. Germany, Russia, Holland, were uneasy and distressed. Even India shared in the trouble: she had been exporting wheat enough to require fleets for its conveyance; a fall of 10s. a quarter severely tried the producers, notwithstanding the mitigation by the fall in the value of silver. Besides this, the low price of calico was so injurious to the Indian makers, that of the many mills lately established in Bombay, numbers had become unprofitable and were closed.

Among ourselves the farmers' losses by inclement weather were aggravated by foreign competition: the prices of wheat fell to a level unknown during the present century: over-production abroad was the cause of the mischief. No one acquainted with the great towns can doubt that they had suffered nearly ten years of bad trade.

It appears that the fall in the *value* of our exports in 13 years had been more than a fourth (population considered): it is alleged that the *quantities* had not diminished, but that it is only the price which had fallen. It is not pretended that prices have fallen mostly through improved processes in manufacture; how great then must have been the excess of supply over effectual demand to cause such a diminution in wages and profits!

The theoretical economists have their remedy at hand. "Disengage your capital from its present employment, and apply it to the pursuit in which it is wanted; change your business, and you will again earn the profits you have lately missed."

How is it that this theory never appears in a practical form? Let the orthodox economists condescend to particulars: let them say that such and such businesses have been overlooked, and that these neglected businesses are sufficient to employ the 1500 or 2000 millions £ of British capital invested abroad at 4 or 5 per cent. I defy them to do this: I challenge them to find at home for one tenth part of these millions, employment offering a chance of profit.

Again; do these men know anything of business? Do they know that a large part of the capital of the country is in such a form that it cannot be devoted to purposes other than those it now serves? Factories, machinery, plant, tools, patterns, invented and manufactured for the purpose of producing one commodity, cannot at will be devoted to the production of something else. So also skilled workmen can only obtain employment in their own trade; often they are restricted to one particular branch of a trade: their labour at any other trade is not worth half so much as at their own. Thus if a trade becomes unprofitable, either because it is overstocked, or because the demand for its produce falls off, its machinery, plant, tools, patterns become worthless; much of the capital invested in it shrinks or actually disappears, whilst the skilled workmen hitherto employed in it are thrown out of employment without much hope of obtaining work elsewhere, and at any rate with a certainty of a very large reduction in their wages.

Over-production then is the result of making more commodities than are in effective demand; *i.e.* more than the public can and will pay for in order to consume them. Granting that however vast the quantity of commodities, all of them *can* be, it does not follow that all of them *will* be consumed. We see then what it is that causes over-production: it is the employment of too much *re*productive capital and labour.

The evils from which we are suffering then, are superabundant capital and labour, causing production in excess of actual consumption.

Remedies may be found in destruction of capital, new channels for the profitable application of the surplus capital, new markets or increased consumption.

One hardly likes to apply to war so favourable a name as *remedy*; though in fact nothing else so rapidly disperses, or so effectually prevents accumulation.

There is a better, and a peaceful remedy; but one which must arise of itself, the opportunity of turning unfixed capital into fixed; *i.e.* the diversion of surplus accumulations into new and profitable channels. This might occur on so large a scale as to clear the market, as happened after 1842-3, a time of depressed trade, over-production, gluts. The recent success of the railways between Manchester, Liverpool, Birmingham, and London had excited hopes of great profits by constructing further lines: the railway mania which followed absorbed the available unfixed capital, so that between 1845 and

1847 the British supply of unfixed capital was unequal to the demand. Instances of how this might again occur may be seen in the possible application of increased capital to land and farming, so far rendered impossible by the feeling of insecurity as to landed property, induced by the serious discussion of the crazy schemes of Henry George, the Irish Nationalists, and others. Also in the construction of railways in China, and elsewhere; irrigation and other works in India; the development in various ways of our vast colonial possessions. These would not only swallow up our unfixed capital, but would open up vast new markets, and thus whilst diminishing over-production would increase consumption.

Failing these, or even in addition to these, remedies could be found in an increased expenditure. As regards private life, this may seem a lamentable conclusion; since it is the vast savings and accumulations of principal which have given free play to human enterprise, which have covered the land with railways, and the ocean with steamers. But we might benefit largely by the application of our savings to works which, though not directly profitable would indirectly be of great value to us: the construction of works for the defence of the various parts of the empire, of coaling stations, of harbours of refuge, and the due increase of the army and still more of the navy.

II.

SUMMARY.

MY argument then, is this.

If a nation consume too much of its wealth, its productions will be lessened: but if it consume too little, capital will be unduly increased and over-production and gluts will result; for to diminish self-maintenance which is not reproductive, and to apply the saving as capital which is reproductive, increases production without increasing consumption or effective demand. Human Productions therefore should be duly apportioned between self-maintenance and capital.

This doctrine is denied by the orthodox political economists, who do not perceive that though potential consumption may be unlimited, effective demand may be restricted. They assert that general over-production is impossible, though they allow that it may occur in particular trades, in which case, say they, withdraw your capital from the unprofitable business, and apply it elsewhere. Such a recommendation however, is unpractical, unless those who make it can show how it should be carried out. This I challenge them to do. I challenge them to point out any profitable business in which sufficient capital has not been already embarked, or to find in

England profitable occupation for one-tenth of the British capital invested abroad. Moreover, it shows a lamentable ignorance to recommend a course which must entail serious loss, if not ruin, both on capitalist and workman.

Of late years bad trade has coincided with or followed excessive production throughout the civilized world. The cause is superabundance of capital and labour.

Remedies might be found in the destruction of capital by war (the greater evil swallowing up the less), the diversion of unfixed capital into new and profitable channels, which would absorb the surplus and lead to increased consumption, and in an increased expenditure in ways indirectly valuable, though not directly profitable.

THE END.

GENERAL INDEX.

A

	PAGE
Accumulation desire	335
Act, Education, 1870	106
Acts of Parliament, beneficent, condemned	18, 20, 24
Adam Smith (S.)	
Agricultural Improvements	255
Alice, Princess	179
Allotments	84
Alms and profusion compared	6
,, indiscriminate	173
,, judicious defended	7
Anabaptists	90
Appreciation, gold. See Enhancement.	
Arch, Joseph	82
Aristocracy	87
Arkwright	42, 67
,, son	46, 67
Atoms, indivisible	122
Austrian, squalor	9

B

Bank, unlimited, failure	3
,, profits	226
Barbarism defined	123
Barbarity defined	124
Bastiat	51, 334
Beggars, England	159
,, France	147-8, 153, 159
Belper, Lord	67
Benevolence	4
Bentham, J.	1, 5, 33
,, ability	131
,, on charity	124-5
"Benthamese"	130
Birth, influence	41
,, satirized	70
Black Country	208
Blanc, Louis	33
Bombay manufactures	338

	PAGE
Bonelace	260
Boryslaw bedrooms	11
Bread prices	272
,, ,, possible	257
"Breathes there the man"	273
Bright, John	274, 286-7
Buddha	177
Budgets	31
Butterine	74
Buzot	36

C

Cade, Jack	90
Cairns, Lord, Act	94
California	79
Canada, fertile region of	271
Cannibalism	197
Capital	54-5-6-8, 60, 293
,, not land	55
,, not faculties	57
,, ex. of benefit	186
,, fixed	339, 340
,, unfixed	301
,, ,, employs labour	307
,, said excess impossible	335-6
,, national	323
Carinthia, squalor	9
Carlyle, T.	1
Carthaginians	68
Catallactics	62
Chalmers, Dr.	332
Chambers of commerce, reciprocity	277
Chances, doctrine of	141
Chaplains, public	25-6
Charity defined	123
,, indiscriminate	181
,, denounced	4
Chartism	74
"Cheap Bread!"	272
Chevalier, M.	334

	PAGE
Children, young, work	10
China	81
Chinese immigrants	78-9
,, pauper	11, 81
,, two scourges	237
,, literati	109
,, maxims	38
,, reverie	144
,, railways	234
Cholesbury Poor Law	12, 39
Chrematistics	62
Christianity condemned	137
Ciudad Jean	188
Civil Service Stores	222
Class jealousy	186
Coal, rise in price	51
Cobden	287
,, Club	277-8, 290
Coin wear	241
,, life of	242
,, actual age	244
Coined quantities	245
Colbert	266
Coleridge	41
Colonies' claims	286
Commission on Depression in Trade	200
Common, rights of	75
Common sense	175
Competition, unjust	107
Confucius	177
Consumption necessary	330, 333
Convents' alms	162
Coöperative societies	206, 223
"Corn Laws," no!	273
,, ,, former	273
,, ,, repeal, results	288
Cotton trade	206, 208
,, wool	270
Court of Requests	75
Coventry	282
Cows promised	84
Cromwell	103
Curates' stipends	76

D

D'Alembert	136
Darmstadt	177, 198
Debt to employers	10
Definitions—Malthus, 1827	54
Democracy, limited	84, 87
,, United States	91
,, England	104
Depression, trade	200
,, ,, Europe and U.S.	231, 337

	PAGE
Depression, trade, Remedies	232, 252
,, ,, Railways	234
,, ,, Loans	237
,, ,, War	238
,, ,, Revulsions	253
Descartes	175
Desire of accumulation	335
Diderot	136
Dinan	154
Dinners, 1d. ½d. ¼d.	212
Dismal Science!	1
Dissenters misled	133
Dixwell	278
Dragonnades	49
Du Camp, Max	142
,, reverie	145
Du Guesclin	154
Dulness	3
Dunoyer	52
Dutch patricians	107

E

Économistes, the	2
Edie Ochiltree	152
Education, Government aid	22
,, Act, 1870	106
,, ,, defence	23
,, dissenters refused Government aid	26
,, compulsory	27
,, injustice	28
Egypt	80
Elizabeth, Queen	162
Emigration	99
,, homes	180
Encyclopædia Americana	59
Entails	93
Envy	70
Expending	314
Expediency	4, 164
Exports	203
,, quantities	205, 238

F

Factory Acts	18, 19
Fair Trade	230, 286
Fallibility, human	122
Fanaticism (Philosoph.)	173
Farm machinery	78
Farmers, distress	338
,, failures	202
,, suicides	201
Field for employment	229, 232, 301
Fifth-Monarchy Men	90
First Principles	63

	PAGE
Fittest (survival)	
,, to die	178
Flaubert, Gustave	143
Foreign Loans	237
Fortune Robert	80
Fortunes, great	66
,, ,, mitigation	68
Fortunes of Nigel	197
Forster, W. E., Act, 1870	24, 26
France, former distress	69
France, anti-clerical fanaticism	155
,, division of property at death	95
,, condition labourers	95
Free Libraries H. S. condemns	24
Free Trade not generally adopted	264
,, ,, explained	287
,, ,, Peel and Cobden's prophecy	277
,, ,, and Democracy	278-9

G

Galicia	11
Garter, The	70
George, Henry	254
Gibbon's reverie	144
Gifts of Nature	54, 296
Gluts universal possible	231, 251, 334, 339, 340
Gold, alleged enhancement	239
,, quantities	241
,, used in manufactures	244
,, new currencies	246
,, stocks of	250
Goldsmith	41
Goschen, G. J.	200
Gournay	2
Government, a free	36
,, Paternal	16, 21
,, Functions	36-7
,, 3 Principles	182
,, Factories	88
Greeley, Horace	278, 290
Gregg, Paradox	72
Grey, Lord	33
Grimm, Melchior	136
Guinness & Co.	224

H

Hardware Trades	207-8
Harmonies Economiques	51
Harrington's Oceana	110
Harrison, F.	121
Hindoos have no Poor-Law	6
,, Famines	8

	PAGE
Hobbes	65
Hodgson, W. B.	292
"Homo sum"	176
Hon. and Rt. Hon.	70
Horace content	71
Hospitaliers, Paris	188
Hours of work	10, 19
How can improve	44
Hugo, Victor	197
Human Productions	54, 296
Hume, Joseph	33
Huskisson, silks	282
Hutton, William	19, 125
,, Court of Requests	75

I

Iddesleigh, Lord	73
Importation, artificial, proposed	45
Improvement of condition, direct, proposed	44, 105
Income defined	314
Incomes, actual, 2s.6d. to £200 a day	67
Income of German Baron	68
Income-tax	214
,, retailers	218
,, summary	227
India our Government	16, 273-4
,, widows, ill treatment	274
,, amount of trade	273
Induction	1
Inequalities of fortune	41, 66
Infanticide	198
Instruct by interesting	59
Insurance natural	166
Interest rate, Holland	107
Ireland	80
,, population	100
,, famine	8
,, emigration	102
,, without a Poor-Law	5
,, increased pasture	101
,, priests	102-3
,, decay of Roman Catholics	103
,, Land Acts	101
Italy	80

J

Jacquerie	90
Jealousy, class	186
Jevons, Professor	59, 61
Jews, the	176
Johnson, Dr.	2
Jugan, Jeanne	147
Juries disparaged	131

K

	PAGE
Kennedy, Dr.	71

L

	PAGE
Labour dependent on what?	300
Labourers can rise	84
,, well treated	85
,, earnings	85
,, grievances	86
Laicisation	155
Laissez-faire	5
Land not Capital	55
,, tenure	92
,, nationalization	132
Lay nurses	155
Leeds Bank failure	69
Le Pailleur	151
" Liberty "	29
Liberty, Equality, Fraternity	95
Life of a machine	242
,, ,, sovereign	242
Little Sisters of the Poor	143
,, ,, smiles	155
Loans	312
,, definition	313
Locke, John	36
Loudon's Agriculture	4
Louis Blanc	33, 170
Louvois	49
Lucian's slave	175
Lunacy treatment	176
Luxuries, extravagant	30

M

McCulloch	59, 125
Machinery, farm	78
,, Sismondi and over-production	336
Madness (Lunacy)	—
Mæcenas	71
" Magnanimity " in Cobden Club	291
Malthus	1, 4, 5, 52, 59
,, Poor Law	126
Manchou Dynasty	81
Married Women's Property	93
Mary, Queen of England	161
Mason, Sir J.	7
Maxime (Du Camp)	—
Mazdakites	90
Melbourne, Lord	33
Merimée, Prosper	143
Middlemore, John	178
Mill, James	1, 3, 59
Mill, J. S.	1, 2, 59

	PAGE
Mill on independence	83
Mines, bad	10
Moderation wanted	107
Monarchy	86
Money, if without	322, 326-7
Montgomery	241
Montyon Fund	150
Moors Spanish	49
Murder, legal proposed	198

N

National Insurance Fund	68
Negroes, United States	47
New Academy	43, 108
New Lanark (Owen)	19
Newton Principia	196
Nonconformists education (1841)	26
Not-Capital	54, 297
Not-Wheat	298
Notre Dame	197
Nuneaton	282
Nurses, lay	155

O

Oceana	110
O'Connell	104
Ogle, Dr.	201
Oligarchy	86
Opulence, causes of	325-6
Order of Merit	108
Orders, Religious, France	190-2
Orissa Famine	141
Outcasts from the better classes	156
Over-production said impossible	231, 251, 334, 339, 340
Owen, Robert	19
Oxford P. E. Club	63
Ox-head theft	139

P

Palmerston, Lord	281
Panics	253
Parks, British	95
Parliament, Our	15
Parrot cries	265
Paternal Government	16, 21
Patriotism	273
Pauperism	211
Peasant Proprietors	82
Peel, Sir Robert (the first)	19
Penny Dinners	212
Philosophical Radicals	52
,, ,, fanatical	173
Philosophy, practical	70

	PAGE
Pleurisy	90
Poetical temperament	41
Poor Laws denounced	4, 38, 39, 166
,, ,, defended	187
,, ,, necessary	9
,, ,, abuses	12, 13
,, ,, proposed for gentry	40, 48
,, ,, French	160
,, ,, Parisian	160
,, ,, ,, reasons	160
Population increase	5, 250
Prices, extravagant	30
,, do not fall as cost falls	219
,, e. g. coal, meat	220
,, milk	222
,, beer	224
Principal	313
Principles (First)	
Private Interest	110
Productive Forces	38, 315, 324
Production "wrong"	334
Property	54
,, sacredness	89
Protective duties, various countries	268
,, ,, U. S.	268, 278
,, ,, France, 1848	279
,, ,, remedies	270
Purse and Cashbox 54, and chap. VI	

Q

Quakers	26
,, philosophy	274-5
Qualities of men	51
Quartering Royal arms	71
Quesnay	2
Queensland	80

R

Railway mania	235-6
,, United States	236
Rank	41
Rayleigh, Lord	67
Reason, pure, &c.	175
Recoinage	243-4
Reform-Bill (1885)	86
Reformatory and Industrial Schools	174
Relief Works	36, 39, 45
Remedy for Inequalities	99
Rennes	153, 162
Rent, Differential, Theory	54
Rents, rate of	77
Restrictions, legal, in past centuries	18

	PAGE
Reproduction	53-5-6, 333
Retaliation	252, 264, and chap. V
Reveries	144-5
Revolution, a safe one	27
Revulsions	253
Reybaud, Louis	14
Ricardo	1, 3, 337
Rising possible for labourers	84-5
Robespierre defence	169
Rogers, Thorold	67
Roland, Madame	29, 36
Romans, the	176
Royal Arms	71
Russian Pauper	157
Rye, Miss	179

S

Sand, Georges	146
To Save	313
Saving	308, 313
Savings	210
,, Banks	210
Say, J. B.	2, 334
Security, sense of	93, 102
Seigneurs	89
Selfishness, Philosophical	1
Self-Maintenance	55, 303, 306, 311
,, ,, servants'	309
,, ,, Mediate or Final	312, 322
Self-respect	86
Sempstress, a	309, 310
Sense, Common	175
Servants No.	303
,, Maintenance	309
Settlement, Law of	4, 124-5
,, of Land	87, 92
,, ,, French marriage	92
Sheridan	41
Skill not Capital	57
Slaves are things	57, 317, 318
Slavery, British, late	10
Smith, Adam	1, 2, 4, 5, 33, 59
,, on Charity	124
,, successors	3
Smith, Sydney, on M. C.	271
Social Importance	41
Socialism	9, 14, 32, 87—90, 187
Sovereign (coin), life of	242
South Australia	279, 284
Spain, Protection	275—7
Spectator	191
Spending and Saving	308—313
Spencer, Herbert	1, 17, 120
,, argument	20
,, Government Education	133

GENERAL INDEX.

Spencer, Man and the State	195
,, is morbid	29
Spinning jenny	67
Squalor	9
Stephen, Mr. Justice	94
St. Malo	147
Stock	296
St. Servan	147, 162
Strutt	67
Sugar refining	46
Suicides	201
Supply and Demand	141
Survival of the Fittest	134, 138, 163, 168, 171, 195
Swedish Pastor	155

T

Taille, the	89
Taxes said fall on rent	2
,, amount	31-2
,, direct or —	182
Taylor, Sir H.	38
Teazle, Lady	71
Tcheng-Ki-Tong	7, 37, 40
Teaching order	64
Teleologic Value	62
Temple, Sir W.	107
Terms, technical	62
Terms and Definitions	62
Textile Trades	206
Theory of Political Economy	53
Thiers	38
Tolerance why?	121
Tourguéneff	158
Trade Unions	81, 135
Trade with United States	269
Treaties, Commercial, A. Smith	279
,, present	285
Treaty, French, Cobden	275, 280-1

U

United States population; troubles	47
,, ,, Railway-mania	51

V

Vagrants, French	162
"Valuable"	310
Vanderbilt	91
Verification	3, 140
Vicar of Wakefield	29
Victor Hugo	197
Voters, new	84

W

Wages, rates	73, 75
,, labourers	304
,, artizans	78
,, low	10, 12
,, higher wanted	46
,, how regulated	49, 82
,, when fixed by law	75
"Wanted" definition of	335
War great cost	68
Warburton	2, 3
Waterloo	52
Wealth (opulence)	—
,, of England	30
,, excessive, pursuit	42
Wesley, John	185
Westminster Review	1, 166
Whately, Archbishop	61, 173
Wheat, prices	74, 338
,, supply	275
,, in different hands	308
Whewell	140
Whist chances	141
Wills hereafter	96
Woollen Trade	208
Work and Wages wanted	46
Workmen are Productive Forces	315

X

Xavier	178

Y

Young, Arthur	12, 78, 101

Printed by ROBERT BIRBECK, Birmingham.

www.ingramcontent.com/pod-product-compliance
Lightning Source LLC
Chambersburg PA
CBHW030427300426
44112CB00009B/893